Praise for Donna and Heather's Gluten-Free Cookbooks

"I just read *125 Best Gluten-Free Bread Machine Recipes* cover to cover. I especially appreciated the section teaching how to use the bread machine, as well as the section on the specific flours: Amazing! It made a *huge* difference in the outcome of my bread. Thank you!"

— *L. Gaines, Los Angeles, California*

"I have made several of the basic sandwich and multigrain breads from *125 Best Gluten-Free Bread Machine Recipes* with my Breadman 2700. Each has turned out perfectly. The directions are very specific, and include options if you want to make substitutions. My gluten-tolerant husband is pleased with the taste and texture, which says a lot because he is very picky! I look forward to trying the other recipes in the book."

— *J. Dotson, Cleveland, Tennessee*

"I have been a full-blown celiac for some time and am delighted to discover flours other than rice. I have four of your cookbooks and truly believe they are the best out there. I have finally started to make my own bread with good results. Thanks for your help and keep churning the cookbooks out. They just get better and better."

— *Dianne Birrell, Port Hope, Ontario*

"I have been using *125 Best Gluten-Free Bread Machine Recipes* for 3 months and love it. I have tried many of the recipes and marked my family's favorites. The very first basic recipe is the best so far. The authors recommend using an instant-read thermometer, and that has been the best thing I bought. This is a must-have cookbook."

— *Nana M., North Carolina*

"I want to commend you on your wonderful gluten-free cookbooks! I recently found out, after years of problems, that I am sensitive to gluten, but am still at the stage of being overwhelmed and feeling that I will never eat anything good ever again. A couple of weeks ago, I was lucky to stumble upon one of your books. (I have since bought a second.) I have made bread, muffins and breakfast squares, and they all taste amazing, even better than the originals. I have always loved bread and muffins, but have been unable to eat them for a long time, so what a treat for me. I would feed them to any gluten-tolerant person. Thank you, thank you! Please keep up your wonderful work — you are a blessing to us gluten-sensitive people!"

— *Lorie Morrison, Almonte, Ontario*

"I purchased *125 Best Gluten-Free Bread Machine Recipes* and have made the Country Harvest Bread and the Mock Swedish Limpa. Both have fabulous flavor and texture. I am absolutely thrilled to enjoy a slice of freshly baked bread again. This morning another success: I made the Triple-Seed Brown Bread. Wonderful texture, flavor and aroma."

— *Betty Blake, Stanmore Bay, New Zealand*

"I purchased my first bread machine about 5 weeks ago. I was a little afraid to use the Gluten-Free Cycle, as I have to warm the water and the eggs. For the beginner I am, this was one more important step not to forget. I decided to use the Dough and Bake cycles. I succeeded quite well, thanks to your tips. I have baked three breads so far: Maritime Brown Bread, Orange Chocolate Chip Loaf and Sandwich Bread. They are all good, but I fell in love with the Sandwich Bread. Toasted, with chicken and honey-Dijon mustard, it is outstanding and it does not crumble. Until I had my bread machine, I ate purchased breads with slices the size of my palm. I am so delighted to eat normal-size slices again."

— *Monique Dubois, Saint-Lambert, Quebec*

"Look no further than Washburn and Butt's books at www.bestbreadrecipes.com. They started out as bakers with expertise in bread machines and got hooked on gluten-free."

— *Ellen Bayens, The Celiac Scene*

"I want to thank you for the *Complete Gluten-Free Cookbook*. My wife has many food restrictions, and your book has helped so much. The recipes work so well. Almost all the bread we eat is made from your cookbook, and it is so good. Gluten-free breads generally leave much to be desired, but yours are excellent — I eat it even though I can eat regular bread. Thanks!"

— *Jim Elphinstone, Lac La Biche, Alberta*

"Donna and Heather's cookbooks are a great addition to the Specialty Food Shop! I do not hesitate to recommend them to customers looking for quality gluten-free cookbooks that offer appetizing and nutritious recipes."

— *Cristina Cicco, RD, Hospital for Sick Children, Toronto, Ontario*

"I love and completely agree with your approach of emphasizing whole grains and nutritious ingredients. You've *proved* that a large percentage of starch in a GF flour blend is not necessary. Your recipes taste delicious, and I believe the hearty flavor of the whole grains actually makes them tastier than the counterpart made with a traditional rice/starch GF flour mix. My favorite bread recipe is the Ancient Grains Bread. I make this regularly, and my kids (non-celiacs, ages 6 and 8) actually prefer it to wheat bread. The Honey Walnut Bread is wonderful too."

— *C. Coffey, GIG Support Group, Rochester, New York*

"Your cookbooks are amazing and inspiring! Everything I have tried is delicious, and my family appreciates it too. I was diagnosed with celiac disease last year. I have always had a passion to be in the kitchen, whether cooking or baking. When I found out I could no longer enjoy the same foods, I was very disappointed. I didn't know if I could obey the rules. After receiving your cookbooks as gifts, I began to read and learn, and I went shopping for the various types of flours, etc. Since I've tried baking your bread recipes, I will never buy frozen gluten-free bread again! Your recipes (not just the bread) are wonderful. Pizza is great. My son, Marc, approves, and he was giving me a hard time about the gluten-free diet. I feel it is a healthier way of life, and for this reason, I *only* cook and bake gluten-free for the whole family, rather than just for myself. My health has since improved dramatically."

— *A Simonetta, Richmond Hill, Ontario*

"I'm interested in recipes that are gluten-free but are also nutritious. Many recipes use white rice flour and large amounts of cornstarch. There is a recipe in *125 Best Gluten-Free Bread Machine Recipes* for 'white' bread that has a mixture of nutritious flours, and it turns out great! There are instructions for how to make it as a mix, so I make a mix for 6 loaves at a time. In my opinion, this bread tastes better than any at the store, and has way more nutrition. I love it!"

— *C. Connally, Fort Collins, Colorado*

Great Gluten-Free Whole-Grain Bread Machine recipes

Featuring **150** delicious recipes

Donna Washburn & Heather Butt

Great Gluten-Free Whole-Grain Bread Machine Recipes
Text copyright © 2013 Donna Washburn and Heather Butt
Photographs copyright © 2013 Robert Rose Inc.
Cover and text design copyright © 2013 Robert Rose Inc.

For complete cataloguing information, see page 311.

Disclaimer
The recipes in this book have been carefully tested by our kitchen and our tasters. To the best of our knowledge, they are safe and nutritious for ordinary use and users. For those people with food or other allergies, or who have special food requirements or health issues, please read the suggested contents of each recipe carefully and determine whether or not they may create a problem for you. All recipes are used at the risk of the consumer. Consumers should always consult their bread machine manufacturer's manual for recommended procedures and cooking times.

We cannot be responsible for any hazards, loss or damage that may occur as a result of any recipe use.

For those with special needs, allergies, requirements or health problems, in the event of any doubt, please contact your medical adviser prior to the use of any recipe.

Design and Production: Daniella Zanchetta/PageWave Graphics Inc.
Editors: Sue Sumeraj and Jennifer MacKenzie
Proofreader: Sheila Wawanash
Indexer: Gillian Watts
Photographer: Colin Erricson
Associate Photographer: Matt Johannsson
Food Stylist: Kathryn Robertson
Prop Stylist: Charlene Erricson

Cover image: Figgy Apricot Bread (page 150)

We acknowledge the financial support of the Government of Canada through the Book Publishing Industry Development Program (BPIDP) for our publishing activities.

Published by Robert Rose Inc.
120 Eglinton Avenue East, Suite 800, Toronto, Ontario, Canada M4P 1E2
Tel: (416) 322-6552 Fax: (416) 322-6936
www.robertrose.ca

Printed and bound in Canada

1 2 3 4 5 6 7 8 9 FP 21 20 19 18 17 16 15 14 13

"A friend is one of the nicest things you can have,
and one of the best things you can be."

We dedicate this book to our friends —
many of whom happen to be gluten-intolerant.

Contents

Acknowledgments

This book has had the support and assistance of many from its inception to the final reality. We want to thank those who helped us along the way.

Our thanks to the following people and companies for supplying products for recipe development: Doug Yuen of Dainty Foods for brown rice flour and rice bran; George Birinyi Jr. of Grain Process Enterprises Ltd. for potato starch, tapioca starch, sorghum flour, amaranth flour, almond meal and xanthan gum; Howard Selig of Valley Flaxflour Ltd. for flax flour and flaxseed, both brown and golden; CanMar Grain Products Ltd. for roasted lentil flour and roasted flaxseed; John Weninger of Jamestown Mills for Beta-Pro Sweet Potato Flour; Cuisine Soleil for lentil flour, buckwheat flour, chickpea flour, millet flour and brown rice flour; Michel Dion of Lallamand Inc., for Eagle Instaferm® yeast; Beth Armour and Tracy Perry of Cream Hill Estates Ltd. for oat flour and rolled oats; Tilley Wiens of Avena Foods Ltd. for Only Oats oat bran, oat flour, steel-cut oats and rolled oats; Margaret Hughes of Best Cooking Pulses Inc. for BEST Whole Yellow Pea Flour, BEST Chickpea Flour, BEST Laird Lentil Flour and BEST Pea Fiber; Northern Quinoa Corp. for NorQuin Brand golden quinoa flour and Canadian-grown Norquin Brand quinoa; Richardson Oilseed, Richardson International Ltd., for Canola Harvest canola oil; Workinesh Spice Blends Inc., for teff flour; and Margaret Hudson of Burnbrae Farms Ltd. for Naturegg Simply Whites and Break-Free liquid eggs.

Thank you to the many manufacturers of bread machines who continue to supply our test kitchen with the latest models: Zojirushi; Cuisinart; Spectrum Brands Breadman® and Hamilton Beach Brands.

A huge thank you to the members of our focus group, who faithfully and tirelessly tasted and tested gluten-free recipes and products from the beginning to end of recipe development. Your comments, suggestions and critical analysis were invaluable and helped make this a better book.

We want to express our appreciation to photographer Colin
Erricson; associate photographer Matt Johannsson; food stylist
Kathryn Robertson; and prop stylist Charlene Erricson. Thank you
for making our gluten-free breads look delicious.

Bob Dees, our publisher; Marian Jarkovich, Director, Sales
and Marketing; Martine Quibell, Manager, Publicity; and Nina
McCreath, Manager, Corporate Accounts and International Sales
at Robert Rose Inc. deserve special thanks for their ongoing support.

To Daniella Zanchetta of PageWave Graphics, thank you for
working through this cookbook's design, layout and production.
Thank you to Sue Sumeraj and Jennifer MacKenzie, our editors.
A very special thanks to Magda Fahmy-Turnbull, RD, for her work
on the nutritional analysis. She has been an invaluable resource
throughout this project.

Thank you to our families: you helped bring balance to our
lives when we became too focused on our work.

And finally, to you who must follow a gluten-free diet, we
sincerely hope these recipes help make your life easier and more
enjoyable. We developed them with you in mind.

— *Donna and Heather*

Introduction

Remember the song about "those lazy, hazy, crazy days of summer"? As we write this book, we are enjoying spending time outside, sitting by the pool and reading. However, both the United States and Canada are in the midst of one of the hottest, driest summers on record. Our gardens are really suffering, as the rain barrels are long empty. We have decided not to turn the oven on this summer. Barbecues, slow cookers, panini grills and toaster ovens have rounded out salads for almost every meal. What a perfect time for breads made in the bread machine! Just measure the ingredients and set the cycles. How easy is that? But, of course, freshly made bread is a wonderful treat all year long.

You hear a lot these days about the importance of whole grains in your diet. Many people think wheat is the only whole grain available. How mistaken they are — some of the most nutritious and delicious whole-grain flours are gluten-free. Among them are amaranth, buckwheat, corn (including whole cornmeal), millet, GF oats (including oatmeal), quinoa, rice (both brown and colored), wild rice, sorghum and teff. It seems like every time we open a magazine, we see an article on adding these flours to your diet. We've been using these nutritious flours in our recipes for quite some time — we're ahead of the times!

In this collection, we have included recipes you requested, from flatbreads to sourdoughs to panini. Every day we receive emails asking for substitutions for eggs, nuts and specific flours, and you told us you especially enjoy our mixes, so we have included nut-free, rice-free and cornbread mixes, and a wide variety of egg-free recipes. Once again, we've provided a nutritional analysis for every recipe.

We really enjoy talking to everyone at trade shows and conferences, as well as receiving your emails. You continue to inspire us, so stay in touch.

Donna J. Washburn, P.H.Ec., and Heather L. Butt, P.H.Ec.
Quality Professional Services
1655 County Road 2
Mallorytown, Ontario K0E 1R0
Website: www.bestbreadrecipes.com
Email: bread@ripnet.com

Speaking Our Language: Are We All on the Same Page?

- "GF" means "gluten-free," such as GF sour cream, GF oat bran, etc., when both gluten-free and gluten-containing products are available. We recommend that you read package labels every time you purchase a GF product. Manufacturers frequently change the ingredients.
- "EF" means recipes are egg-free.

Keeping the following points in mind as you prepare our recipes will help you get the same great results we did:

- We selected specific GF flour combinations for individual recipes based on the desired texture and flavor of the final product. Unless mentioned as a variation, we have not tested other GF flours in the recipes. Substituting other flours may adversely affect the results.
- We used large eggs, liquid honey, light (fancy) molasses, bread machine or instant yeast, unsweetened fruit juice (not fruit drinks) and salted butter. We know you'll get the same great results if you bake with these, but expect slightly different results if you make substitutions.
- We tested with 2%, 1% or nonfat milk, yogurt and sour cream, but our recipes will work with other fat levels.
- Unless otherwise stated in the recipe or your bread machine manual, eggs and dairy products are used cold from the refrigerator. If the manufacturer recommends warming the eggs and heating the liquid to a specific temperature, be sure to follow their directions or the loaf will be short and raw in middle.
- All foods that require washing are washed before preparation. Foods such as bananas are peeled, but apples, rhubarb and zucchini are not (unless specified).
- If the preparation method (chopped, melted, diced, sliced) is listed before the food, it means that you prepare the food before measuring. If it is listed after the food, measure first, then prepare. Examples are "melted butter" vs. "butter, melted"; "ground flaxseed" vs. "flaxseed, ground"; and "cooked quinoa" vs. "quinoa, cooked."
- If in doubt about a food term, a piece of equipment or a specific recipe technique, refer to the glossaries, located on pages 298 to 309.

Using Your Bread Machine for Gluten-Free Baking

We have worked with many different brands and models of bread machines over the years, and we enjoy the challenges presented by the fact that each is so individual. Some bread machines on the market today have a longer and more vigorous knead than others, which results in slightly different loaves from the same recipe. We baked eight loaves in eight different bread machines using the White Bread mix, and got eight different results. The manual for your bread machine will help you become familiar with your make and model. Read it before you attempt to bake a loaf of bread: happy baking depends on it.

When purchasing a new bread machine, make sure it has at least one of the following choices: both a Dough Cycle and a Bake Cycle; a Programmable Cycle; or a dedicated Gluten-Free Cycle. Neither the 58-minute nor the 70-minute Rapid Cycles are long enough to rise and bake loaves successfully. The old 2-Hour Rapid Cycle works well, but this machine is no longer available. If you are using an older bread machine that doesn't have any of these options, try baking the loaves using a Basic or White Cycle.

The recipes in this book were developed for $1^1/_2$-lb (750 g) or 2-lb (1 kg) bread machines with either one or two kneading blades. These are the only ones you will have success with. The larger-capacity bread machines (those that bake $2^1/_2$-lb/1.25 kg or 3-lb/1.5 kg loaves) are too large to properly knead the amount of dough in our recipes. Expect shorter loaves when you use a bread machine with two paddles and a larger pan.

Getting to Know Your Bread Machine

Before you bake your first gluten-free loaf, it is important to become familiar with your bread machine, since models vary so much. Here's what we recommend. Standing in front of your machine, manual in hand, fill the baking pan with 1 inch (2.5 cm) of water. Observe and record the digital readout for the beginning of each operation as you determine the answers to the following questions.

What size bread machine do I need to make your recipes? Do I need a two-paddle machine?

We developed the recipes in this book for $1^1/_2$-lb (750 g) or 2-lb (1 kg) bread machines with either one or two kneading blades.

My new bread machine won't turn on and there is nothing in the display window. What do I do?

There are a couple of things to check before returning the machine. First, be sure the outlet is live. If so, check to see if the machine has an on/off switch — we found one that did. Look for it on the back of the machine, near the bottom, just above the cord.

Does the manual recommend warming the liquids and eggs?

Some machines advise warming liquids to between 110°F and 115°F (43°C and 46°C) if you're using the Gluten-Free Cycle, or to between 80°F and 90°F (27°C and 32°C) if you're using the Dough Cycle. In addition, some suggest warming eggs to room temperature (see the Technique Glossary, page 307.)

Does the machine have a Preheat Cycle? If so, how long is it?

Some machines start immediately, while others delay up to 25 minutes. Write the length of the Preheat Cycle on a label and stick it to your bread machine.

How long is the mixing stage?

Some machines mix for 1 to 2 minutes; others for up to 4 minutes. Write how long the mixing stage takes on the label you stuck to your bread machine when answering the previous question.

How long does the kneading take? Is it constant or intermittent?

The kneading stage varies from to 15 to 35 minutes. Add this information to the label you stuck to the bread machine. When you're making dough that won't be baked in the machine, we suggest removing it as soon as the kneading portion of the cycle is complete, simply because doing so speeds up the bread-baking process. If you forget and the machine finishes the cycle, don't worry about it.

Does the machine alert me when it's time to remove the kneading blade?

Most bread machines have an audible signal that tells you when to remove the blade. If yours doesn't, remove it at the end of the long knead (unless you're using the Programmable Cycle; see page 17).

Do I really have to remove the kneading blade?

Lately we have been experimenting and, with many loaves, the top will collapse slightly if the blade is not removed. For some, we had to remove the blade for the Gluten-Free Cycle so we didn't get a sinkhole; for others, we could leave it in. Remove the blade the next time you make a loaf if you find that the loaf collapses slightly and/or the blade leaves a hole. The real advantages to removing the blade are that no gobs of bread get baked onto it and every slice is complete, without a large hole at the bottom, so cleanup and slicing are much easier.

What do I do if the blade is stuck in the baked loaf? How do I get it out?

Glad you asked. We have had people email us who forgot about the blade and ruined a knife while slicing the loaf. We find that a plastic crochet hook — not a knife — inserted into the bottom of the loaf works best for removing the blade.

My bread machine has a Dough Cycle but no Bake Cycle. Can I still use the Dough Cycle/Bake Cycle method?

Yes, if your bread machine has a Programmable Cycle. When prompted, set all cycles to 0, eliminating the extra cycles until you come to Bake. Set Bake to 60 minutes at 350°F (180°C).

At the end of the Dough Cycle, does the machine shut off automatically or stay on?

Look for a flashing colon, which will tell you it is still on.

Is the time for the Bake Cycle preset?

Some machines have the baking time preset to 10 minutes and you'll need to set it by 10-minute intervals. Others are preset to 90 minutes and need to be adjusted to 60 minutes. To adjust the time, move the timer arrows up or down.

Can the Bake Cycle be immediately set for more time at the end of the cycle?

Before turning the machine off, take the internal temperature of the loaf with an instant-read thermometer. It should be 200°F (100°C). If it's below 180°F (85°C), you'll need to reset the Bake Cycle and check the internal temperature every 10 minutes.

Can the baking time for the Gluten-Free Cycle be extended?

If not, turn on the Bake Cycle and check the internal temperature every 10 minutes.

Does the machine have a Keep Warm Cycle? How long is it?

Most machines have a 1-hour Keep Warm Cycle, which is a handy feature if the bread is between 180°F (85°C) and 200°F (100°C) after 60 minutes on the Bake Cycle. Simply leave the machine on the Keep Warm Cycle until the bread reaches 200°F (100°C).

Choosing What Cycles to Use

To use the dedicated Gluten-Free Cycle

Read the manufacturer's manual for information about the Gluten-Free Cycle. Some ingredients, including liquids and eggs, may need to be warmed, not used directly from the refrigerator. It is not necessary to warm them unless the manufacturer recommends doing so. (See the Techniques Glossary, page 207, for information on safely warming eggs).

Select the Gluten-Free Cycle, removing the kneading blade when the machine signals or at the end of the long knead. Consult your manual for the timing of this signal. Removing the blade may prevent the collapse of the top crust.

To use the Dough Cycle, then the Bake Cycle

Select the Dough Cycle first. Remove the kneading blade at the end of the long knead, then allow the cycle to finish. Immediately select the Bake Cycle, setting it to 350°F or 360°F (180°C or 185°C) for 60 minutes. Allow the Bake Cycle to finish.

It is important to get to know your own bread machine. For instance, we have one that is a lot hotter than the rest, and we find that we have to lower the baking temperature; however, with other machines of the same make and model, the loaf bakes with a thin, tender crust. In most machines, the default temperature is 350°F (180°C). Check your manual to learn how to change time and temperature.

To use the Programmable Cycle

Read your owner's manual to learn how to set the Programmable Cycle. Select a short knead of 2 minutes (the machine stirs slowly, allowing for the addition of dry ingredients). Then set a knead of 20 minutes, then a rise of 70 minutes and a 60-minute Bake Cycle at 350°F (180°C). When prompted, set all other cycles to 0, eliminating the extra cycles. There's no need to remove the blade. If your machine allows you to select the temperature of the rise, choose the hotter option. You only need to program the machine once, as it will remember your settings until you change them.

To use the Basic or White Cycle (not a preferred method)

Some new machines on the market have neither a Bake Cycle nor a dedicated Gluten-Free Cycle. It is still possible to make GF bread in these machines using the Basic or White Cycle. Read your manual and figure out when the long knead is completed. If your manual does not contain this information, pour 1 inch (2.5 cm) of water into the baking pan and turn on the machine. Record the time for each operation to learn when kneading is complete. At that point, remove the kneading blade and let the machine complete the loaf. You may need to adjust the amount of yeast if the loaf collapses once baked. Do not use a Rapid or White/Quick/Express Cycle of under 2 hours or the loaf will not be baked at the end of the time.

Tips for Successful Gluten-Free Bread Machine Baking

- Read through the recipe before beginning, then gather the equipment and ingredients and wash anything that needs it.
- We selected specific flour combinations for individual recipes based on the desired texture and flavor of the final product. Rather than using a standard mix of flours, we like to vary the proportions of flours and starches so that each recipe is unique. Unless mentioned as a variation, we have not tested other GF flours in the recipes. Substituting other flours may adversely affect the results.
- Select either metric or imperial measures and stick to your choice for the entire recipe.
- Gluten-free recipes can be temperamental, so be sure to measure all ingredients accurately. Even an extra tablespoon (15 mL) of water in a baked product can cause the recipe to fail. Use a clear, graduated liquid measuring cup for all liquids. Place it on a flat surface and read it at eye level.
- Select the correct dry measures. For example, when the recipe calls for ¾ cup, use a ½-cup measure and a ¼-cup measure (for 175 mL, use a 125 mL measure and a 50 mL measure). Use the "spoon lightly, heap and level once" method of measuring for accuracy and perfect products. Use measuring spoons, not kitchen cutlery, for small amounts. There are also sets of long-handled, narrow spoons made especially to fit into spice jars. These are accurate and fun to use.

- Remove the baking pan from the bread machine when adding liquid ingredients. Do not measure over the bread pan.
- Gluten-free flours and starches must be well mixed or sifted together before they are slowly added to liquids, as they have a fine powder-like consistency and lump easily.
- If your bread machine has a Preheat Cycle, keep the top down until mixing starts, so the heat does not escape. As soon as the liquids begin to mix, add the dry ingredients, scraping the corners, sides and bottom of the baking pan and the kneading blade while adding. Watch that the rubber spatula does not get caught under the rotating blade. Continue scraping until no dry ingredients remain and the dough is well mixed. Some machines require more "help" mixing than others.
- The consistency of the dough is closer to a cake batter than the traditional yeast dough ball. You should see the motion of the kneading blade turning. The mixing mark of the kneading blade remains on top of the dough. Some doughs are thicker than others, but do not adjust by adding more liquid or dry ingredients.
- The kneading blade needs to be removed at the end of the long knead to prevent the collapse of the final loaf. However, some bread machines knead intermittently rather than continuously, so the first few times you use a new machine, listen carefully for the sounds of the different cycles. Make notes of the times the cycles change. We note the times for start of mixing and end of long knead right on the machine. Use either a label or permanent marker to write them on the machine. Then set an auxiliary timer for the time the kneading finishes and the rising starts. This will alert you to when to remove the kneading blade. The dough is sticky, so rinse the rubber spatula and your hand with cold water before removing the blade. Smooth the top of the loaf quickly.
- Some bread machines and some recipes bake darker-colored crusts than others. If you find certain loaves are too dark, next time set the Bake Cycle temperature lower. When baking on a Gluten-Free Cycle, a Basic Cycle or a 2-Hour Rapid Cycle, select a lighter crust setting, if possible.
- At the end of the baking cycle, before turning the machine off, take the temperature of the loaf using an instant-read thermometer. It should read 200°F (100°C). If it's between 180°F (85°C) and 200°F (100°C), leave the machine on the Keep Warm Cycle until the loaf is baked. If it's below 180°F (85°C), turn on the Bake Cycle and check the internal temperature every 10 minutes. (Some bread machines are automatically set for 60 minutes; others need to be set by 10-minute intervals.)

- Slice the cooled baked loaf with an electric knife or bread knife with a serrated blade. Place one or two slices in individual plastic bags, then place bags in a larger sealable bag. Freeze for up to 3 weeks. Remove a slice or two at a time.

Using an Instant-Read Thermometer

When we bake gluten-free, it is important to use a thermometer to test foods for doneness, as it is more difficult to tell when they are baked: the outside of the bread may look browned enough when the inside is still raw. The indicators you may be used to looking for when baking with wheat may not be reliable, as gluten-free foods often have a different appearance. A thermometer is the only accurate way to be sure the food is done.

Purchasing

The best thermometer for this purpose is a bimetallic stemmed thermometer often called an instant-read or chef's thermometer. It has a round head at the top, a long metal stem and a pointed end that senses the temperature. There are both digital and dial versions available. Check the temperature range to be sure it covers the temperatures you need. Instant-read thermometers are widely available in department stores, some grocery stores, specialty shops and box stores, and can also be purchased online.

Use

To test bread for doneness, insert the thermometer into the center of the loaf. Gluten-free breads are baked at 200°F (100°C). Do not leave the thermometer in the loaf during baking, as the plastic cover will melt, ruining the thermometer.

Clean the probe thoroughly after each use and store the thermometer in the plastic sleeve that came with it. Some of the more expensive ones (but not all) are dishwasher-safe. Read the manufacturer's instructions.

How to Calibrate Your Thermometer

It is important to make sure your thermometer is reading temperatures accurately, so you'll want to test it periodically. There are two ways of doing this and either will work, though we prefer the boiling-water method.

- **Boiling-water method:** Bring a pot of water to a boil. Insert the thermometer probe into the boiling water, making sure it doesn't touch the pot. It should read 212°F or 100°C. (Be careful not to burn yourself on the steam; we hold the thermometer with needle-nose pliers.)
- **Ice-water method:** Fill a container with crushed ice and cold water (mostly ice; just use water to fill the gaps). Insert the thermometer probe into the center of the ice water, making sure it doesn't touch the container. It should read 32°F or 0°C.

If the temperature reading is not exact, hold the calibration nut (found right under the round head) with a wrench and rotate the head until it reads the correct number of degrees.

Understanding Whole Grains

"A whole grain is the entire seed, including the naturally occurring nutrients of an edible plant. The size, shape and color of the seed, also referred to as the 'kernel,' vary with the species. A grain is considered a whole grain when it contains all three seed parts: bran, germ and endosperm."

— *Whole Grains Council (www.wholegrainscouncil.org)*

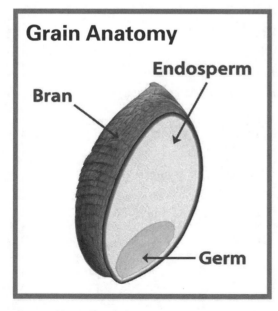

Source: Whole Grains Council. Used with permission.

What Is Meant by "Whole Grain"?

As the preceding quote explains, a whole grain consists of three parts: the bran, the germ and the endosperm. The **bran**, or outer coating, is made up of several layers. It is rich in insoluble fiber and contains antioxidants and B vitamins. Just beneath the bran layers is a small structure called the **germ**. The germ is rich in healthy oils, B vitamins, minerals including magnesium and iron, and some protein. The **endosperm** is the largest portion of the grain. It contains starch, protein, soluble fiber and small amounts of vitamins and minerals.

Whole grains contain all three parts, whereas refined grains (white rice, defatted soy, degerminated cornmeal) have the bran and germ removed, leaving only the endosperm. Refined grains are not as nutritious as whole grains. Some refined grains may be enriched (some of the nutrients that were removed are added back), but few GF grains, flours or products are enriched. It is very important to read labels every time when purchasing products made commercially with GF flours.

Whole grains can be eaten whole, cracked, ground or milled into flour. A whole grain that has been processed (cracked, crushed, ground, milled, rolled, extruded and/or cooked) still contains approximately the same nutrients found in the original grain seed.

Flour is the ground form of a grain. It can be milled from the whole grain or may be a refined and processed grain. Many gluten-free flours are whole grains.

GF Whole Grains

- amaranth
- buckwheat
- corn, including whole cornmeal
- millet
- GF oats, including oatmeal
- quinoa
- rice, both brown and colored
- wild rice
- sorghum
- teff

Amaranth

Amaranth seeds (also known as whole-grain amaranth) are off-white, golden, tan or light brown in color and are about the size of poppy seeds. The flavor ranges from mild, slightly sweet and nutty to a more robust, peppery whole-grain taste. Use amaranth seeds raw or cooked in crackers and sweet loaves with molasses or honey.

   Amaranth flour is very fine and has a light cream color and a pleasant, nutty taste. Because of its high moisture content, use it in combination with other flours. It produces baked goods that are moist and dense, but added starch helps to lighten the texture. The grain of the bread is more open, the texture not as silky and the crumb color slightly darker than wheat flour breads. Amaranth flour tends to form a crust on the outside of a product during baking, sealing the outside before the product is completely cooked on the inside, so use the smallest amount of liquid you can and allow for slightly longer baking times than you might otherwise. Products baked with amaranth flour tend to brown quickly and may need to be tented with foil during the last third of the baking time. Check to make sure the internal temperature of the baked bread reaches 200°F (100°C), as it may look baked on the outside before the center is done.

Buckwheat

Buckwheat groats are the hulled, white to cream-colored, triangular-shaped kernels of the buckwheat (saracen corn) plant. Soft in texture and bitter in flavor, they are available whole or cracked into coarse, medium or fine grinds. Finely cracked groats (grits) may be labeled "cream of buckwheat."

   Buckwheat flakes (oatmeal-style buckwheat) are rolled flakes made from buckwheat groats treated with hot steam. These small, brittle flakes look like small rolled oats, but have a slightly sweeter flavor and a slightly browner color. Those who can't tolerate oatmeal can substitute buckwheat flakes.

   Buckwheat flour is very fine, with a unique, strong, musty, slightly sour, slightly nutty flavor. For light buckwheat flour, the hull is removed before the groats are ground. Dark buckwheat flour is made of unhulled groats; it is grayish, with tiny black specks of hull, and has a strong, earthy taste. Buckwheat flour tends to make baked goods heavier and give them a distinctive, stronger taste. It is usually blended with other flours.

Corn

Cornmeal is milled from corn. It has larger granules than regular flour and can be yellow, white, red or blue. Although these varieties are slightly different in texture and flavor, one can be substituted for the other. The coarser the grind, the more granular the texture of the finished product and the more intense the corn flavor. Cornmeal is sometimes used to dust a greased pan, which helps keep the product from sticking to the pan and gives the crust extra crunch and a hint of flavor.

Degerminated cornmeal is ground between massive steel rollers. The fiber and corn germ are separated out, leaving a less nutritious and less flavorful grain. When you're looking for whole-grain cornmeal, avoid products that are labeled "degerminated."

Corn flour is more finely ground than cornmeal. Baked goods made using corn flour have a lighter texture than those made with cornmeal. Cornbread made with corn flour is richer and less crumbly.

Millet

Millet grain is not a true grain but is closely related to corn and sorghum. It is yellow or white, small and round, with a mild, delicate, corn-like flavor and a texture much like that of brown rice. Millet takes on the flavor of whatever it is cooked with. We like to add dry millet grain to yeast breads for a crunchy texture.

Millet grits are coarsely ground millet grain; **millet meal** is more finely ground and has a slightly sweet flavor, similar to that of corn.

Millet flour is made from finely ground millet grain. It can be substituted for rice flour in small amounts in most recipes and adds a lovely cream color to baked goods. Millet flour can be used in flatbreads.

Oats (pure, uncontaminated GF only)

Rolled oats (oat flakes or oatmeal) result when oat groats (the whole-grain form of oats, with the hull removed) are steamed and then rolled to flatten. Some rolled oats are also roasted to provide more flavor. These large, separate flakes are called old-fashioned, thick-cut or porridge oats; they take longer to cook than quick-cooking oats (which are cut into smaller pieces to reduce the cooking time), but they retain more flavor and nutrition. This is what most people think of as "oatmeal." **Steel-cut oats** are the whole raw oat cut into smaller chunks.

Oat flour is made from finely ground groats, which contain much of the bran. Depending on how it is ground, the flour can be almost as nutritious as the whole grain itself (it is heat during grinding that causes nutrient loss). The high oil content provides a sweet, nutty flavor.

Oat flour makes baked items moist and more crumbly, but the products stay fresh longer than items baked with wheat flour.

Oat bran is the outer layer of the oat groat, the part of the grain that contains soluble fiber, which is known to lower cholesterol. Light tan in color, it provides a distinctive texture and a rich, nutty flavor. When used in breads, it increases their fiber content. Breads can also be dusted with oat bran before they are baked, to create a flavorful topping.

Quinoa

Quinoa seeds are small and flat, with a pointed oval shape, and can be white, red, black or mixed — the darker the color, the nuttier the flavor. Quinoa must be washed and rinsed in a fine-mesh sieve to remove the bitter, toxic outer saponin coating. We recommend this step even if the label states "prewashed." Quinoa can also be soaked overnight (see the Technique Glossary, page 309) before it is added raw to breads.

As quinoa cooks, the outer germ around each grain twists outward, forming a small white spiraled tail that is attached to the kernel. The grain itself is soft and delicate, while the tail is crunchy. Cooked quinoa has a fluffy consistency and is excellent in yeast breads. For information on cooking quinoa, see the Technique Glossary, page 309.

Quinoa flakes are whole quinoa kernels rolled flat into flakes of $1/8$ to $1/4$ inch (3 to 5 mm) in diameter. Quinoa flakes can replace GF oatmeal or buckwheat flakes in recipes.

Quinoa flour is finely ground and tan-colored, with a strong, slightly nutty flavor. Because of its strong flavor, use it in small amounts. Breads made with quinoa flour have a tender, moist crumb and keep well.

Rice Flours

Brown rice flour is milled from the whole grain. It has a grainy texture and provides more fiber and nutrients than white rice flour. It is only a shade darker than white rice flour and has a mild, nutty flavor. Brown rice flour results in a product with a grainy texture and a fine, dry crumb. Use it in recipes calling for rice flour.

Rice bran and **rice polish** are the two outer parts of the rice kernel, removed during milling for white rice flour. Rice bran is the outermost layer. When bran and polish are added in small amounts to recipes, the fiber content is increased. They are interchangeable in recipes. **Stabilized rice bran** has undergone a process to ensure it remains fresh without refrigeration.

Sweet rice flour (glutinous rice flour, mochiko flour, sticky rice flour, mochi flour, sushi rice flour) is made from short-grain rice. It contains more starch than brown or white rice flour. There are two grades: one is beige, grainy and sandy-textured; the other is white, starchy, sticky and less expensive. The latter works better in recipes. We use it to dust baking pans or our fingers for easier handling of sticky dough.

Wild rice flour is gray-brown to black and has a nutty flavor and an interesting texture.

Sorghum

Sorghum flour ranges in color from a gray-tan to eggshell white, and the grinds vary from coarse (stone-ground) to very fine. Because its flavor is neutral, it absorbs other flavors well. The most wheat-like of all GF flours, it is the best general-purpose flour, giving baked items a warm, creamy color. Sorghum flour adds protein to breads. We love the results we get when we use a mixture of sorghum flour and bean flour with strong flavors such as pumpkin, chocolate, molasses, dates and rhubarb.

Sorghum should not be used as a sprouting grain, as the young shoots are very poisonous.

Teff

Teff grain is the smallest grain in the world, tinier than a poppy seed and only twice the size of the period at the end of this sentence. A hundred and fifty teff seeds weigh as much as one kernel of wheat; seven grains will fit onto the head of a pin. The seeds can be white, ivory or brown. Brown teff has a subtle hazelnut, almost chocolate-like flavor; white teff has a chestnut-like flavor; ivory teff has a mild, slightly molasses-like sweetness and nutty taste. The darker varieties are earthier-tasting. Raw teff grain can substitute for some of the seeds, nuts or other small grains in bread recipes. Due to its small size, use only $1/2$ cup (125 mL) of teff to replace 1 cup (250 mL) of sesame seeds.

Teff grain cooks quickly. Cook it just long enough to open the grain. For extra flavor, toast the grains first. Cooked teff can be seasoned with cinnamon, ginger, garlic, cardamom, chiles, basil or cilantro. Ethiopians use teff as the main ingredient in their staple bread, injera.

Teff flour milled from brown teff has a sweet, nutty flavor, while flour from white teff is milder. Teff flour has excellent baking qualities.

Storing Whole Grains and Whole-Grain Flours

Whole grain or whole-grain flour	Room temperature*	Refrigerator	Freezer	Additional information
Amaranth seeds	1 month	6 months	1 year	Refrigerate cooked seeds for up to 3 days or freeze for up to 6 months.
Amaranth flour		6 months	1 year	
Buckwheat groats	1 year			
Buckwheat flakes	2 years			
Buckwheat flour		2 months	6 months	
Cornmeal/corn flour	1 month	6 months	1 year	
Degerminated cornmeal	6 months			
Millet grain, grits, meal and flour		6 months	1 year	
Oat groats and rolled oats	2 months		6 months	
Oat flour	3 months		6 months	
Oat bran		6 months	1 year	
Quinoa flakes	2 months			
Quinoa flour		6 months	1 year	
Brown rice**		6 months		Refrigerate cooked rice for up to 7 days or freeze for up to 6 months.
Rice flours	1 year		1 year	
Rice bran and rice polish		6 months	1 year	
Sorghum flour	1 month	6 months	1 year	
Teff grain and flour	1 month	6 months	1 year	Refrigerate cooked teff grain for up to 3 days or freeze for up to 6 months.

*   All gluten-free grains and flours should be stored in airtight containers in a cool, dry, dark place.
** The bran layers in brown rice contain oil that could become rancid; thus, brown rice must be refrigerated.

Nutrient Content of Gluten-Free Flours and Starches

Gluten-free flour (per 1 cup/250 mL)	Protein (g)	Fat (g)	Carbohydrates (g)	Fiber (g)	Calcium (mg)	Iron (mg)
Whole-grain flours						
Amaranth flour	17	8	80	18	51	9.1
Brown rice flour	11	4	124	7	17	3.1
Oat flour	21	9	78	12	50	7.2
Quinoa flour	13	8	84	6	61	9.4
Sorghum flour	12	4	88	8	35	5.7
Teff flour	16	4	88	16	201	7.0
Other flours and starches						
Almond flour	24	56	24	12	750	5.4
Cornstarch	0	0	117	1	3	0.6
Flax flour	24	45	38	36	332	7.5
Garfava flour	35	6	72	12	104	7.9
Soy flour (low-fat)	47	6	38	18	241	9.2

Sources: USDA, Case Nutrition Consulting Inc., Bob's Red Mill, Nu-World Amaranth, Northern Quinoa Corp., Twin Valley Mills and Nutrition Data.

Protein helps us maintain and repair body tissues. Complete proteins (meat, fish, poultry, milk and milk products and eggs) provide all the amino acids necessary for a healthy body; incomplete proteins (grains, legumes, vegetables) lack some of the essential amino acids. However, the body has the ability to use amino acids from a variety of sources to form complete proteins. Here are some suggested combinations: beans and rice, cereals and milk, nuts and grains; whole-grain breads and legumes. All grains are not created equal: some contain more and higher levels of essential amino acids than others. It is therefore important to bake with a variety of nutritious grains.

Fat provides the essential fatty acids that the body cannot produce. It protects the organs and muscles with padding and insulation. Although fats are necessary for a healthy diet, they have two and a half times as many calories per gram as protein and carbohydrates, so the amount of fat consumed should be controlled.

Carbohydrates are the primary source of energy for the body. They provide fuel as the body breaks down complex carbohydrates into simple sugars.

UNDERSTANDING WHOLE GRAINS

Fiber is found only in plants and plays a significant role in keeping us healthy. Insoluble fiber aids in digestion, while soluble fiber can lower cholesterol. Sources of insoluble fiber include rice bran, brown rice, almond meal and legumes. Sources of soluble fiber include flaxseed and pears. Oat bran, whole-grain oats and soybeans contain both types. When increasing fiber in the diet, do so gradually.

Calcium helps the body build strong bones and teeth. It is also required for blood clotting and nerve and muscle function.

Iron is necessary for the formation of hemoglobin in red blood cells. It also helps the immune system function.

Other Gluten-Free Baking Ingredients

Coconut Flour

Coconut flour is made from dried, ground-up coconut meat, usually defatted by the removal of the coconut oil and milk. It is a very low-calorie food because most of the carbohydrate it contains is fiber, which cannot be digested. It is also a good source of protein.

Coconut flour is fine, dense, pale yellow, smells like coconut and tastes slightly sweet. It brings out the flavors of chocolate and vanilla.

Batter made with coconut flour will thicken in the few minutes after you add the flour mixture to the liquid in the bread machine. As it tends to clump, the batter needs to be mixed very well to make sure all the lumps are removed.

Breads made with coconut flour are dense and filling. It is often a good idea to make them in smaller loaf pans.

Fats

Fat gives the crust its tenderness and the loaf its softness. It also helps to retain moisture, which keeps the loaf from going stale too quickly. The type of fat used is a matter of preference and can include vegetable oil, butter, shortening or margarine. (Your choice may have some effect on the loaf, however.) Do not use low-calorie margarine, as its high water content will affect the size and texture of the loaf.

Cheese and egg yolk contribute to the fat in some recipes. When measuring shredded cheese, do not pack. Weight is a more accurate measure than volume. If desired, small cubes of cheese can replace shredded, since cheese melts during baking.

Flaxseed

Whole flaxseed (also known as linseed) refers to the unbroken seed. The seeds are small, flat and tear-shaped. They range in color from dark reddish-brown to golden and have a nutty flavor and a crisp, yet chewy texture.

Cracked flaxseed is not sold in stores but can be prepared at home: use a coffee grinder to crack the outer coating of the seed slightly, resulting in pieces of different sizes and textures. Cracked flaxseed is easier to digest than whole flaxseed. For extra crunch, add slightly cracked flaxseed to yeast breads.

Ground flaxseed is sold as flax flour, milled flaxseed or sprouted flax flour. All forms of ground flaxseed are interchangeable in recipes. You can prepare your own by grinding whole flaxseed to a gold to medium brown powder with slightly darker flecks. Grind to the consistency you want for your recipe. For optimum freshness, grind it as you need it. Refrigerate any extra.

Legume Flours

Legumes (also called pulses) include peas, beans, lentils and peanuts. Legume flours combine well with other GF flours. All legume flours are a shade of yellow and have a very fine texture. They complement recipes made with molasses, brown sugar, chocolate, pumpkin, applesauce and rhubarb.

- **Fava bean flour** is made from earthy-flavored fava beans.
- **Chickpea flour** (garbanzo bean flour, gram, besan, chana dal) has a mild, nut-like taste, with a hint of lemon. It adds a rich, sweet flavor to baked foods.
- **Garfava flour** (sold as garbanzo-fava bean flour in Canada) is a blend of garbanzo bean (chickpea) flour and fava bean flour. It has a nutty taste.
- **Whole bean flour** is made from Romano beans (also called cranberry beans or speckled sugar beans). The dried beans are cooked (heat-treated, micronized) to help reduce flatulence, then stone-ground to a uniform, fine, dark, strong-tasting flour. When one of our recipes calls for whole bean flour, use this one; however, if it's not available, any bean or pea flour can be substituted.
- **White (navy) bean flour** is made from small white round or oval beans. The white flour has a mild flavor and a powdery texture.
- **Pinto bean flour** has a slightly pink tinge, although the pinto beans it is made from have a spotty beige and brown color.
- **Pea flours** are produced from dried field peas with the bran (hull) removed. Green pea flour has a sweeter flavor than yellow pea flour. Pea flours keep baked products softer longer and

improve dough made in a bread machine. Pea flours complement recipes made with banana, peanut butter and strong spices such as cloves. All types of bean flours (except soy flour) can be used interchangeably with pea flours in our recipes.

- **Lentil flour** is made by grinding dried red, green, yellow, brown or cream-colored lentils. It has a nutty, earthy flavor and a pale yellow color. It holds baked goods together and doesn't leave a noticeable flavor or extra color in the finished product.

- **Soy flour** (soya flour), made from soybeans, is powdery fine, with a pungent, nutty, slightly bitter flavor that is enhanced by the flavors of accompanying flours. Soy flour is available in full-fat (natural), low-fat (our preference) and defatted versions. The higher the fat content, the deeper the color. Full-fat soy flour contains the natural oils found in the soybean; defatted soy flour has had the oils removed during processing. Soy flour has a strong odor when wet that disappears with baking. It adds rich color, fine texture, a pleasant nutty flavor, tenderness and moistness to baked goods. Products containing soy flour bake faster and tend to brown quickly, so the baking time may need to be shortened or the oven temperature lowered. Tenting oven-baked breads with foil partway through the baking time also helps.

Nut Flours and Meals

Nut flours and meals are made from very finely ground nuts such as almonds, hazelnuts and pecans. They are not as smooth or as fine as grain flours. Nut flours can be purchased, or you can grind them yourself (see the Technique Glossary, page 308). Grind the nuts when you're ready to prepare the recipe. We like to toast them first, for a nuttier flavor (see page 308). Toasting also dries nut flour, helping to prevent clumping.

- **Almond flour**, or almond meal, is made from blanched almonds and is creamy white. Sugar or flour is sometimes added during grinding to absorb the oil from the almonds and prevent clumping, so check purchased almond flour to be sure it is gluten-free. Combine almond flour with rice flour or amaranth flour when a white, delicate-flavored product is desired.

- **Hazelnut flour** is a creamy color with dark brown to black flecks. It has a full, rich flavor that is sweet and nutty. We enjoy it with orange or chocolate.

- **Pecan meal** is a warm brown, similar in color to ground flaxseed. It complements recipes made with maple, pumpkin and dried fruits such apricots and dates.

Salt

While we have used only small amounts of salt in our recipes, the salt is necessary, as it controls the yeast's activity and prevents the loaf from over-rising and collapsing. Breads made without salt are very bland and over-risen. Do not omit the salt, even if you are on a low-sodium diet.

Starches

Starches, which are complex carbohydrates, lighten gluten-free breads.

- **Arrowroot** (arrowroot starch, arrowroot powder, arrowroot starch flour) is a fine, white, tasteless starchy powder with a mild aroma. Arrowroot is more expensive and may be more difficult to find than other starches. When mixed with GF flours, arrowroot helps bread bind better and lightens the finished product.
- **Cornstarch** (corn flour, maize, *crème de maïs*) is a fine, silky, white, tasteless starchy powder. When mixed with GF flours, cornstarch helps bread bind better and lightens the finished product. If you cannot tolerate corn, substitute an equal amount of any other starch you can tolerate that is not already in the ingredient list of the recipe.
- **Potato flour** is made from the whole potato, including the skin. Because it has been cooked, it absorbs large amounts of water. Potato flour is much denser and heavier than potato starch and has a definite potato flavor. Potato flour is not used like other flours in baking as it would absorb too much liquid and make the product gummy, but small amounts can be used in breads to hold them together. We rarely use potato flour.
- **Potato starch** (potato starch flour) is made from only the starch of potatoes, and is therefore less expensive than potato flour. It is a very fine, silky, white powder with a bland taste. It lumps easily and must be sifted frequently. When combined with GF flours, it adds moistness and gives a light and airy texture. It also causes breads to rise higher. Potato starch is often confused with potato flour, but one cannot be substituted for the other. A permitted ingredient for Passover (unlike cornstarch and other non-kosher grain-based foods), potato starch is often found with kosher products in supermarkets.
- **Tapioca starch** (tapioca flour, tapioca starch flour, cassava flour, yucca starch, manioc, manihot, *almídon de yucca*) is powdery fine, white and mildly sweet. Tapioca starch lightens baked goods and gives them a slightly sweet, chewy texture.

Sugars

Sugar provides food for the yeast and adds flavor to the dough. Granulated sugar, packed brown sugar, liquid honey, pure maple syrup, corn syrup and light (fancy) molasses can be used interchangeably, though the results will vary slightly in color, flavor and texture.

Aspartame-based sugar substitutes can be used, but not those based on saccharin. Substitute an equal amount for the sugar in the recipe. Loaves will be lighter in color than when sugar is used.

Sweet Potato Flour

Made from white sweet potatoes, sweet potato flour ranges in color from white to a warm, deep tan. It holds moisture well and brings rich flavor and a little extra sweetness to baked goods, including breads. High in fiber, vitamin A, beta carotene, potassium, iron and calcium, sweet potato flour contains more carbohydrates than many other flours, but less protein. Despite the "sweet" in its name, studies have shown that it helps stabilize blood sugar levels, as it has a low glycemic index.

Xanthan Gum

Xanthan gum is a natural carbohydrate made from a microscopic organism called *Xanthomonas campestris*. It is produced from the fermentation of corn sugar. It helps prevent baked goods from crumbling, gives them greater volume, improves their texture and extends their shelf life. Do not omit xanthan gum from a recipe.

Xanthan gum can be purchased at health food stores, online or where you purchase other gluten-free ingredients. Before working with xanthan gum, be sure to wipe counters and containers with a dry cloth. When it comes in contact with water, it becomes slippery, slimy and almost impossible to wipe up.

According to TIC Gums Inc., a major xantham gum manufacturer, "Due to processing, there aren't any proteins from the corn left in the finished product; therefore, xantham gum does not contain a corn allergen and is suitable for those sensitive to corn."

Guar gum is also gluten-free, but it may act as a laxative in some people. It can be substituted for xanthan gum in an equal amount.

Yeast

Yeast converts the carbohydrates in flour and sugar to produce the carbon dioxide gas that causes dough to rise. The recipes in this cookbook were developed using bread machine (instant) yeast. We always recommend using the type of yeast called for in the recipe.

Bread machine (instant) yeast is a very active strain of yeast that can be added directly to the bread machine without the need for pre-activating.

The expiry date on a package of yeast indicates that it should be opened before that date and used within a 2-month period. Yeast should be kept in an airtight container in the freezer, and there's no need to defrost before measuring. Do not transfer yeast from one container to another; exposing it to air can shorten its life.

Perform this test for freshness if you suspect yeast has become less active: Dissolve 1 tsp (5 mL) granulated sugar in $\frac{1}{2}$ cup (125 mL) lukewarm water. Add 2 tsp (10 mL) yeast and stir gently. In 10 minutes, the mixture should have a strong yeasty smell and be foamy. If it doesn't, the yeast is too old — time to buy fresh yeast!

Storing Other Gluten-Free Baking Ingredients

Ingredient	Room temperature*	Refrigerator	Freezer	Additional information
Coconut flour	6 months			
Flaxseed, whole	1 year			
Flaxseed, cracked or ground		6 months	1 year	For optimum freshness, grind only as needed.
Legume flours		6 months	1 year	
Nut flours and meals**		3 months	1 year	Store away from foods with strong odors, such as fish and onions.
Nuts, unshelled**	6 months		1 year	
Seeds (pumpkin, poppy, sesame and sunflower)**		6 months	1 year	
Soy flour, full-fat		6 months	1 year	
Soy flour, defatted	1 year			
Starches	Indefinitely			
Sweet potato flour		6 months	1 year	
Xanthan gum and guar gum	6 months		Indefinitely	
Yeast (bread machine and instant)	2 months		12 months	Open before expiry date.

 * All gluten-free baking ingredients should be stored in airtight containers in a cool, dry, dark place.

** Because of their high oil content, seeds, nuts and nut flours tend to become rancid quickly. Purchase in small quantities and taste before using.

The Classics

This chapter contains all the basic recipes you need to get started with whole-grain gluten-free bread machine baking. Fans of our previous gluten-free bread machine book may find some of the recipes familiar. You're right! Several of the recipes in this chapter are true classics that no gluten-free bread book would be complete without. These recipes have proved so popular with our loyal fans that we decided to repeat them here so our new readers could enjoy them too.

White Bread

This moist, all-purpose yeast bread is always a big hit with our fans. We know you'll enjoy it, whether for sandwiches or to accompany your favorite salad.

Tips

To ensure success, see page 14 for information on using your bread machine and page 18 for general tips on bread machine baking.

Remember to thoroughly mix the dry ingredients before adding them to the liquids — they are powder-fine and could clump together.

2¼ cups	brown rice flour	550 mL
⅔ cup	potato starch	150 mL
⅓ cup	tapioca starch	75 mL
¼ cup	nonfat dry milk or skim milk powder	60 mL
¼ cup	granulated sugar	60 mL
2½ tsp	xanthan gum	12 mL
1¼ tsp	bread machine or instant yeast	6 mL
1¾ tsp	salt	8 mL
1¼ cups	water	300 mL
¼ cup	vegetable oil	60 mL
1 tsp	cider vinegar	5 mL
2	eggs, lightly beaten	2
2	egg whites, lightly beaten	2

1. In a large bowl or plastic bag, combine brown rice flour, potato starch, tapioca starch, dry milk, sugar, xanthan gum, yeast and salt; mix well and set aside.

2. Pour water, oil and vinegar into the bread machine baking pan. Add eggs and egg whites.

3. Select the **Gluten-Free Cycle**. As the bread machine is mixing, gradually add the dry ingredients, scraping bottom and sides of pan with a rubber spatula. Try to incorporate all the dry ingredients within 1 to 2 minutes. When the mixing and kneading are complete, remove the kneading blade, leaving the bread pan in the bread machine. Quickly smooth the top of the loaf. Allow the cycle to finish.

4. At the end of the cycle, take the temperature of the loaf using an instant-read thermometer. It is baked at 200°F (100°C). If it's between 180°F (85°C) and 200°F (100°C), leave machine on the **Keep Warm Cycle** until baked. If it's below 180°F (85°C), turn on the **Bake Cycle** and check the internal temperature every 10 minutes. (Some bread machines are automatically set for 60 minutes; others need to be set by 10-minute intervals.)

5. Once the loaf has reached 200°F (100°C), remove it from the pan immediately and let cool completely on a rack.

NUTRITIONAL VALUES
per serving

Calories	183
Fat, total	5 g
Fat, saturated	1 g
Cholesterol	22 mg
Sodium	297 mg
Carbohydrate	33 g
Fiber	1 g
Protein	4 g
Calcium	18 mg
Iron	1 mg

Tip
Use any leftovers to make bread crumbs (see the Technique Glossary, page 306).

Variation
Add 1¼ cups (300 mL) milk instead of the water and nonfat dry milk or skim milk powder.

Dough Cycle and Bake Cycle

If your bread machine does not have a Gluten-Free Cycle, use the Dough Cycle followed by the Bake Cycle.

1. In a large bowl or plastic bag, combine brown rice flour, potato starch, tapioca starch, dry milk, sugar, xanthan gum, yeast and salt; mix well and set aside.

2. Pour water, oil and vinegar into the bread machine baking pan. Add eggs and egg whites.

3. Select the **Dough Cycle**. As the bread machine is mixing, gradually add the dry ingredients, scraping bottom and sides of pan with a rubber spatula. Try to incorporate all the dry ingredients within 1 to 2 minutes. When the mixing and kneading are complete, remove the kneading blade, leaving the bread pan in the bread machine. Quickly smooth the top of the loaf. Allow the cycle to finish. Turn off the bread machine.

4. Select the **Bake Cycle**. Set time to 60 minutes and temperature to 350°F (180°C). Allow the cycle to finish. Do not turn machine off before taking the internal temperature of the loaf with an instant-read thermometer. It should be 200°F (100°C). If it's between 180°F (85°C) and 200°F (100°C), leave machine on the **Keep Warm Cycle** until baked. If it's below 180°F (85°C), turn on the **Bake Cycle** and check the internal temperature every 10 minutes. (Some bread machines are automatically set for 60 minutes; others need to be set by 10-minute intervals.)

5. Once the loaf has reached 200°F (100°C), remove it from the pan immediately and let cool completely on a rack.

Buttermilk Bread

Here's a warm, soft, creamy loaf for those who enjoy white bread.

Tips

To ensure success, see page 14 for information on using your bread machine and page 18 for general tips on bread machine baking.

You can purchase buttermilk powder in bulk stores and health food stores.

1¼ cups	brown rice flour	300 mL
1 cup	amaranth flour	250 mL
½ cup	almond flour	125 mL
⅓ cup	tapioca starch	75 mL
½ cup	buttermilk powder	125 mL
1 tbsp	xanthan gum	15 mL
2 tsp	bread machine or instant yeast	10 mL
¾ tsp	salt	3 mL
1⅓ cups	water	325 mL
3 tbsp	vegetable oil	45 mL
3 tbsp	liquid honey	45 mL
1 tsp	cider vinegar	5 mL
2	eggs, lightly beaten	2
2	egg whites, lightly beaten	2

1. In a large bowl or plastic bag, combine brown rice flour, amaranth flour, almond flour, tapioca starch, buttermilk powder, xanthan gum, yeast and salt; mix well and set aside.

2. Pour water, oil, honey and vinegar into the bread machine baking pan. Add eggs and egg whites.

3. Select the **Gluten-Free Cycle**. As the bread machine is mixing, gradually add the dry ingredients, scraping bottom and sides of pan with a rubber spatula. Try to incorporate all the dry ingredients within 1 to 2 minutes. When the mixing and kneading are complete, remove the kneading blade, leaving the bread pan in the bread machine. Quickly smooth the top of the loaf. Allow the cycle to finish.

4. At the end of the cycle, take the temperature of the loaf using an instant-read thermometer. It is baked at 200°F (100°C). If it's between 180°F (85°C) and 200°F (100°C), leave machine on the **Keep Warm Cycle** until baked. If it's below 180°F (85°C), turn on the **Bake Cycle** and check the internal temperature every 10 minutes. (Some bread machines are automatically set for 60 minutes; others need to be set by 10-minute intervals.)

5. Once the loaf has reached 200°F (100°C), remove it from the pan immediately and let cool completely on a rack.

NUTRITIONAL VALUES
per serving

Calories	173
Fat, total	6 g
Fat, saturated	1 g
Cholesterol	25 mg
Sodium	160 mg
Carbohydrate	25 g
Fiber	2 g
Protein	6 g
Calcium	76 mg
Iron	1 mg

For whiter bread, purchase almond flour made from almonds with the skin removed.

Remember to thoroughly mix the dry ingredients before adding them to the liquids — they are powder-fine and could clump together.

Dough Cycle and Bake Cycle

If your bread machine does not have a Gluten-Free Cycle, use the Dough Cycle followed by the Bake Cycle.

1. In a large bowl or plastic bag, combine brown rice flour, amaranth flour, almond flour, tapioca starch, buttermilk powder, xanthan gum, yeast and salt; mix well and set aside.

2. Pour water, oil, honey and vinegar into the bread machine baking pan. Add eggs and egg whites.

3. Select the **Dough Cycle**. As the bread machine is mixing, gradually add the dry ingredients, scraping bottom and sides of pan with a rubber spatula. Try to incorporate all the dry ingredients within 1 to 2 minutes. When the mixing and kneading are complete, remove the kneading blade, leaving the bread pan in the bread machine. Quickly smooth the top of the loaf. Allow the cycle to finish. Turn off the bread machine.

4. Select the **Bake Cycle**. Set time to 60 minutes and temperature to 350°F (180°C). Allow the cycle to finish. Do not turn machine off before taking the internal temperature of the loaf with an instant-read thermometer. It should be 200°F (100°C). If it's between 180°F (85°C) and 200°F (100°C), leave machine on the **Keep Warm Cycle** until baked. If it's below 180°F (85°C), turn on the **Bake Cycle** and check the internal temperature every 10 minutes. (Some bread machines are automatically set for 60 minutes; others need to be set by 10-minute intervals.)

5. Once the loaf has reached 200°F (100°C), remove it from the pan immediately and let cool completely on a rack.

Brown Bread

This basic brown sandwich bread is rich, golden, wholesome and nutritious. It's a true classic!

Tips

To ensure success, see page 14 for information on using your bread machine and page 18 for general tips on bread machine baking.

Pea flour, like soy flour, has a distinctive odor when wet that disappears with baking.

1¼ cups	sorghum flour	300 mL
1 cup	pea flour	250 mL
½ cup	tapioca starch	125 mL
⅓ cup	rice bran	75 mL
2 tbsp	packed brown sugar	30 mL
1 tbsp	xanthan gum	15 mL
2 tsp	bread machine or instant yeast	10 mL
1½ tsp	salt	7 mL
1⅔ cups	water	400 mL
2 tbsp	vegetable oil	30 mL
2 tbsp	light (fancy) molasses	30 mL
1 tsp	cider vinegar	5 mL
2	eggs, lightly beaten	2
2	egg whites, lightly beaten	2

1. In a large bowl or plastic bag, combine sorghum flour, pea flour, tapioca starch, rice bran, brown sugar, xanthan gum, yeast and salt; mix well and set aside.

2. Pour water, oil, molasses and vinegar into the bread machine baking pan. Add eggs and egg whites.

3. Select the **Gluten-Free Cycle**. As the bread machine is mixing, gradually add the dry ingredients, scraping bottom and sides of pan with a rubber spatula. Try to incorporate all the dry ingredients within 1 to 2 minutes. When the mixing and kneading are complete, remove the kneading blade, leaving the bread pan in the bread machine. Quickly smooth the top of the loaf. Allow the cycle to finish.

4. At the end of the cycle, take the temperature of the loaf using an instant-read thermometer. It is baked at 200°F (100°C). If it's between 180°F (85°C) and 200°F (100°C), leave machine on the **Keep Warm Cycle** until baked. If it's below 180°F (85°C), turn on the **Bake Cycle** and check the internal temperature every 10 minutes. (Some bread machines are automatically set for 60 minutes; others need to be set by 10-minute intervals.)

5. Once the loaf has reached 200°F (100°C), remove it from the pan immediately and let cool completely on a rack.

NUTRITIONAL VALUES
per serving

Calories	166
Fat, total	4 g
Fat, saturated	1 g
Cholesterol	25 mg
Sodium	292 mg
Carbohydrate	28 g
Fiber	6 g
Protein	7 g
Calcium	16 mg
Iron	2 mg

Variations

Any type of bean flour can be substituted for the pea flour.

Substitute GF oat bran for the rice bran.

For a slightly sweeter flavor, substitute liquid honey or packed brown sugar for the molasses.

Dough Cycle and Bake Cycle

If your bread machine does not have a Gluten-Free Cycle, use the Dough Cycle followed by the Bake Cycle.

1. In a large bowl or plastic bag, combine sorghum flour, pea flour, tapioca starch, rice bran, brown sugar, xanthan gum, yeast and salt; mix well and set aside.

2. Pour water, oil, molasses and vinegar into the bread machine baking pan. Add eggs and egg whites.

3. Select the **Dough Cycle**. As the bread machine is mixing, gradually add the dry ingredients, scraping bottom and sides of pan with a rubber spatula. Try to incorporate all the dry ingredients within 1 to 2 minutes. When the mixing and kneading are complete, remove the kneading blade, leaving the bread pan in the bread machine. Quickly smooth the top of the loaf. Allow the cycle to finish. Turn off the bread machine.

4. Select the **Bake Cycle**. Set time to 60 minutes and temperature to 350°F (180°C). Allow the cycle to finish. Do not turn machine off before taking the internal temperature of the loaf with an instant-read thermometer. It should be 200°F (100°C). If it's between 180°F (85°C) and 200°F (100°C), leave machine on the **Keep Warm Cycle** until baked. If it's below 180°F (85°C), turn on the **Bake Cycle** and check the internal temperature every 10 minutes. (Some bread machines are automatically set for 60 minutes; others need to be set by 10-minute intervals.)

5. Once the loaf has reached 200°F (100°C), remove it from the pan immediately and let cool completely on a rack.

Herb Bread

This ever-popular classic loaf has a fragrant aroma that makes waiting for it to bake extremely difficult. Serve it alongside soup, salad or your entrée.

Tips

To ensure success, see page 14 for information on using your bread machine and page 18 for general tips on bread machine baking.

This is an excellent loaf to use for making croutons and bread crumbs. See the Technique Glossary, page 306, for information about bread crumbs.

1½ cups	sorghum flour	375 mL
¾ cup	whole bean flour	175 mL
½ cup	potato starch	125 mL
¼ cup	tapioca starch	60 mL
⅓ cup	granulated sugar	75 mL
1 tbsp	xanthan gum	15 mL
1½ tsp	bread machine or instant yeast	7 mL
1½ tsp	salt	7 mL
½ cup	snipped fresh parsley	125 mL
⅓ cup	snipped fresh marjoram	75 mL
⅓ cup	snipped fresh thyme	75 mL
1¼ cups	water	300 mL
⅓ cup	vegetable oil	75 mL
1 tsp	cider vinegar	5 mL
2	eggs, lightly beaten	2

1. In a large bowl or plastic bag, combine sorghum flour, whole bean flour, potato starch, tapioca starch, sugar, xanthan gum, yeast, salt, parsley, marjoram and thyme; mix well and set aside.

2. Pour water, oil and vinegar into the bread machine baking pan. Add eggs.

3. Select the **Gluten-Free Cycle**. As the bread machine is mixing, gradually add the dry ingredients, scraping bottom and sides of pan with a rubber spatula. Try to incorporate all the dry ingredients within 1 to 2 minutes. When the mixing and kneading are complete, remove the kneading blade, leaving the bread pan in the bread machine. Quickly smooth the top of the loaf. Allow the cycle to finish.

4. At the end of the cycle, take the temperature of the loaf using an instant-read thermometer. It is baked at 200°F (100°C). If it's between 180°F (85°C) and 200°F (100°C), leave machine on the **Keep Warm Cycle** until baked. If it's below 180°F (85°C), turn on the **Bake Cycle** and check the internal temperature every 10 minutes. (Some bread machines are automatically set for 60 minutes; others need to be set by 10-minute intervals.)

5. Once the loaf has reached 200°F (100°C), remove it from the pan immediately and let cool completely on a rack.

Bake an extra loaf to make bread crumbs for a stuffing or dressing for beef, pork or poultry.

See the Technique Glossary, page 307, for information about working with fresh herbs.

Variation
Substitute one-third the amount of dried herbs for the fresh.

Dough Cycle and Bake Cycle

If your bread machine does not have a Gluten-Free Cycle, use the Dough Cycle followed by the Bake Cycle.

1. In a large bowl or plastic bag, combine sorghum flour, whole bean flour, potato starch, tapioca starch, sugar, xanthan gum, yeast, salt, parsley, marjoram and thyme; mix well and set aside.

2. Pour water, oil and vinegar into the bread machine baking pan. Add eggs.

3. Select the **Dough Cycle**. As the bread machine is mixing, gradually add the dry ingredients, scraping bottom and sides of pan with a rubber spatula. Try to incorporate all the dry ingredients within 1 to 2 minutes. When the mixing and kneading are complete, remove the kneading blade, leaving the bread pan in the bread machine. Quickly smooth the top of the loaf. Allow the cycle to finish. Turn off the bread machine.

4. Select the **Bake Cycle**. Set time to 60 minutes and temperature to 350°F (180°C). Allow the cycle to finish. Do not turn machine off before taking the internal temperature of the loaf with an instant-read thermometer. It should be 200°F (100°C). If it's between 180°F (85°C) and 200°F (100°C), leave machine on the **Keep Warm Cycle** until baked. If it's below 180°F (85°C), turn on the **Bake Cycle** and check the internal temperature every 10 minutes. (Some bread machines are automatically set for 60 minutes; others need to be set by 10-minute intervals.)

5. Once the loaf has reached 200°F (100°C), remove it from the pan immediately and let cool completely on a rack.

Oatmeal Bread

*Everyone loves a warm
slice of oatmeal bread.
It's so sweet, yet with a
delightful crunch!*

Tips

To ensure success, see
page 14 for information on
using your bread machine
and page 18 for general tips
on bread machine baking.

The batter will appear
thinner than most as you
are incorporating the dry
ingredients, but it will
thicken; don't adjust any of
the ingredient amounts.

1¾ cups	sorghum flour	425 mL
⅓ cup	GF oats	75 mL
⅓ cup	GF oat flour	75 mL
⅓ cup	GF steel-cut oats	75 mL
⅓ cup	tapioca starch	75 mL
3 tbsp	packed brown sugar	45 mL
1 tbsp	xanthan gum	15 mL
1 tbsp	bread machine or instant yeast	15 mL
1¼ tsp	salt	6 mL
1½ cups	milk, warmed to room temperature	375 mL
2 tbsp	vegetable oil	30 mL
2 tsp	cider vinegar	10 mL
2	eggs, lightly beaten	2

1. In a large bowl or plastic bag, combine sorghum flour, oats, oat flour, steel-cut oats, tapioca starch, brown sugar, xanthan gum, yeast and salt; mix well and set aside.

2. Pour milk, oil and vinegar into the bread machine baking pan. Add eggs.

3. Select the **Gluten-Free Cycle**. As the bread machine is mixing, gradually add the dry ingredients, scraping bottom and sides of pan with a rubber spatula. Try to incorporate all the dry ingredients within 1 to 2 minutes. When the mixing and kneading are complete, remove the kneading blade, leaving the bread pan in the bread machine. Quickly smooth the top of the loaf. Allow the cycle to finish.

4. At the end of the cycle, take the temperature of the loaf using an instant-read thermometer. It is baked at 200°F (100°C). If it's between 180°F (85°C) and 200°F (100°C), leave machine on the **Keep Warm Cycle** until baked. If it's below 180°F (85°C), turn on the **Bake Cycle** and check the internal temperature every 10 minutes. (Some bread machines are automatically set for 60 minutes; others need to be set by 10-minute intervals.)

5. Once the loaf has reached 200°F (100°C), remove it from the pan immediately and let cool completely on a rack.

NUTRITIONAL VALUES per serving	
Calories	144
Fat, total	4 g
Fat, saturated	1 g
Cholesterol	23 mg
Sodium	217 mg
Carbohydrate	24 g
Fiber	3 g
Protein	5 g
Calcium	40 mg
Iron	1 mg

Tips
For instructions on warming milk, see the Technique Glossary, page 308.

You can use ½ cup (125 mL) liquid whole eggs, if you prefer.

Dough Cycle and Bake Cycle

If your bread machine does not have a Gluten-Free Cycle, use the Dough Cycle followed by the Bake Cycle.

1. In a large bowl or plastic bag, combine sorghum flour, oats, oat flour, steel-cut oats, tapioca starch, brown sugar, xanthan gum, yeast and salt; mix well and set aside.

2. Pour milk, oil and vinegar into the bread machine baking pan. Add eggs.

3. Select the **Dough Cycle**. As the bread machine is mixing, gradually add the dry ingredients, scraping bottom and sides of pan with a rubber spatula. Try to incorporate all the dry ingredients within 1 to 2 minutes. When the mixing and kneading are complete, remove the kneading blade, leaving the bread pan in the bread machine. Quickly smooth the top of the loaf. Allow the cycle to finish. Turn off the bread machine.

4. Select the **Bake Cycle**. Set time to 60 minutes and temperature to 350°F (180°C). Allow the cycle to finish. Do not turn machine off before taking the internal temperature of the loaf with an instant-read thermometer. It should be 200°F (100°C). If it's between 180°F (85°C) and 200°F (100°C), leave machine on the **Keep Warm Cycle** until baked. If it's below 180°F (85°C), turn on the **Bake Cycle** and check the internal temperature every 10 minutes. (Some bread machines are automatically set for 60 minutes; others need to be set by 10-minute intervals.)

5. Once the loaf has reached 200°F (100°C), remove it from the pan immediately and let cool completely on a rack.

Mock Rye Loaf

When considering what recipes to include in our Classics chapter, we couldn't leave this one out. It's perfect for making delicious sandwiches from leftover roast beef.

Tip

To ensure success, see page 14 for information on using your bread machine and page 18 for general tips on bread machine baking.

1 cup	sorghum flour	250 mL
¾ cup	whole bean flour	175 mL
½ cup	quinoa flour	125 mL
½ cup	tapioca starch	125 mL
¼ cup	packed brown sugar	60 mL
1 tbsp	xanthan gum	15 mL
1¼ tsp	bread machine or instant yeast	6 mL
1¼ tsp	salt	6 mL
2 tbsp	caraway seeds	30 mL
1¼ cups	water	300 mL
2 tbsp	vegetable oil	30 mL
1 tsp	cider vinegar	5 mL
2	eggs, lightly beaten	2
2	egg whites, lightly beaten	2

1. In a large bowl or plastic bag, combine sorghum flour, whole bean flour, quinoa flour, tapioca starch, brown sugar, xanthan gum, yeast, salt and caraway seeds; mix well and set aside.

2. Pour water, oil and vinegar into the bread machine baking pan. Add eggs and egg whites.

3. Select the **Gluten-Free Cycle**. As the bread machine is mixing, gradually add the dry ingredients, scraping bottom and sides of pan with a rubber spatula. Try to incorporate all the dry ingredients within 1 to 2 minutes. When the mixing and kneading are complete, remove the kneading blade, leaving the bread pan in the bread machine. Quickly smooth the top of the loaf. Allow the cycle to finish.

4. At the end of the cycle, take the temperature of the loaf using an instant-read thermometer. It is baked at 200°F (100°C). If it's between 180°F (85°C) and 200°F (100°C), leave machine on the **Keep Warm Cycle** until baked. If it's below 180°F (85°C), turn on the **Bake Cycle** and check the internal temperature every 10 minutes. (Some bread machines are automatically set for 60 minutes; others need to be set by 10-minute intervals.)

5. Once the loaf has reached 200°F (100°C), remove it from the pan immediately and let cool completely on a rack.

NUTRITIONAL VALUES per serving	
Calories	137
Fat, total	4 g
Fat, saturated	0 g
Cholesterol	22 mg
Sodium	213 mg
Carbohydrate	22 g
Fiber	3 g
Protein	5 g
Calcium	19 mg
Iron	1 mg

Tips
Thoroughly mix the dry ingredients before adding them to the liquids — they are powder-fine and could clump together.

Slice this or any bread with an electric knife for thin, even sandwich slices.

Dough Cycle and Bake Cycle

If your bread machine does not have a Gluten-Free Cycle, use the Dough Cycle followed by the Bake Cycle.

1. In a large bowl or plastic bag, combine sorghum flour, whole bean flour, quinoa flour, tapioca starch, brown sugar, xanthan gum, yeast, salt and caraway seeds; mix well and set aside.

2. Pour water, oil and vinegar into the bread machine baking pan. Add eggs and egg whites.

3. Select the **Dough Cycle**. As the bread machine is mixing, gradually add the dry ingredients, scraping bottom and sides of pan with a rubber spatula. Try to incorporate all the dry ingredients within 1 to 2 minutes. When the mixing and kneading are complete, remove the kneading blade, leaving the bread pan in the bread machine. Quickly smooth the top of the loaf. Allow the cycle to finish. Turn off the bread machine.

4. Select the **Bake Cycle**. Set time to 60 minutes and temperature to 350°F (180°C). Allow the cycle to finish. Do not turn machine off before taking the internal temperature of the loaf with an instant-read thermometer. It should be 200°F (100°C). If it's between 180°F (85°C) and 200°F (100°C), leave machine on the **Keep Warm Cycle** until baked. If it's below 180°F (85°C), turn on the **Bake Cycle** and check the internal temperature every 10 minutes. (Some bread machines are automatically set for 60 minutes; others need to be set by 10-minute intervals.)

5. Once the loaf has reached 200°F (100°C), remove it from the pan immediately and let cool completely on a rack.

Cinnamon Raisin Bread

Our cinnamon raisin bread is an all-time favorite among our readers. Once you've mastered this basic version, you might enjoy trying Grainy Cinnamon Raisin Bread (page 94) or Banana Raisin Bread (page 160).

Tips

To ensure success, see page 14 for information on using your bread machine and page 18 for general tips on bread machine baking.

Thoroughly mix the dry ingredients before adding them to the liquids — they are powder-fine and can clump together.

1¾ cups	brown rice flour	425 mL
½ cup	potato starch	125 mL
¼ cup	tapioca starch	60 mL
½ cup	granulated sugar	125 mL
¼ cup	nonfat dry milk or skim milk powder	60 mL
1 tbsp	xanthan gum	15 mL
1½ tsp	bread machine or instant yeast	7 mL
1¼ tsp	salt	6 mL
1 tbsp	ground cinnamon	15 mL
1½ cups	raisins	375 mL
1 cup	water	250 mL
2 tbsp	vegetable oil	30 mL
2 tsp	cider vinegar	10 mL
2	eggs, lightly beaten	2
2	egg whites, lightly beaten	2

1. In a large bowl or plastic bag, combine brown rice flour, potato starch, tapioca starch, sugar, dry milk, xanthan gum, yeast, salt, cinnamon and raisins; mix well and set aside.

2. Pour water, oil and vinegar into the bread machine baking pan. Add eggs and egg whites.

3. Select the **Gluten-Free Cycle**. As the bread machine is mixing, gradually add the dry ingredients, scraping bottom and sides of pan with a rubber spatula. Try to incorporate all the dry ingredients within 1 to 2 minutes. When the mixing and kneading are complete, remove the kneading blade, leaving the bread pan in the bread machine. Quickly smooth the top of the loaf. Allow the cycle to finish.

4. At the end of the cycle, take the temperature of the loaf using an instant-read thermometer. It is baked at 200°F (100°C). If it's between 180°F (85°C) and 200°F (100°C), leave machine on the **Keep Warm Cycle** until baked. If it's below 180°F (85°C), turn on the **Bake Cycle** and check the internal temperature every 10 minutes. (Some bread machines are automatically set for 60 minutes; others need to be set by 10-minute intervals.)

5. Once the loaf has reached 200°F (100°C), remove it from the pan immediately and let cool completely on a rack.

NUTRITIONAL VALUES
per serving

Calories	205
Fat, total	3 g
Fat, saturated	0 g
Cholesterol	22 mg
Sodium	223 mg
Carbohydrate	42 g
Fiber	2 g
Protein	4 g
Calcium	31 mg
Iron	1 mg

Dough Cycle and Bake Cycle

If your bread machine does not have a Gluten-Free Cycle,
use the Dough Cycle followed by the Bake Cycle.

1. In a large bowl or plastic bag, combine brown rice flour,
   potato starch, tapioca starch, sugar, dry milk, xanthan
   gum, yeast, salt, cinnamon and raisins; mix well and
   set aside.

2. Pour water, oil and vinegar into the bread machine
   baking pan. Add eggs and egg whites.

3. Select the **Dough Cycle**. As the bread machine is
   mixing, gradually add the dry ingredients, scraping
   bottom and sides of pan with a rubber spatula. Try
   to incorporate all the dry ingredients within 1 to
   2 minutes. When the mixing and kneading are
   complete, remove the kneading blade, leaving the
   bread pan in the bread machine. Quickly smooth
   the top of the loaf. Allow the cycle to finish. Turn off
   the bread machine.

4. Select the **Bake Cycle**. Set time to 60 minutes and
   temperature to 350°F (180°C). Allow the cycle to
   finish. Do not turn machine off before taking the
   internal temperature of the loaf with an instant-read
   thermometer. It should be 200°F (100°C). If it's
   between 180°F (85°C) and 200°F (100°C), leave
   machine on the **Keep Warm Cycle** until baked. If
   it's below 180°F (85°C), turn on the **Bake Cycle** and
   check the internal temperature every 10 minutes. (Some
   bread machines are automatically set for 60 minutes;
   others need to be set by 10-minute intervals.)

5. Once the loaf has reached 200°F (100°C), remove it
   from the pan immediately and let cool completely on
   a rack.

Cheese Bread

We knew a whole new batch of readers would want to try our fantastic cheese bread. It's a perfect accompaniment to homemade chili or beef stew.

Tips

To ensure success, see page 14 for information on using your bread machine and page 18 for general tips on bread machine baking.

For the amount of cheese to purchase, see the weight/volume equivalents in the Ingredient Glossary, page 301.

1²⁄₃ cups	brown rice flour	400 mL
²⁄₃ cup	sorghum flour	150 mL
¹⁄₃ cup	tapioca starch	75 mL
²⁄₃ cup	buttermilk powder	150 mL
2 tbsp	granulated sugar	30 mL
1 tbsp	xanthan gum	15 mL
1¹⁄₂ tsp	bread machine or instant yeast	7 mL
1¹⁄₄ tsp	salt	6 mL
1 cup	shredded sharp (old) Cheddar cheese	250 mL
¹⁄₄ cup	freshly grated Parmesan cheese	60 mL
¹⁄₄ tsp	dry mustard	1 mL
1¹⁄₄ cups	water	300 mL
2 tsp	cider vinegar	10 mL
2	eggs, lightly beaten	2
2	egg whites, lightly beaten	2

1. In a large bowl or plastic bag, combine brown rice flour, sorghum flour, tapioca starch, buttermilk powder, sugar, xanthan gum, yeast, salt, Cheddar, Parmesan and mustard; mix well and set aside.

2. Pour water and vinegar into the bread machine baking pan. Add eggs and egg whites.

3. Select the **Gluten-Free Cycle**. As the bread machine is mixing, gradually add the dry ingredients, scraping bottom and sides of pan with a rubber spatula. Try to incorporate all the dry ingredients within 1 to 2 minutes. When the mixing and kneading are complete, remove the kneading blade, leaving the bread pan in the bread machine. Quickly smooth the top of the loaf. Allow the cycle to finish.

4. At the end of the cycle, take the temperature of the loaf using an instant-read thermometer. It is baked at 200°F (100°C). If it's between 180°F (85°C) and 200°F (100°C), leave machine on the **Keep Warm Cycle** until baked. If it's below 180°F (85°C), turn on the **Bake Cycle** and check the internal temperature every 10 minutes. (Some bread machines are automatically set for 60 minutes; others need to be set by 10-minute intervals.)

5. Once the loaf has reached 200°F (100°C), remove it from the pan immediately and let cool completely on a rack.

NUTRITIONAL VALUES
per serving

Calories	171
Fat, total	5 g
Fat, saturated	2 g
Cholesterol	34 mg
Sodium	325 mg
Carbohydrate	26 g
Fiber	2 g
Protein	8 g
Calcium	153 mg
Iron	1 mg

Tip

This bread slices well and stays moist for a second day.

Variation

You can replace the Cheddar cheese with Monterey Jack or Swiss cheese. Or try a combination, but do not exceed the total volume in the recipe or the loaf will be short and heavy.

Dough Cycle and Bake Cycle

If your bread machine does not have a Gluten-Free Cycle, use the Dough Cycle followed by the Bake Cycle.

1. In a large bowl or plastic bag, combine brown rice flour, sorghum flour, tapioca starch, buttermilk powder, sugar, xanthan gum, yeast, salt, Cheddar, Parmesan and mustard; mix well and set aside.

2. Pour water and vinegar into the bread machine baking pan. Add eggs and egg whites.

3. Select the **Dough Cycle**. As the bread machine is mixing, gradually add the dry ingredients, scraping bottom and sides of pan with a rubber spatula. Try to incorporate all the dry ingredients within 1 to 2 minutes. When the mixing and kneading are complete, remove the kneading blade, leaving the bread pan in the bread machine. Quickly smooth the top of the loaf. Allow the cycle to finish. Turn off the bread machine.

4. Select the **Bake Cycle**. Set time to 60 minutes and temperature to 350°F (180°C). Allow the cycle to finish. Do not turn machine off before taking the internal temperature of the loaf with an instant-read thermometer. It should be 200°F (100°C). If it's between 180°F (85°C) and 200°F (100°C), leave machine on the **Keep Warm Cycle** until baked. If it's below 180°F (85°C), turn on the **Bake Cycle** and check the internal temperature every 10 minutes. (Some bread machines are automatically set for 60 minutes; others need to be set by 10-minute intervals.)

5. Once the loaf has reached 200°F (100°C), remove it from the pan immediately and let cool completely on a rack.

Twice-Baked Potato Bread

This flavorful loaf with a warm, creamy color is a perfect way to use fresh herbs from your garden.

Tip

To ensure success, see page 14 for information on using your bread machine and page 18 for general tips on bread machine baking.

1⅓ cups	brown rice flour	325 mL
1 cup	almond flour	250 mL
¾ cup	amaranth flour	175 mL
1 tbsp	xanthan gum	15 mL
1 tbsp	bread machine or instant yeast	15 mL
1½ tsp	salt	7 mL
⅓ cup	snipped fresh chives	75 mL
¼ cup	snipped fresh parsley	60 mL
1¼ cups	water	300 mL
2 tbsp	extra virgin olive oil	30 mL
3 tbsp	liquid honey	45 mL
1 tbsp	cider vinegar	15 mL
1 cup	mashed baked potato (see tip, at right)	250 mL
2	eggs, lightly beaten	2
2	egg whites, lightly beaten	2

1. In a large bowl or plastic bag, combine brown rice flour, almond flour, amaranth flour, xanthan gum, yeast, salt, chives and parsley; mix well and set aside.

2. Pour water, oil, honey, vinegar and potato into the bread machine baking pan. Add eggs and egg whites.

3. Select the **Gluten-Free Cycle**. As the bread machine is mixing, gradually add the dry ingredients, scraping bottom and sides of pan with a rubber spatula. Try to incorporate all the dry ingredients within 1 to 2 minutes. When the mixing and kneading are complete, remove the kneading blade, leaving the bread pan in the bread machine. Quickly smooth the top of the loaf. Allow the cycle to finish.

4. At the end of the cycle, take the temperature of the loaf using an instant-read thermometer. It is baked at 200°F (100°C). If it's between 180°F (85°C) and 200°F (100°C), leave machine on the **Keep Warm Cycle** until baked. If it's below 180°F (85°C), turn on the **Bake Cycle** and check the internal temperature every 10 minutes. (Some bread machines are automatically set for 60 minutes; others need to be set by 10-minute intervals.)

5. Once the loaf has reached 200°F (100°C), remove it from the pan immediately and let cool completely on a rack.

NUTRITIONAL VALUES per serving	
Calories	189
Fat, total	8 g
Fat, saturated	1 g
Cholesterol	22 mg
Sodium	389 mg
Carbohydrate	26 g
Fiber	3 g
Protein	6 g
Calcium	41 mg
Iron	1 mg

Tips

One large potato yields about 1 cup (250 mL) mashed. Do not add butter or salt when mashing.

The mashed potato contains enough starch that we did not have to add more. Choose older (not new) potatoes for a higher starch content.

Dough Cycle and Bake Cycle

If your bread machine does not have a Gluten-Free Cycle, use the Dough Cycle followed by the Bake Cycle.

1. In a large bowl or plastic bag, combine brown rice flour, almond flour, amaranth flour, xanthan gum, yeast, salt, chives and parsley; mix well and set aside.

2. Pour water, oil, honey, vinegar and potato into the bread machine baking pan. Add eggs and egg whites.

3. Select the **Dough Cycle**. As the bread machine is mixing, gradually add the dry ingredients, scraping bottom and sides of pan with a rubber spatula. Try to incorporate all the dry ingredients within 1 to 2 minutes. When the mixing and kneading are complete, remove the kneading blade, leaving the bread pan in the bread machine. Quickly smooth the top of the loaf. Allow the cycle to finish. Turn off the bread machine.

4. Select the **Bake Cycle**. Set time to 60 minutes and temperature to 350°F (180°C). Allow the cycle to finish. Do not turn machine off before taking the internal temperature of the loaf with an instant-read thermometer. It should be 200°F (100°C). If it's between 180°F (85°C) and 200°F (100°C), leave machine on the **Keep Warm Cycle** until baked. If it's below 180°F (85°C), turn on the **Bake Cycle** and check the internal temperature every 10 minutes. (Some bread machines are automatically set for 60 minutes; others need to be set by 10-minute intervals.)

5. Once the loaf has reached 200°F (100°C), remove it from the pan immediately and let cool completely on a rack.

French Baguette

MAKES TWO 12-INCH (30 CM) LOAVES, 12 SLICES EACH (1 slice per serving)

Everyone needs a baguette recipe in their repertoire. Like countless fans of our previous book, you'll be amazed by the texture of this crusty loaf.

Tips

To ensure success, see page 14 for information on using your bread machine and page 18 for general tips on bread machine baking.

See the Equipment Glossary, page 298, for information about baguette pans.

◆ **Baguette pan or baking sheet, lightly greased, then lined with parchment paper and sprinkled with cornmeal**

2 cups	brown rice flour	500 mL
2/3 cup	potato starch	150 mL
2 tsp	granulated sugar	10 mL
2 tsp	xanthan gum	10 mL
2 tsp	bread machine or instant yeast	10 mL
1 1/2 tsp	salt	7 mL
1 1/2 cups	water	375 mL
2 tsp	cider vinegar	10 mL
2	egg whites, lightly beaten	2

1. In a large bowl or plastic bag, combine brown rice flour, potato starch, sugar, xanthan gum, yeast and salt; mix well and set aside.

2. Pour water and vinegar into the bread machine baking pan. Add egg whites.

3. Select the **Dough Cycle**. As the bread machine is mixing, gradually add the dry ingredients, scraping bottom and sides of pan with a rubber spatula. Try to incorporate all the dry ingredients within 1 to 2 minutes. Stop bread machine as soon as the kneading portion of the cycle is complete. Do not let bread machine finish the cycle.

NUTRITIONAL VALUES per serving	
Calories	110
Fat, total	1 g
Fat, saturated	0 g
Cholesterol	0 mg
Sodium	244 mg
Carbohydrate	25 g
Fiber	1 g
Protein	2 g
Calcium	1 mg
Iron	0 mg

Tips

Be sure to store this bread loosely covered in a paper bag to maintain the crisp crust.

Use an electric or serrated bladed knife to thickly slice these loaves on the diagonal.

Slice leftover loaf into 1-inch (2.5 cm) thick slices to use for Classic French Onion Soup (see our recipe in *250 Gluten-Free Favorites*, page 120).

Variation

Make 6 mini loaves or 1 large loaf. Bake large loaf for 30 to 35 minutes or minis for 20 to 25 minutes or until internal temperature registers 200°F (100°C).

4. Divide dough in half and place into each half of prepared pan or onto the baking sheet in the shape of a baguette. Place parallel to each other in prepared pan, at least 3 inches (7.5 cm) apart. Using the edge of a moistened rubber spatula or a sharp knife, draw three or four diagonal lines, $1/4$ inch (0.5 cm) deep, across the top of each loaf. Let rise, uncovered, in a warm, draft-free place for 50 minutes. Meanwhile, preheat oven to 425°F (220°C).

5. Bake for 20 to 23 minutes or until internal temperature of loaves registers 200°F (100°C) on an instant-read thermometer. Remove from the pan immediately and let cool completely on a rack.

Challah

A braided egg bread, challah is traditionally served for the Jewish Sabbath. Our version, baked in a round pan, is closer to the traditional Jewish New Year crown shape.

Tips

To ensure success, see page 14 for information on using your bread machine and page 18 for general tips on bread machine baking.

It is important to tent this bread with foil; otherwise, the crust becomes very dark and could burn.

Variation

Add ¾ cup (175 mL) raisins with the dry ingredients.

NUTRITIONAL VALUES
per serving

Calories	137
Fat, total	5 g
Fat, saturated	0 g
Cholesterol	21 mg
Sodium	169 mg
Carbohydrate	22 g
Fiber	1 g
Protein	3 g
Calcium	35 mg
Iron	1 mg

◆ **8-inch (20 cm) round baking pan, lightly greased**

1 cup	brown rice flour	250 mL
⅓ cup	quinoa flour	75 mL
¼ cup	almond flour	60 mL
⅓ cup	tapioca starch	75 mL
¼ cup	potato starch	60 mL
1 tbsp	xanthan gum	15 mL
1 tbsp	bread machine or instant yeast	15 mL
1 tsp	salt	5 mL
½ cup	nonfat dry milk or skim milk powder	125 mL
1 cup	water	250 mL
3 tbsp	vegetable oil	45 mL
⅓ cup	liquid honey	75 mL
1 tsp	cider vinegar	5 mL
2	eggs, lightly beaten	2

1. In a large bowl or plastic bag, combine brown rice flour, quinoa flour, almond flour, tapioca starch, potato starch, xanthan gum, yeast, salt and dry milk; mix well and set aside.

2. Pour water, oil, honey and vinegar into the bread machine baking pan. Add eggs.

3. Select the **Dough Cycle**. As the bread machine is mixing, gradually add the dry ingredients, scraping bottom and sides of pan with a rubber spatula. Try to incorporate all the dry ingredients within 1 to 2 minutes. Stop bread machine as soon as the kneading portion of the cycle is complete. Do not let bread machine finish the cycle.

4. Gently transfer dough to prepared pan and spread to edges with a moistened rubber spatula. Let rise, uncovered, in a warm, draft-free place for 45 to 55 minutes or until risen almost to the top of the pan. Meanwhile, preheat oven to 350°F (180°C).

5. Bake for 30 to 35 minutes, tenting with foil after 15 minutes, until internal temperature of loaf registers 200°F (100°C) on an instant-read thermometer. Remove from the pan immediately and let cool completely on a rack.

Hamburger Buns

**MAKES 6
HAMBURGER BUNS
(1 per serving)**

Here's another classic recipe, as basic white bread rolls are always in demand. Though formed into the traditional shape for hamburger buns, these rolls are also great for sandwiches or as a dinner accompaniment.

Tips

To ensure success, see page 14 for information on using your bread machine and page 18 for general tips on bread machine baking.

If you don't have a hamburger bun pan, try a cast-iron corncob-shaped bread pan or English muffin rings, or make free-form buns on a lightly greased baking sheet. Decrease the water by 2 tbsp (30 mL) for free-form buns.

NUTRITIONAL VALUES per serving	
Calories	413
Fat, total	12 g
Fat, saturated	1 g
Cholesterol	55 mg
Sodium	645 mg
Carbohydrate	72 g
Fiber	3 g
Protein	8 g
Calcium	46 mg
Iron	1 mg

◆ **Hamburger bun baking pan, lightly greased**

1¾ cups	brown rice flour	425 mL
⅔ cup	potato starch	150 mL
⅓ cup	tapioca starch	75 mL
¼ cup	nonfat dry milk or skim milk powder	60 mL
¼ cup	granulated sugar	60 mL
2½ tsp	xanthan gum	12 mL
1 tbsp	bread machine or instant yeast	15 mL
1½ tsp	salt	7 mL
1¼ cups	water	300 mL
¼ cup	vegetable oil	60 mL
1 tsp	cider vinegar	5 mL
2	eggs, lightly beaten	2
2	egg whites, lightly beaten	2

1. In a large bowl or plastic bag, combine brown rice flour, potato starch, tapioca starch, dry milk, sugar, xanthan gum, yeast and salt; mix well and set aside.

2. Pour water, oil and vinegar into the bread machine baking pan. Add eggs and egg whites.

3. Select the **Dough Cycle**. As the bread machine is mixing, gradually add the dry ingredients, scraping bottom and sides of pan with a rubber spatula. Try to incorporate all the dry ingredients within 1 to 2 minutes. Stop bread machine as soon as the kneading portion of the cycle is complete. Do not let bread machine finish the cycle.

4. Spoon ⅔ cup (150 mL) dough into each cup of prepared pan (see tip, at left), mounding toward the center of each bun. Smooth the tops with a moistened rubber spatula. Let rise in a warm, draft-free place for 30 to 45 minutes or until the dough has almost doubled in volume. Do not allow dough to over-rise. Meanwhile, preheat oven to 350°F (180°C).

5. Bake for 18 to 23 minutes or until internal temperature of buns registers 200°F (100°C) on an instant-read thermometer. Remove from the pan immediately and let cool completely on a rack.

Yogurt Pan Rolls

These soft-sided rolls have the slight tang of yogurt.

Tips

To ensure success, see page 14 for information on using your bread machine and page 18 for general tips on bread machine baking.

◆ **9-inch (23 cm) square baking pan, lightly greased**

1 cup	almond flour	250 mL
1 cup	brown rice flour	250 mL
½ cup	amaranth flour	125 mL
½ cup	potato starch	125 mL
2½ tsp	xanthan gum	12 mL
2 ½ tsp	bread machine or instant yeast	12 mL
1¼ tsp	salt	6 mL
1½ cups	plain yogurt	375 mL
¼ cup	vegetable oil	60 mL
3 tbsp	liquid honey	45 mL
2	eggs, lightly beaten	2
2	egg whites, lightly beaten	2

1. In a large bowl or plastic bag, combine almond flour, brown rice flour, amaranth flour, potato starch, xanthan gum, yeast and salt; mix well and set aside.

2. Pour yogurt, oil and honey into the bread machine baking pan. Add eggs and egg whites.

3. Select the **Dough Cycle**. As the bread machine is mixing, gradually add the dry ingredients, scraping bottom and sides of pan with a rubber spatula. Try to incorporate all the dry ingredients within 1 to 2 minutes. Stop bread machine as soon as the kneading portion of the cycle is complete. Do not let bread machine finish the cycle.

4. Using a ¼-cup (60 mL) scoop, divide dough into 16 equal amounts and arrange in four rows of four in prepared pan. Let rise, uncovered, in a warm, draft-free place for 60 minutes. Meanwhile, preheat oven to 350°F (180°C).

5. Bake for 22 to 24 minutes or until internal temperature of rolls registers 200°F (100°C) on an instant-read thermometer. Remove from the pan immediately and let cool completely on a rack.

NUTRITIONAL VALUES per serving	
Calories	178
Fat, total	8 g
Fat, saturated	1 g
Cholesterol	22 mg
Sodium	218 mg
Carbohydrate	22 g
Fiber	2 g
Protein	5 g
Calcium	66 mg
Iron	1 mg

Artisan Breads

Once you've mastered the basic recipes in our Classics chapter, it's time to expand your taste horizons, with tangy sourdoughs, hearty batards and other artisan delights, from loaves and mini loaves to buns and rolls.

Teff Sourdough Starter

3 cups	warm water	750 mL
2 tbsp	granulated sugar	30 mL
2 tbsp	bread machine or instant yeast	30 mL
3 cups	teff flour	750 mL

You loved our sourdough breads in 125 Best Gluten-Free Bread Machine Recipes, *but many of you wondered how you could make them even more nutritious. The answer is teff flour!*

Tips

If the starter liquid turns green, pink or orange — or develops mold — throw it out and start again.

During hot weather, use a triple layer of cheesecloth to cover the sourdough starter when it is at room temperature. A loose-fitting lid on a large casserole dish works well too.

1. In a very large glass bowl, combine water and sugar. Sprinkle with yeast, gently stir to moisten and let stand for 10 minutes.

2. Add teff flour and whisk until smooth.

3. Cover with a double layer of cheesecloth or a loose-fitting lid. Secure so that it is not touching the starter. Let stand at room temperature for 2 to 4 days, stirring two to three times a day. When ready to use, starter has a sour smell, with small bubbles rising to the surface.

4. Store, loosely covered, in the refrigerator until needed. If not used regularly, stir in 1 tsp (5 mL) granulated sugar every 10 days.

NUTRITIONAL VALUES per serving	
Calories	435
Fat, total	4 g
Fat, saturated	0 g
Cholesterol	0 mg
Sodium	24 mg
Carbohydrate	85 g
Fiber	15 g
Protein	16 g
Calcium	176 mg
Iron	8 mg

Tips for Successful Starters

Using the Starter

- It is normal for a starter to separate. The grayish liquid rises to the top, while the very thick part settles to the bottom of the storage container. Stir well before each use.

- The starter should have the consistency of pancake batter. If it's too thick, add a small amount of water before measuring.

- After refrigerating, bring the starter to room temperature by placing it in a bowl of warm water for 15 minutes before measuring.

- Until the starter becomes established and is working well, remove only 1 cup (250 mL) at a time.

- Make sure all utensils and pans that come into contact with the starter go through the dishwasher or are sanitized with a mild solution of water and bleach.

Feeding the Starter

- To replace each cup (250 mL) of starter used in preparing a recipe, add to the remaining starter:

¾ cup	water	175 mL
¾ cup	teff flour	175 mL
1 tsp	granulated sugar	5 mL

  Stir well, cover with a double layer of cheesecloth or a loose-fitting lid and let stand at room temperature for at least 24 hours or until bubbly and sour-smelling. Refrigerate, loosely covered.

- If not used regularly, stir in 1 tsp (5 mL) granulated sugar every 10 days.

Sourdough Teff Loaf

Our basic sourdough loaf is only improved by the use of good-for-you teff flour, which gives the bread a warm chocolate color if you use brown teff.

Tip

To ensure success, see page 14 for information on using your bread machine, page 18 for general tips on bread machine baking and page 61 for tips on using and feeding the starter.

1 cup	brown rice flour	250 mL
2/3 cup	teff flour	150 mL
1/2 cup	potato starch	125 mL
2 tbsp	granulated sugar	30 mL
1 tbsp	xanthan gum	15 mL
1 tbsp	bread machine or instant yeast	15 mL
1 1/2 tsp	salt	7 mL
1 cup	Teff Sourdough Starter (page 60), at room temperature	250 mL
1/2 cup	water	125 mL
1/4 cup	vegetable oil	60 mL
2	eggs, lightly beaten	2
2	egg whites, lightly beaten	2

1. In a large bowl or plastic bag, combine brown rice flour, teff flour, potato starch, sugar, xanthan gum, yeast and salt; mix well and set aside.

2. Pour sourdough starter, water and oil into the bread machine baking pan. Add eggs and egg whites.

3. Select the **Gluten-Free Cycle**. As the bread machine is mixing, gradually add the dry ingredients, scraping bottom and sides of pan with a rubber spatula. Try to incorporate all the dry ingredients within 1 to 2 minutes. When the mixing and kneading are complete, remove the kneading blade, leaving the bread pan in the bread machine. Quickly smooth the top of the loaf. Allow the cycle to finish.

4. At the end of the cycle, take the temperature of the loaf using an instant-read thermometer. It is baked at 200°F (100°C). If it's between 180°F (85°C) and 200°F (100°C), leave machine on the **Keep Warm Cycle** until baked. If it's below 180°F (85°C), turn on the **Bake Cycle** and check the internal temperature every 10 minutes. (Some bread machines are automatically set for 60 minutes; others need to be set by 10-minute intervals.)

5. Once the loaf has reached 200°F (100°C), remove it from the pan immediately and let cool completely on a rack.

NUTRITIONAL VALUES
per serving

Calories	161
Fat, total	5 g
Fat, saturated	1 g
Cholesterol	22 mg
Sodium	254 mg
Carbohydrate	26 g
Fiber	3 g
Protein	4 g
Calcium	26 mg
Iron	1 mg

Dough Cycle and Bake Cycle

If your bread machine does not have a Gluten-Free Cycle, use the Dough Cycle followed by the Bake Cycle.

1. In a large bowl or plastic bag, combine brown rice flour, teff flour, potato starch, sugar, xanthan gum, yeast and salt; mix well and set aside.

2. Pour sourdough starter, water and oil into the bread machine baking pan. Add eggs and egg whites.

3. Select the **Dough Cycle**. As the bread machine is mixing, gradually add the dry ingredients, scraping bottom and sides of pan with a rubber spatula. Try to incorporate all the dry ingredients within 1 to 2 minutes. When the mixing and kneading are complete, remove the kneading blade, leaving the bread pan in the bread machine. Quickly smooth the top of the loaf. Allow the cycle to finish. Turn off the bread machine.

4. Select the **Bake Cycle**. Set time to 60 minutes and temperature to 350°F (180°C). Allow the cycle to finish. Do not turn machine off before taking the internal temperature of the loaf with an instant-read thermometer. It should be 200°F (100°C). If it's between 180°F (85°C) and 200°F (100°C), leave machine on the **Keep Warm Cycle** until baked. If it's below 180°F (85°C), turn on the **Bake Cycle** and check the internal temperature every 10 minutes. (Some bread machines are automatically set for 60 minutes; others need to be set by 10-minute intervals.)

5. Once the loaf has reached 200°F (100°C), remove it from the pan immediately and let cool completely on a rack.

Sourdough Teff Brown Bread

If you liked our Sourdough Brown Bread, you're going to absolutely love this version, made with teff flour in the starter.

Tips

To ensure success, see page 14 for information on using your bread machine, page 18 for general tips on bread machine baking and page 61 for tips on using and feeding the starter.

Don't forget about the sourdough starter sitting in your refrigerator. If you haven't used it to make a loaf in the last 10 days, see page 61 for information on feeding it.

1 cup	sorghum flour	250 mL
2/3 cup	whole bean flour	150 mL
1/3 cup	tapioca starch	75 mL
1 tbsp	xanthan gum	15 mL
1 tbsp	bread machine or instant yeast	15 mL
1¼ tsp	salt	6 mL
1 cup	Teff Sourdough Starter (page 60), at room temperature	250 mL
½ cup	water	125 mL
2 tbsp	vegetable oil	30 mL
3 tbsp	liquid honey	45 mL
2 tbsp	light (fancy) molasses	30 mL
2	eggs, lightly beaten	2

1. In a large bowl or plastic bag, combine sorghum flour, whole bean flour, tapioca starch, xanthan gum, yeast and salt; mix well and set aside.

2. Pour sourdough starter, water, oil, honey and molasses into the bread machine baking pan. Add eggs.

3. Select the **Gluten-Free Cycle**. As the bread machine is mixing, gradually add the dry ingredients, scraping bottom and sides of pan with a rubber spatula. Try to incorporate all the dry ingredients within 1 to 2 minutes. When the mixing and kneading are complete, remove the kneading blade, leaving the bread pan in the bread machine. Quickly smooth the top of the loaf. Allow the cycle to finish.

4. At the end of the cycle, take the temperature of the loaf using an instant-read thermometer. It is baked at 200°F (100°C). If it's between 180°F (85°C) and 200°F (100°C), leave machine on the **Keep Warm Cycle** until baked. If it's below 180°F (85°C), turn on the **Bake Cycle** and check the internal temperature every 10 minutes. (Some bread machines are automatically set for 60 minutes; others need to be set by 10-minute intervals.)

5. Once the loaf has reached 200°F (100°C), remove it from the pan immediately and let cool completely on a rack.

NUTRITIONAL VALUES
per serving

Calories	147
Fat, total	3 g
Fat, saturated	0 g
Cholesterol	22 mg
Sodium	207 mg
Carbohydrate	25 g
Fiber	3 g
Protein	5 g
Calcium	29 mg
Iron	2 mg

Tip

It is easier to measure honey and molasses if they are warmed in the microwave for a few seconds, or set in a pan of hot water for a few minutes. Measure the oil first, then measure the honey and molasses; they will slide off the measuring spoon more easily that way.

Variation

Substitute ¼ cup (60 mL) packed brown sugar for the honey and the molasses.

Dough Cycle and Bake Cycle

If your bread machine does not have a Gluten-Free Cycle, use the Dough Cycle followed by the Bake Cycle.

1. In a large bowl or plastic bag, combine sorghum flour, whole bean flour, tapioca starch, xanthan gum, yeast and salt; mix well and set aside.

2. Pour sourdough starter, water, oil, honey and molasses into the bread machine baking pan. Add eggs.

3. Select the **Dough Cycle**. As the bread machine is mixing, gradually add the dry ingredients, scraping bottom and sides of pan with a rubber spatula. Try to incorporate all the dry ingredients within 1 to 2 minutes. When the mixing and kneading are complete, remove the kneading blade, leaving the bread pan in the bread machine. Quickly smooth the top of the loaf. Allow the cycle to finish. Turn off the bread machine.

4. Select the **Bake Cycle**. Set time to 60 minutes and temperature to 350°F (180°C). Allow the cycle to finish. Do not turn machine off before taking the internal temperature of the loaf with an instant-read thermometer. It should be 200°F (100°C). If it's between 180°F (85°C) and 200°F (100°C), leave machine on the **Keep Warm Cycle** until baked. If it's below 180°F (85°C), turn on the **Bake Cycle** and check the internal temperature every 10 minutes. (Some bread machines are automatically set for 60 minutes; others need to be set by 10-minute intervals.)

5. Once the loaf has reached 200°F (100°C), remove it from the pan immediately and let cool completely on a rack.

Sourdough Teff Walnut Raisin Bread

MAKES 15 SLICES
(1 per serving)

Our original Sourdough Walnut Bread was already packed with nutritious goodness, but this new version offers added protein, calcium, thiamin, iron and fiber, thanks to the teff flour, and a boost of antioxidants from the raisins.

Tip

To ensure success, see page 14 for information on using your bread machine, page 18 for general tips on bread machine baking and page 61 for tips on using and feeding the starter.

1¼ cups	amaranth flour	300 mL
⅔ cup	teff flour	150 mL
⅔ cup	tapioca starch	150 mL
¼ cup	packed brown sugar	60 mL
1 tbsp	xanthan gum	15 mL
1 tbsp	bread machine or instant yeast	15 mL
1¼ tsp	salt	6 mL
1 cup	coarsely chopped toasted walnuts	250 mL
½ cup	raisins	125 mL
1 cup	Teff Sourdough Starter (page 60), at room temperature	250 mL
⅔ cup	water	150 mL
2 tbsp	vegetable oil	30 mL
2	eggs, lightly beaten	2
2	egg whites, lightly beaten	2

1. In a large bowl or plastic bag, combine amaranth flour, teff flour, tapioca starch, brown sugar, xanthan gum, yeast, salt, walnuts and raisins; mix well and set aside.

2. Pour sourdough starter, water and oil into the bread machine baking pan. Add eggs and egg whites.

3. Select the **Gluten-Free Cycle**. As the bread machine is mixing, gradually add the dry ingredients, scraping bottom and sides of pan with a rubber spatula. Try to incorporate all the dry ingredients within 1 to 2 minutes. When the mixing and kneading are complete, remove the kneading blade, leaving the bread pan in the bread machine. Quickly smooth the top of the loaf. Allow the cycle to finish.

4. At the end of the cycle, take the temperature of the loaf using an instant-read thermometer. It is baked at 200°F (100°C). If it's between 180°F (85°C) and 200°F (100°C), leave machine on the **Keep Warm Cycle** until baked. If it's below 180°F (85°C), turn on the **Bake Cycle** and check the internal temperature every 10 minutes. (Some bread machines are automatically set for 60 minutes; others need to be set by 10-minute intervals.)

5. Once the loaf has reached 200°F (100°C), remove it from the pan immediately and let cool completely on a rack.

NUTRITIONAL VALUES per serving	
Calories	209
Fat, total	8 g
Fat, saturated	1 g
Cholesterol	0 mg
Sodium	210 mg
Carbohydrate	31 g
Fiber	4 g
Protein	6 g
Calcium	46 mg
Iron	2 mg

See the Technique Glossary, page 308, for information on toasting walnuts. Don't skip this step, as it really makes a difference to the flavor of the loaf.

Always store bread at room temperature or wrapped airtight in the freezer. The refrigerator accelerates the staling process.

Dough Cycle and Bake Cycle

If your bread machine does not have a Gluten-Free Cycle, use the Dough Cycle followed by the Bake Cycle.

1. In a large bowl or plastic bag, combine amaranth flour, teff flour, tapioca starch, brown sugar, xanthan gum, yeast, salt, walnuts and raisins; mix well and set aside.

2. Pour sourdough starter, water and oil into the bread machine baking pan. Add eggs and egg whites.

3. Select the **Dough Cycle**. As the bread machine is mixing, gradually add the dry ingredients, scraping bottom and sides of pan with a rubber spatula. Try to incorporate all the dry ingredients within 1 to 2 minutes. When the mixing and kneading are complete, remove the kneading blade, leaving the bread pan in the bread machine. Quickly smooth the top of the loaf. Allow the cycle to finish. Turn off the bread machine.

4. Select the **Bake Cycle**. Set time to 60 minutes and temperature to 350°F (180°C). Allow the cycle to finish. Do not turn machine off before taking the internal temperature of the loaf with an instant-read thermometer. It should be 200°F (100°C). If it's between 180°F (85°C) and 200°F (100°C), leave machine on the **Keep Warm Cycle** until baked. If it's below 180°F (85°C), turn on the **Bake Cycle** and check the internal temperature every 10 minutes. (Some bread machines are automatically set for 60 minutes; others need to be set by 10-minute intervals.)

5. Once the loaf has reached 200°F (100°C), remove it from the pan immediately and let cool completely on a rack.

Sourdough Teff Savory Ciabatta

Our Sourdough Savory Ciabatta gets rave reviews, and the addition of teff flour only makes it that much better!

Tips

To ensure success, see page 14 for information on using your bread machine, page 18 for general tips on bread machine baking and page 61 for tips on using and feeding the starter.

We like this ciabatta best served hot out of the oven.

◆ **8-inch (20 cm) round baking pan, lightly greased and floured with teff flour**

1/2 cup	amaranth flour	125 mL
1/3 cup	teff flour	75 mL
1/4 cup	tapioca starch	60 mL
1 tbsp	granulated sugar	15 mL
2 tsp	xanthan gum	10 mL
2 tbsp	bread machine or instant yeast	30 mL
1/2 tsp	salt	2 mL
1/3 cup	packed fresh savory leaves (see tip, at right), snipped	75 mL
1 cup	Teff Sourdough Starter (page 60), at room temperature	250 mL
1/4 cup	water	60 mL
2 tbsp	extra virgin olive oil	30 mL
2	eggs, lightly beaten	2
1 to 2 tbsp	teff flour	15 to 30 mL

1. In a large bowl or plastic bag, combine amaranth flour, teff flour, tapioca starch, sugar, xanthan gum, yeast, salt and savory; mix well and set aside.

2. Pour sourdough starter, water and oil into the bread machine baking pan. Add eggs.

3. Select the **Dough Cycle**. As the bread machine is mixing, gradually add the dry ingredients, scraping bottom and sides of pan with a rubber spatula. Try to incorporate all the dry ingredients within 1 to 2 minutes. Stop bread machine as soon as the kneading portion of the cycle is complete. Do not let bread machine finish the cycle.

Tips

If fresh savory is not available, use one-third the amount of dried savory. Or substitute an equal amount of your favorite herb — rosemary, thyme or cilantro work well, to name a few.

When dusting with teff flour, use a flour sifter for a light, even sprinkle.

This bread freezes well. Cut into wedges and freeze individually for sandwiches.

4. Gently transfer dough to prepared pan and spread evenly to the edges, leaving the top rough and uneven. Lightly dust top with teff flour. With well-floured fingers, make deep indents all over the dough, pressing all the way down to the pan. Let rise, uncovered, in a warm, draft-free place for 40 to 50 minutes or until almost doubled in volume. Meanwhile, preheat oven to 425°F (220°C).

5. Bake for 14 to 16 minutes or until top is golden. Remove from the pan immediately and let cool on a rack. Cut into 8 wedges and serve warm.

Teff Baguette

These loaves are just what you think of when you hear the word "baguette": crunchy on the outside, but with a softer interior. If you use brown teff flour, the dough will be the color of a milk chocolate cake batter.

Tips

To ensure success, see page 14 for information on using your bread machine and page 18 for general tips on bread machine baking.

See the Equipment Glossary, page 298, for information about baguette pans.

◆ **Baguette pan or baking sheet, lightly greased, then lined with parchment paper and sprinkled with cornmeal**

1½ cups	teff flour	375 mL
½ cup	brown rice flour	125 mL
⅔ cup	potato starch	150 mL
2 tsp	granulated sugar	10 mL
2 tsp	xanthan gum	10 mL
1 tbsp	bread machine or instant yeast	15 mL
1½ tsp	salt	7 mL
1½ cups	water	375 mL
2 tsp	cider vinegar	10 mL
2	egg whites, lightly beaten	2

1. In a large bowl or plastic bag, combine teff flour, brown rice flour, potato starch, sugar, xanthan gum, yeast and salt; mix well and set aside.

2. Pour water and vinegar into the bread machine baking pan. Add egg whites.

3. Select the **Dough Cycle**. As the bread machine is mixing, gradually add the dry ingredients, scraping bottom and sides of pan with a rubber spatula. Try to incorporate all the dry ingredients within 1 to 2 minutes. Stop bread machine as soon as the kneading portion of the cycle is complete. Do not let bread machine finish the cycle.

NUTRITIONAL VALUES per serving	
Calories	75
Fat, total	0 g
Fat, saturated	0 g
Cholesterol	0 mg
Sodium	183 mg
Carbohydrate	16 g
Fiber	2 g
Protein	2 g
Calcium	16 mg
Iron	1 mg

Tips

Be sure to store this bread loosely covered in a paper bag to maintain the crisp crust.

Use an electric or serrated bladed knife to thickly slice these loaves on the diagonal.

Variation

Make 6 mini loaves or 1 large loaf. Bake the large loaf for 30 to 35 minutes, or the minis for 20 to 25 minutes, until internal temperature registers 200°F (100°C).

4. Divide dough in half and form each half into the shape of a baguette. Place parallel to each other in prepared pan, at least 3 inches (7.5 cm) apart. Using the edge of a moistened rubber spatula or a sharp knife, draw three or four diagonal lines, $1/4$ inch (0.5 cm) deep, across the top of each loaf. Let rise, uncovered, in a warm, draft-free place for 50 minutes. Meanwhile, preheat oven to 425°F (220°C).

5. Bake for 20 to 23 minutes or until internal temperature of loaves registers 200°F (100°C) on an instant-read thermometer. Remove from the pan immediately and let cool completely on a rack.

Après Ski Batard

*Heather's sister, Bonnie,
enjoys the crunch of
millet, flax and pumpkin
seeds in a baguette. She
uses slices of this bread as
a base for hors d' oeuvres.*

Tips

To ensure success, see
page 14 for information on
using your bread machine
and page 18 for general tips
on bread machine baking.

See the Equipment Glossary,
page 298, for information
about baguette pans.

◆ **Baguette pan or baking sheet, lined with parchment
paper**

1½ cups	sorghum flour	375 mL
½ cup	quinoa flour	125 mL
⅔ cup	potato starch	150 mL
2 tsp	xanthan gum	10 mL
1 tbsp	bread machine or instant yeast	15 mL
1½ tsp	salt	7 mL
⅓ cup	millet seed	75 mL
⅓ cup	cracked flaxseed	75 mL
¼ cup	unsalted green pumpkin seeds	60 mL
1½ cups	water	375 mL
2 tbsp	vegetable oil	30 mL
1 tbsp	liquid honey	15 mL
2 tsp	cider vinegar	10 mL
2	egg whites, lightly beaten	2

1. In a large bowl or plastic bag, combine sorghum flour,
quinoa flour, potato starch, xanthan gum, yeast, salt, millet
seed, flaxseed and pumpkin seeds; mix well and set aside.

2. Pour water, oil, honey and vinegar into the bread machine
baking pan. Add egg whites.

3. Select the **Dough Cycle**. As the bread machine is mixing,
gradually add the dry ingredients, scraping bottom and
sides of pan with a rubber spatula. Try to incorporate all
the dry ingredients within 1 to 2 minutes. Stop bread
machine as soon as the kneading portion of the cycle is
complete. Do not let bread machine finish the cycle.

NUTRITIONAL VALUES per serving	
Calories	102
Fat, total	3 g
Fat, saturated	0 g
Cholesterol	0 mg
Sodium	153 mg
Carbohydrate	17 g
Fiber	2 g
Protein	3 g
Calcium	8 mg
Iron	1 mg

Tips

Store this bread loosely covered in a paper bag to maintain the crisp crust.

Use an electric or serrated knife to thickly slice these sticks on the diagonal.

Variation

Make 6 mini loaves or 1 large loaf. Bake the large loaf for 30 to 35 minutes, or the minis for 20 to 25 minutes, until internal temperature registers 200°F (100°C).

4. Divide dough in half and form each half into the shape of a batard (wide baguette). Place parallel to each other in prepared pan, at least 3 inches (7.5 cm) apart. Using the edge of a moistened rubber spatula or a sharp knife, draw three or four diagonal lines, ¼ inch (0.5 cm) deep, across the top of each loaf. Let rise, uncovered, in a warm, draft-free place for 75 minutes. Meanwhile, preheat oven to 425°F (220°C).

5. Bake for 22 to 25 minutes or until internal temperature of loaves registers 200°F (100°C) on an instant-read thermometer. Remove from the pan immediately and let cool completely on a rack.

Rice-Free Multi-Seed Batard

MAKES TWO 12-INCH (30 CM) LOAVES, 12 SLICES EACH
(1 slice per serving)

You asked for a rice-free version of our batard — try this one! Toasting the seeds makes all the difference in the flavor.

Tips

To ensure success, see page 14 for information on using your bread machine and page 18 for general tips on bread machine baking.

For information on toasting seeds, see the Technique Glossary, page 309.

◆ **Baguette pan or baking sheet, lightly greased, then lined with parchment paper**

1½ cups	sorghum flour	375 mL
½ cup	quinoa flour	125 mL
⅔ cup	potato starch	150 mL
2 tsp	granulated sugar	10 mL
2 tsp	xanthan gum	10 mL
1 tbsp	bread machine or instant yeast	15 mL
¾ tsp	salt	3 mL
⅓ cup	unsalted green pumpkin seeds	75 mL
⅓ cup	unsalted raw sunflower seeds, toasted	75 mL
¼ cup	sesame seeds, toasted	60 mL
1½ cups	water	375 mL
2 tbsp	cider vinegar	30 mL
2	egg whites, lightly beaten	2

1. In a large bowl or plastic bag, combine sorghum flour, quinoa flour, potato starch, sugar, xanthan gum, yeast, salt, pumpkin seeds, sunflower seeds and sesame seeds; mix well and set aside.

2. Pour water and vinegar into the bread machine baking pan. Add egg whites.

3. Select the **Dough Cycle**. As the bread machine is mixing, gradually add the dry ingredients, scraping bottom and sides of pan with a rubber spatula. Try to incorporate all the dry ingredients within 1 to 2 minutes. Stop bread machine as soon as the kneading portion of the cycle is complete. Do not let bread machine finish the cycle.

NUTRITIONAL VALUES per serving	
Calories	91
Fat, total	3 g
Fat, saturated	0 g
Cholesterol	0 mg
Sodium	82 mg
Carbohydrate	14 g
Fiber	2 g
Protein	3 g
Calcium	8 mg
Iron	1 m

See the Equipment Glossary, page 298, for information about baguette pans.

Store this bread loosely covered in a paper bag to maintain the crisp crust.

Use an electric or serrated knife to thickly slice these loaves on the diagonal.

4. Divide dough in half and form each half into the shape of a batard (wide baguette). Place parallel to each other in prepared pan, at least 3 inches (7.5 cm) apart. Using the edge of a moistened rubber spatula or a sharp knife, draw three or four diagonal lines, $\frac{1}{4}$ inch (0.5 cm) deep, across the top of each loaf. Let rise, uncovered, in a warm, draft-free place for 75 minutes. Meanwhile, preheat oven to 425°F (220°C).

5. Bake for 22 to 25 minutes or until internal temperature of loaves registers 200°F (100°C) on an instant-read thermometer. Remove from the pan immediately and let cool completely on a rack.

Russian Black Bread

MAKES 15 SLICES
(1 per serving)

This heavy, dense bread has a deeper flavor than most pumpernickels, thanks to the coffee, cocoa, molasses and caraway.

Tips

To ensure success, see page 14 for information on using your bread machine and page 18 for general tips on bread machine baking

Sift the cocoa powder before measuring.

1 cup	whole bean flour	250 mL
1 cup	yellow pea flour	250 mL
½ cup	potato starch	125 mL
⅓ cup	tapioca starch	75 mL
½ cup	buttermilk powder	125 mL
3 tbsp	packed brown sugar	45 mL
2½ tsp	xanthan gum	12 mL
1 tbsp	bread machine or instant yeast	15 mL
1½ tsp	salt	7 mL
1 tbsp	unsweetened cocoa powder, sifted	15 mL
2 tbsp	caraway seeds	30 mL
1½ cups	freshly brewed coffee, at room temperature	375 mL
3 tbsp	vegetable oil	45 mL
3 tbsp	light (fancy) molasses	45 mL
2 tbsp	cider vinegar	30 mL
2	eggs, lightly beaten	2
2	egg whites, lightly beaten	2

1. In a large bowl or plastic bag, combine whole bean flour, yellow pea flour, potato starch, tapioca starch, buttermilk powder, brown sugar, xanthan gum, yeast, salt, cocoa and caraway seeds; mix well and set aside.

2. Pour coffee, oil, molasses and vinegar into the bread machine baking pan. Add eggs and egg whites.

3. Select the **Gluten-Free Cycle**. As the bread machine is mixing, gradually add the dry ingredients, scraping bottom and sides of pan with a rubber spatula. Try to incorporate all the dry ingredients within 1 to 2 minutes. When the mixing and kneading are complete, remove the kneading blade, leaving the bread pan in the bread machine. Quickly smooth the top of the loaf. Allow the cycle to finish.

4. At the end of the cycle, take the temperature of the loaf using an instant-read thermometer. It is baked at 200°F (100°C). If it's between 180°F (85°C) and 200°F (100°C), leave machine on the **Keep Warm Cycle** until baked. If it's below 180°F (85°C), turn on the **Bake Cycle** and check the internal temperature every 10 minutes. (Some bread machines are automatically set for 60 minutes; others need to be set by 10-minute intervals.)

NUTRITIONAL VALUES per serving	
Calories	187
Fat, total	5 g
Fat, saturated	1 g
Cholesterol	25 mg
Sodium	277 mg
Carbohydrate	29 g
Fiber	5 g
Protein	8 g
Calcium	85 mg
Iron	2 mg

Tip

Measuring the oil before the molasses ensures that the molasses slides out of the measure. If the molasses is really thick or is straight out of the refrigerator, warm it slightly in the microwave before measuring.

Variation

For an even deeper flavor, add an extra 1 to 2 tsp (5 to 10 mL) of unsweetened cocoa powder.

5. Once the loaf has reached 200°F (100°C), remove it from the pan immediately and let cool completely on a rack.

Dough Cycle and Bake Cycle

If your bread machine does not have a Gluten-Free Cycle, use the Dough Cycle followed by the Bake Cycle.

1. In a large bowl or plastic bag, combine whole bean flour, yellow pea flour, potato starch, tapioca starch, buttermilk powder, brown sugar, xanthan gum, yeast, salt, cocoa and caraway seeds; mix well and set aside.

2. Pour coffee, oil, molasses and vinegar into the bread machine baking pan. Add eggs and egg whites.

3. Select the **Dough Cycle**. As the bread machine is mixing, gradually add the dry ingredients, scraping bottom and sides of pan with a rubber spatula. Try to incorporate all the dry ingredients within 1 to 2 minutes. When the mixing and kneading are complete, remove the kneading blade, leaving the bread pan in the bread machine. Quickly smooth the top of the loaf. Allow the cycle to finish. Turn off the bread machine.

4. Select the **Bake Cycle**. Set time to 60 minutes and temperature to 350°F (180°C). Allow the cycle to finish. Do not turn machine off before taking the internal temperature of the loaf with an instant-read thermometer. It should be 200°F (100°C). If it's between 180°F (85°C) and 200°F (100°C), leave machine on the **Keep Warm Cycle** until baked. If it's below 180°F (85°C), turn on the **Bake Cycle** and check the internal temperature every 10 minutes. (Some bread machines are automatically set for 60 minutes; others need to be set by 10-minute intervals.)

5. Once the loaf has reached 200°F (100°C), remove it from the pan immediately and let cool completely on a rack.

Hazelnut Buckwheat Loaf

This warm brown loaf with great buckwheat flavor is studded with tasty chunks of hazelnuts.

Tips

To ensure success, see page 14 for information on using your bread machine and page 18 for general tips on bread machine baking.

Make sure buckwheat is on your list of allowable foods before you try this recipe.

1⅓ cups	whole bean flour	325 mL
¾ cup	buckwheat flour	175 mL
¼ cup	hazelnut flour	60 mL
⅔ cup	tapioca starch	150 mL
1 tbsp	xanthan gum	15 mL
1½ tsp	bread machine or instant yeast	7 mL
1¼ tsp	salt	6 mL
1 tsp	ground nutmeg	5 mL
1 cup	toasted chopped hazelnuts	250 mL
1¾ cups	water	425 mL
¼ cup	vegetable oil	60 mL
3 tbsp	liquid buckwheat honey	45 mL
1 tbsp	light (fancy) molasses	15 mL
1 tsp	cider vinegar	5 mL
2	eggs, lightly beaten	2

1. In a large bowl or plastic bag, combine whole bean flour, buckwheat flour, hazelnut flour, tapioca starch, xanthan gum, yeast, salt, nutmeg and hazelnuts; mix well and set aside.

2. Pour water, oil, buckwheat honey, molasses and vinegar into the bread machine baking pan. Add eggs.

3. Select the **Gluten-Free Cycle**. As the bread machine is mixing, gradually add the dry ingredients, scraping bottom and sides of pan with a rubber spatula. Try to incorporate all the dry ingredients within 1 to 2 minutes. When the mixing and kneading are complete, remove the kneading blade, leaving the bread pan in the bread machine. Quickly smooth the top of the loaf. Allow the cycle to finish.

4. At the end of the cycle, take the temperature of the loaf using an instant-read thermometer. It is baked at 200°F (100°C). If it's between 180°F (85°C) and 200°F (100°C), leave machine on the **Keep Warm Cycle** until baked. If it's below 180°F (85°C), turn on the **Bake Cycle** and check the internal temperature every 10 minutes. (Some bread machines are automatically set for 60 minutes; others need to be set by 10-minute intervals.)

5. Once the loaf has reached 200°F (100°C), remove it from the pan immediately and let cool completely on a rack.

NUTRITIONAL VALUES
per serving

Calories	212
Fat, total	11 g
Fat, saturated	1 g
Cholesterol	22 mg
Sodium	204 mg
Carbohydrate	24 g
Fiber	4 g
Protein	6 g
Calcium	31 mg
Iron	2 mg

See the Technique Glossary, page 308, for information on toasting nuts.

Variations
Substitute orange blossom or regular liquid honey if buckwheat honey isn't available.

Dough Cycle and Bake Cycle

If your bread machine does not have a Gluten-Free Cycle, use the Dough Cycle followed by the Bake Cycle.

1. In a large bowl or plastic bag, combine whole bean flour, buckwheat flour, hazelnut flour, tapioca starch, xanthan gum, yeast, salt, nutmeg and hazelnuts; mix well and set aside.

2. Pour water, oil, buckwheat honey, molasses and vinegar into the bread machine baking pan. Add eggs.

3. Select the **Dough Cycle**. As the bread machine is mixing, gradually add the dry ingredients, scraping bottom and sides of pan with a rubber spatula. Try to incorporate all the dry ingredients within 1 to 2 minutes. When the mixing and kneading are complete, remove the kneading blade, leaving the bread pan in the bread machine. Quickly smooth the top of the loaf. Allow the cycle to finish. Turn off the bread machine.

4. Select the **Bake Cycle**. Set time to 60 minutes and temperature to 350°F (180°C). Allow the cycle to finish. Do not turn machine off before taking the internal temperature of the loaf with an instant-read thermometer. It should be 200°F (100°C). If it's between 180°F (85°C) and 200°F (100°C), leave machine on the **Keep Warm Cycle** until baked. If it's below 180°F (85°C), turn on the **Bake Cycle** and check the internal temperature every 10 minutes. (Some bread machines are automatically set for 60 minutes; others need to be set by 10-minute intervals.)

5. Once the loaf has reached 200°F (100°C), remove it from the pan immediately and let cool completely on a rack.

Chocolate Almond Bread

**MAKES 4 LOAVES,
6 SLICES EACH**
(1 slice per serving)

*The bittersweet
smoothness of chocolate,
the tang of yogurt and
the crunch of almonds
combine to create a loaf
that has become one of
our favorites!*

Tips

To ensure success, see
page 14 for information on
using your bread machine
and page 18 for general tips
on bread machine baking.

You can use mini or jumbo
chocolate chips in place of
the chocolate chunks, or just
stick with the regular size.

See the Technique Glossary,
page 308, for information
on toasting almonds.

◆ **Four 5³⁄4- by 3¹⁄4-inch (14 by 8 cm) loaf pans, lightly
greased**

1¹⁄2 cups	sorghum flour	375 mL
¹⁄2 cup	whole bean flour	125 mL
¹⁄2 cup	tapioca starch	125 mL
1 tbsp	xanthan gum	15 mL
2¹⁄2 tsp	bread machine or instant yeast	12 mL
1¹⁄4 tsp	salt	6 mL
¹⁄4 cup	unsweetened cocoa powder, sifted	60 mL
³⁄4 cup	semisweet or bittersweet (dark) chocolate chunks	175 mL
¹⁄2 cup	toasted slivered almonds	125 mL
2 tbsp	grated orange zest	30 mL
1¹⁄4 cups	plain yogurt	300 mL
¹⁄2 cup	freshly squeezed orange juice	125 mL
¹⁄4 cup	vegetable oil	60 mL
¹⁄3 cup	liquid honey	75 mL
2 tsp	cider vinegar	10 mL
2	eggs, lightly beaten	2
2	egg whites, lightly beaten	2

1. In a large bowl or plastic bag, combine sorghum flour,
   whole bean flour, tapioca starch, xanthan gum, yeast,
   salt, cocoa, chocolate chunks, almonds and orange zest;
   mix well and set aside.

2. Pour yogurt, orange juice, oil, honey and vinegar into the
   bread machine baking pan. Add eggs and egg whites.

NUTRITIONAL VALUES per serving	
Calories	145
Fat, total	6 g
Fat, saturated	2 g
Cholesterol	14 mg
Sodium	141 mg
Carbohydrate	20 g
Fiber	2 g
Protein	4 g
Calcium	35 mg
Iron	1 mg

Tips

Use a zester to make long, thin strips of orange zest. Be sure to remove only the colored outer layer, avoiding the bitter white pith beneath.

Freshly squeezed orange juice enhances the flavor of this loaf. Roll the orange on the counter or between your hands to loosen the juice.

Keep an orange in the freezer. Zest while frozen, then juice after warming in the microwave.

Variations

Use two 7½- by 3½-inch (18 by 8.5 cm) baking pans and bake for 36 to 40 minutes.

For a stronger almond flavor add 2 tsp (10 mL) almond extract.

3. Select the **Dough Cycle**. As the bread machine is mixing, gradually add the dry ingredients, scraping bottom and sides of pan with a rubber spatula. Try to incorporate all the dry ingredients within 1 to 2 minutes. Stop bread machine as soon as the kneading portion of the cycle is complete. Do not let bread machine finish the cycle.

4. Spoon dough into prepared pans, dividing evenly. Let rise, uncovered, in a warm, draft-free place for 60 minutes. Meanwhile, preheat oven to 350°F (180°C).

5. Bake for 33 to 38 minutes or until internal temperature of loaves registers 200°F (100°C) on an instant-read thermometer. Remove from the pan immediately and serve warm.

Crunchy Seed Mini Loaves

**MAKES 4 LOAVES,
6 SLICES EACH**
(1 slice per serving)

*Try these soft-textured
loaves if you enjoy a
bread with some crunch
to it.*

Tips

To ensure success, see
page 14 for information on
using your bread machine
and page 18 for general tips
on bread machine baking.

To prevent seeds from
becoming rancid, store them
in an airtight container in
the refrigerator.

For information on cracking
flaxseed, see the Technique
Glossary, page 307.

NUTRITIONAL VALUES per serving	
Calories	102
Fat, total	5 g
Fat, saturated	0 g
Cholesterol	14 mg
Sodium	134 mg
Carbohydrate	13 g
Fiber	2 g
Protein	4 g
Calcium	19 mg
Iron	1 mg

◆ **Four 5³⁄₄- by 3¹⁄₄-inch (14 by 8 cm) loaf pans, lightly greased**

1 cup	sorghum flour	250 mL
1/2 cup	whole bean flour	125 mL
1/4 cup	flax flour	60 mL
1/2 cup	tapioca starch	125 mL
1/4 cup	packed brown sugar	60 mL
1 tbsp	xanthan gum	15 mL
2 tsp	bread machine or instant yeast	10 mL
1 1/4 tsp	salt	6 mL
1/3 cup	unsalted raw sunflower seeds	75 mL
1/4 cup	cracked flaxseed	60 mL
1/4 cup	unsalted green pumpkin seeds	60 mL
2 tbsp	sesame seeds	30 mL
1 1/4 cups	water	300 mL
2 tbsp	vegetable oil	30 mL
1 tsp	cider vinegar	5 mL
2	eggs, lightly beaten	2
2	egg whites, lightly beaten	2

1. In a large bowl or plastic bag, combine sorghum flour, whole bean flour, flax flour, tapioca starch, brown sugar, xanthan gum, yeast, salt, sunflower seeds, flaxseed, pumpkin seeds and sesame seeds; mix well and set aside.

2. Pour water, oil and vinegar into the bread machine baking pan. Add eggs and egg whites.

Variations

Use two 7$\frac{1}{2}$- by 3$\frac{1}{2}$-inch (18 by 8.5 cm) baking pans and bake for 36 to 40 minutes.

For extra crunch, lightly brush the risen dough with water and sprinkle an extra 1 tsp (5 mL) sesame seeds on top of each loaf just before baking.

3. Select the **Dough Cycle**. As the bread machine is mixing, gradually add the dry ingredients, scraping bottom and sides of pan with a rubber spatula. Try to incorporate all the dry ingredients within 1 to 2 minutes. Stop bread machine as soon as the kneading portion of the cycle is complete. Do not let bread machine finish the cycle.

4. Spoon dough into prepared pans, dividing evenly. Let rise, uncovered, in a warm, draft-free place for 60 to 75 minutes or until dough has mounded slightly over the top of the pans. Meanwhile, preheat oven to 350°F (180°C).

5. Bake for 30 to 35 minutes or until internal temperature of loaves registers 200°F (100°C) on an instant-read thermometer. Remove from the pan immediately and let cool completely on a rack.

Hawaiian Mini Loaves

Bring the fragrance and flavor of the Hawaiian Islands to your table with these light loaves that will remind you of angel food cake.

Tips

To ensure success, see page 14 for information on using your bread machine and page 18 for general tips on bread machine baking.

The candied fruit is added with the liquids, as the sugary syrup coating makes it stick to the dry ingredients.

◆ **Two 7$\frac{1}{2}$- by 3$\frac{1}{2}$-inch (18 by 8.5 cm) loaf pans, lightly greased**

1 cup	brown rice flour	250 mL
$\frac{1}{2}$ cup	coconut flour	125 mL
$\frac{1}{2}$ cup	potato starch	125 mL
1 tbsp	xanthan gum	15 mL
2 tsp	bread machine or instant yeast	10 mL
$\frac{1}{2}$ tsp	salt	2 mL
$\frac{1}{4}$ cup	shredded unsweetened coconut	60 mL
$\frac{1}{4}$ cup	coarsely chopped unsalted macadamia nuts	60 mL
1$\frac{1}{2}$ cups	water	375 mL
2 tbsp	vegetable oil	30 mL
3 tbsp	liquid honey	45 mL
1 tbsp	cider vinegar	15 mL
2 tsp	almond extract	10 mL
2	eggs, lightly beaten	2
2	egg whites, lightly beaten	2
$\frac{1}{2}$ cup	chopped mixed candied fruit	125 mL

1. In a large bowl or plastic bag, combine brown rice flour, coconut flour, potato starch, xanthan gum, yeast, salt, coconut and macadamia nuts; mix well and set aside.

2. Pour water, oil, honey, vinegar and almond extract into the bread machine baking pan. Add eggs, egg whites and candied fruit.

NUTRITIONAL VALUES per serving	
Calories	165
Fat, total	7 g
Fat, saturated	3 g
Cholesterol	21 mg
Sodium	99 mg
Carbohydrate	25 g
Fiber	2 g
Protein	3 g
Calcium	8 mg
Iron	1 mg

Variations

Substitute raisins for some of the candied fruit.

To make these loaves nut-free, omit the nuts and almond extract, and increase the coconut by ¼ cup (60 mL).

To make smaller loaves for gifts, use four 5¾- by 3¼-inch (14 by 8 cm) loaf pans and bake for 33 to 38 minutes.

3. Select the **Dough Cycle**. As the bread machine is mixing, gradually add the dry ingredients, scraping bottom and sides of pan with a rubber spatula. Try to incorporate all the dry ingredients within 1 to 2 minutes. Stop bread machine as soon as the kneading portion of the cycle is complete. Do not let bread machine finish the cycle.

4. Spoon dough into prepared pans, dividing evenly. Let rise, uncovered, in a warm, draft-free place for 75 minutes. Meanwhile, preheat oven to 350°F (180°C).

5. Bake for 38 to 42 minutes or until internal temperature of loaves registers 200°F (100°C) on an instant-read thermometer. Remove from the pan immediately and let cool completely on a rack.

Bacon Cheddar Mini Loaves

**MAKES 2 LOAVES,
8 SLICES EACH
(1 slice per serving)**

The smoky flavor of the bacon and the sharpness of the Cheddar will have you coming back for a second slice.

Tip

To ensure success, see page 14 for information on using your bread machine and page 18 for general tips on bread machine baking.

◆ **Two 7$^{1}/_{2}$- by 3$^{1}/_{2}$-inch (18 by 8.5 cm) loaf pans, lightly greased**

1$^{2}/_{3}$ cups	brown rice flour	400 mL
$^{2}/_{3}$ cup	sorghum flour	150 mL
$^{1}/_{3}$ cup	arrowroot starch	75 mL
$^{1}/_{4}$ cup	nonfat dry milk or skim milk powder	60 mL
2 tbsp	granulated sugar	30 mL
1 tbsp	xanthan gum	15 mL
1$^{1}/_{2}$ tsp	bread machine or instant yeast	7 mL
1$^{1}/_{4}$ tsp	salt	6 mL
1 cup	shredded sharp (old) Cheddar cheese	250 mL
$^{1}/_{4}$ cup	freshly grated Parmesan cheese	60 mL
6	slices GF bacon, cooked crisp and crumbled	6
$^{1}/_{2}$ tsp	dry mustard	2 mL
1$^{1}/_{4}$ cups	water	300 mL
1 tbsp	cider vinegar	15 mL
2	eggs, lightly beaten	2
2	egg whites, lightly beaten	2

1. In a large bowl or plastic bag, combine brown rice flour, sorghum flour, arrowroot starch, dry milk, sugar, xanthan gum, yeast, salt, Cheddar, Parmesan, bacon and mustard; mix well and set aside.

2. Pour water and vinegar into the bread machine baking pan. Add eggs and egg whites.

NUTRITIONAL VALUES per serving	
Calories	159
Fat, total	5 g
Fat, saturated	2 g
Cholesterol	32 mg
Sodium	343 mg
Carbohydrate	23 g
Fiber	2 g
Protein	7 g
Calcium	90 mg
Iron	1 mg

3. Select the **Dough Cycle**. As the bread machine is mixing, gradually add the dry ingredients, scraping bottom and sides of pan with a rubber spatula. Try to incorporate all the dry ingredients within 1 to 2 minutes. Stop bread machine as soon as the kneading portion of the cycle is complete. Do not let bread machine finish the cycle.

4. Spoon dough into prepared pans, dividing evenly. Let rise, uncovered, in a warm, draft-free place for 75 minutes. Meanwhile, preheat oven to 350°F (180°C).

5. Bake for 30 to 35 minutes or until internal temperature of loaves registers 200°F (100°C) on an instant-read thermometer. Remove from the pan immediately and let cool completely on a rack.

Whole-Grain Hamburger Buns

**MAKES 6
HAMBURGER BUNS
(1 per serving)**

*Take advantage of the
extra nutrition in these
whole-grain hamburger
buns. We like to use
them for sandwiches too!*

Tips

To ensure success, see
page 14 for information on
using your bread machine
and page 18 for general tips
on bread machine baking.

Smooth the tops with a
water-moistened rubber
spatula.

If you don't have a
hamburger bun pan, try a
cast-iron corncob-shaped
bread pan or English muffin
rings, or make free-form
buns on a lightly greased
baking sheet. Decrease the
water by 2 tbsp (30 mL) for
free-form buns.

NUTRITIONAL VALUES
per serving

Calories	401
Fat, total	10 g
Fat, saturated	1 g
Cholesterol	55 mg
Sodium	535 mg
Carbohydrate	72 g
Fiber	7 g
Protein	10 g
Calcium	30 mg
Iron	4 mg

◆ **Hamburger bun baking pan, lightly greased**

1½ cups	brown rice flour	375 mL
1 cup	sorghum flour	250 mL
⅓ cup	cornstarch	75 mL
½ cup	rice bran	125 mL
1 tbsp	xanthan gum	15 mL
1½ tsp	bread machine or instant yeast	7 mL
1¼ tsp	salt	6 mL
1¼ cups	water	300 mL
2 tbsp	vegetable oil	30 mL
2 tbsp	liquid honey	30 mL
2 tbsp	light (fancy) molasses	30 mL
1 tsp	cider vinegar	5 mL
2	eggs, lightly beaten	2
2	egg whites, lightly beaten	2

1. In a large bowl or plastic bag, combine brown rice flour, sorghum flour, cornstarch, rice bran, xanthan gum, yeast and salt; mix well and set aside.

2. Pour water, oil, honey, molasses and vinegar into the bread machine baking pan. Add eggs and egg whites.

3. Select the **Dough Cycle**. As the bread machine is mixing, gradually add the dry ingredients, scraping bottom and sides of pan with a rubber spatula. Try to incorporate all the dry ingredients within 1 to 2 minutes. Stop bread machine as soon as the kneading portion of the cycle is complete. Do not let bread machine finish the cycle.

4. Spoon ⅔ cup (150 mL) dough into each cup of prepared pan (see tip, at left), mounding toward the center of each bun. Smooth the tops with a moistened rubber spatula. Let rise in a warm, draft-free place for 30 to 45 minutes or until the dough has almost doubled in volume. Do not allow dough to over-rise. Meanwhile, preheat oven to 350°F (180°C).

5. Bake for 15 to 20 minutes or until internal temperature of buns registers 200°F (100°C) on an instant-read thermometer. Remove from the pan immediately and let cool completely on a rack.

Asiago Herb Pan Rolls

**MAKES 16 ROLLS
(1 per serving)**

Yogurt and Asiago cheese lend these soft-sided rolls a pleasant tang.

Tips

To ensure success, see page 14 for information on using your bread machine and page 18 for general tips on bread machine baking.

For the amount of cheese to purchase, see the weight/volume equivalents in the Ingredient Glossary, page 300.

Variations

Use three 5¾- by 3¼-inch (14 by 8 cm) loaf pans, lightly greased, and bake for 30 to 35 minutes.

To add heat to the bread, add ¼ tsp (1 mL) cayenne pepper.

NUTRITIONAL VALUES
per serving

Calories	191
Fat, total	9 g
Fat, saturated	2 g
Cholesterol	25 mg
Sodium	215 mg
Carbohydrate	24 g
Fiber	2 g
Protein	6 g
Calcium	91 mg
Iron	1 mg

◆ **9-inch (23 cm) square baking pan, lightly greased**

1¼ cups	brown rice flour	300 mL
¾ cup	almond flour	175 mL
½ cup	amaranth flour	125 mL
½ cup	potato starch	125 mL
2½ tsp	xanthan gum	12 mL
2½ tsp	bread machine or instant yeast	12 mL
1 tsp	salt	5 mL
½ cup	shredded Asiago cheese	125 mL
1 tsp	dried basil	5 mL
1 tsp	fennel seeds	5 mL
1 tsp	dried oregano	5 mL
1½ cups	plain yogurt	375 mL
¼ cup	vegetable oil	60 mL
3 tbsp	liquid honey	45 mL
2	eggs, lightly beaten	2
2	egg whites, lightly beaten	2

1. In a large bowl or plastic bag, combine brown rice flour, almond flour, amaranth flour, potato starch, xanthan gum, yeast, salt, Asiago cheese, basil, fennel seeds and oregano; mix well and set aside.

2. Pour yogurt, oil and honey into the bread machine baking pan. Add eggs and egg whites.

3. Select the **Dough Cycle**. As the bread machine is mixing, gradually add the dry ingredients, scraping bottom and sides of pan with a rubber spatula. Try to incorporate all the dry ingredients within 1 to 2 minutes. Stop bread machine as soon as the kneading portion of the cycle is complete. Do not let bread machine finish the cycle.

4. Using a ¼-cup (60 mL) scoop, divide dough into 16 equal amounts and arrange in four rows of four in prepared pan. Let rise, uncovered, in a warm, draft-free place for 60 to 75 minutes or until dough has risen to the top of the pan. Meanwhile, preheat oven to 350°F (180°C).

5. Bake for 22 to 24 minutes or until internal temperature of rolls registers 200°F (100°C) on an instant-read thermometer. Remove from the pan immediately and let cool completely on a rack.

Alpine Rolls

MAKES 12 ROLLS
(1 per serving)

Granola lends these rolls an interesting mix of seeds, nuts and dried fruits.

Tips

To ensure success, see page 14 for information on using your bread machine and page 18 for general tips on bread machine baking.

Choose a lower-fat, unsweetened GF granola for this recipe. Try one of ours, such as Heather's Granola from *250 Gluten-Free Favorites* or Linda's Granola from *Easy Everyday Gluten-Free Cooking.*

Variation

Replace the sunflower seeds with unsalted green pumpkin seeds.

◆ **12-cup muffin tin, lightly greased**

1½ cups	sorghum flour	375 mL
⅓ cup	amaranth flour	75 mL
¾ cup	GF granola	175 mL
⅓ cup	potato starch	75 mL
¼ cup	tapioca starch	60 mL
2½ tsp	xanthan gum	12 mL
1 tbsp	bread machine or instant yeast	15 mL
1¼ tsp	salt	6 mL
½ cup	unsalted raw sunflower seeds	125 mL
1⅓ cups	water	325 mL
2 tbsp	vegetable oil	30 mL
2 tbsp	liquid honey	30 mL
2 tsp	cider vinegar	10 mL
2	eggs, lightly beaten	2
2	egg whites, lightly beaten	2

1. In a large bowl or plastic bag, combine sorghum flour, amaranth flour, granola, potato starch, tapioca starch, xanthan gum, yeast, salt and sunflower seeds; mix well and set aside.

2. Pour water, oil, honey and vinegar into the bread machine baking pan. Add eggs and egg whites.

3. Select the **Dough Cycle**. As the bread machine is mixing, gradually add the dry ingredients, scraping bottom and sides of pan with a rubber spatula. Try to incorporate all the dry ingredients within 1 to 2 minutes. Stop bread machine as soon as the kneading portion of the cycle is complete. Do not let bread machine finish the cycle.

4. Using a ¼-cup (60 mL) scoop, divide dough into 12 equal amounts and place in cups of prepared muffin tin. Let rise, uncovered, in a warm, draft-free place for 45 minutes. Meanwhile, preheat oven to 350°F (180°C).

5. Bake for 20 to 22 minutes or until internal temperature of rolls registers 200°F (100°C) on an instant-read thermometer. Remove from the pan immediately and let cool completely on a rack.

Hearty Whole Grains

These hearty, nutritious breads will stave off hunger longer. They're great for toast in the morning or a packed lunch at noon.

Country Grains Bread

Slices of this nutritious, moist loaf carry easily for lunch.

Tips

To ensure success, see page 14 for information on using your bread machine and page 18 for general tips on bread machine baking.

Measuring the oil before the molasses ensures that the molasses slides out of the measure. If the molasses is really thick or is straight out of the refrigerator, warm it slightly in the microwave before measuring.

1 cup	sorghum flour	250 mL
¾ cup	teff flour	175 mL
¾ cup	cornmeal	175 mL
¼ cup	quinoa flour	60 mL
½ cup	tapioca starch	125 mL
¼ cup	packed brown sugar	60 mL
1 tbsp	xanthan gum	15 mL
¾ tsp	bread machine or instant yeast	3 mL
1½ tsp	salt	7 mL
1¼ cups	water	300 mL
2 tbsp	vegetable oil	30 mL
2 tbsp	light (fancy) molasses	30 mL
1 tsp	cider vinegar	5 mL
2	eggs, lightly beaten	2
2	egg whites, lightly beaten	2

1. In a large bowl or plastic bag, combine sorghum flour, teff flour, cornmeal, quinoa flour, tapioca starch, brown sugar, xanthan gum, yeast and salt; mix well and set aside.

2. Pour water, oil, molasses and vinegar into the bread machine baking pan. Add eggs and egg whites.

3. Select the **Gluten-Free Cycle**. As the bread machine is mixing, gradually add the dry ingredients, scraping bottom and sides of pan with a rubber spatula. Try to incorporate all the dry ingredients within 1 to 2 minutes. When the mixing and kneading are complete, remove the kneading blade, leaving the bread pan in the bread machine. Quickly smooth the top of the loaf. Allow the cycle to finish.

4. At the end of the cycle, take the temperature of the loaf using an instant-read thermometer. It is baked at 200°F (100°C). If it's between 180°F (85°C) and 200°F (100°C), leave machine on the **Keep Warm Cycle** until baked. If it's below 180°F (85°C), turn on the **Bake Cycle** and check the internal temperature every 10 minutes. (Some bread machines are automatically set for 60 minutes; others need to be set by 10-minute intervals.)

5. Once the loaf has reached 200°F (100°C), remove it from the pan immediately and let cool completely on a rack.

NUTRITIONAL VALUES
per serving

Calories	155
Fat, total	3 g
Fat, saturated	0 g
Cholesterol	22 mg
Sodium	254 mg
Carbohydrate	29 g
Fiber	3 g
Protein	4 g
Calcium	26 mg
Iron	2 mg

You can use ½ cup (125 mL) liquid whole eggs and ¼ cup (60 mL) liquid egg whites, if you prefer.

Slice this or any bread with an electric knife for thin, even sandwich slices.

Dough Cycle and Bake Cycle

If your bread machine does not have a Gluten-Free Cycle, use the Dough Cycle followed by the Bake Cycle.

1. In a large bowl or plastic bag, combine sorghum flour, teff flour, cornmeal, quinoa flour, tapioca starch, brown sugar, xanthan gum, yeast and salt; mix well and set aside.

2. Pour water, oil, molasses and vinegar into the bread machine baking pan. Add eggs and egg whites.

3. Select the **Dough Cycle**. As the bread machine is mixing, gradually add the dry ingredients, scraping bottom and sides of pan with a rubber spatula. Try to incorporate all the dry ingredients within 1 to 2 minutes. When the mixing and kneading are complete, remove the kneading blade, leaving the bread pan in the bread machine. Quickly smooth the top of the loaf. Allow the cycle to finish. Turn off the bread machine.

4. Select the **Bake Cycle**. Set time to 60 minutes and temperature to 350°F (180°C). Allow the cycle to finish. Do not turn machine off before taking the internal temperature of the loaf with an instant-read thermometer. It should be 200°F (100°C). If it's between 180°F (85°C) and 200°F (100°C), leave machine on the **Keep Warm Cycle** until baked. If it's below 180°F (85°C), turn on the **Bake Cycle** and check the internal temperature every 10 minutes. (Some bread machines are automatically set for 60 minutes; others need to be set by 10-minute intervals.)

5. Once the loaf has reached 200°F (100°C), remove it from the pan immediately and let cool completely on a rack.

Grainy Cinnamon Raisin Bread

Our friend Anne Wraggett of Victoria, British Columbia, tells us this is her favorite cinnamon raisin loaf.

Tips

To ensure success, see page 14 for information on using your bread machine and page 18 for general tips on bread machine baking.

See the Technique Glossary, page 307, for information on cracking flaxseed.

You can use ½ cup (125 mL) liquid whole eggs and ¼ cup (60 mL) liquid egg whites, if you prefer.

1¼ cups	sorghum flour	300 mL
1 cup	amaranth flour	250 mL
¼ cup	quinoa flour	60 mL
½ cup	cracked brown flaxseed	125 mL
¼ cup	millet seeds	60 mL
½ cup	tapioca starch	125 mL
1 tbsp	xanthan gum	15 mL
1¼ tsp	bread machine or instant yeast	6 mL
1¼ tsp	salt	6 mL
1 tbsp	ground cinnamon	15 mL
1½ cups	raisins	375 mL
1¼ cups	water	300 mL
¼ cup	liquid honey	60 mL
2 tbsp	vegetable oil	30 mL
1 tsp	cider vinegar	5 mL
2	eggs, lightly beaten	2
2	egg whites, lightly beaten	2

1. In a large bowl or plastic bag, combine sorghum flour, amaranth flour, quinoa flour, flaxseed, millet seeds, tapioca starch, xanthan gum, yeast, salt, cinnamon and raisins; mix well and set aside.

2. Pour water, honey, oil and vinegar into the bread machine baking pan. Add eggs and egg whites.

3. Select the **Gluten-Free Cycle**. As the bread machine is mixing, gradually add the dry ingredients, scraping bottom and sides of pan with a rubber spatula. Try to incorporate all the dry ingredients within 1 to 2 minutes. When the mixing and kneading are complete, remove the kneading blade, leaving the bread pan in the bread machine. Quickly smooth the top of the loaf. Allow the cycle to finish.

4. At the end of the cycle, take the temperature of the loaf using an instant-read thermometer. It is baked at 200°F (100°C). If it's between 180°F (85°C) and 200°F (100°C), leave machine on the **Keep Warm Cycle** until baked. If it's below 180°F (85°C), turn on the **Bake Cycle** and check the internal temperature every 10 minutes. (Some bread machines are automatically set for 60 minutes; others need to be set by 10-minute intervals.)

NUTRITIONAL VALUES	
per serving	
Calories	230
Fat, total	6 g
Fat, saturated	1 g
Cholesterol	22 mg
Sodium	218 mg
Carbohydrate	41 g
Fiber	6 g
Protein	6 g
Calcium	39 mg
Iron	2 mg

5. Once the loaf has reached 200°F (100°C), remove it from the pan immediately and let cool completely on a rack.

Dough Cycle and Bake Cycle

If your bread machine does not have a Gluten-Free Cycle, use the Dough Cycle followed by the Bake Cycle.

1. In a large bowl or plastic bag, combine sorghum flour, amaranth flour, quinoa flour, flaxseed, millet seeds, tapioca starch, xanthan gum, yeast, salt, cinnamon and raisins; mix well and set aside.

2. Pour water, honey, oil and vinegar into the bread machine baking pan. Add eggs and egg whites.

3. Select the **Dough Cycle**. As the bread machine is mixing, gradually add the dry ingredients, scraping bottom and sides of pan with a rubber spatula. Try to incorporate all the dry ingredients within 1 to 2 minutes. When the mixing and kneading are complete, remove the kneading blade, leaving the bread pan in the bread machine. Quickly smooth the top of the loaf. Allow the cycle to finish. Turn off the bread machine.

4. Select the **Bake Cycle**. Set time to 60 minutes and temperature to 350°F (180°C). Allow the cycle to finish. Do not turn machine off before taking the internal temperature of the loaf with an instant-read thermometer. It should be 200°F (100°C). If it's between 180°F (85°C) and 200°F (100°C), leave machine on the **Keep Warm Cycle** until baked. If it's below 180°F (85°C), turn on the **Bake Cycle** and check the internal temperature every 10 minutes. (Some bread machines are automatically set for 60 minutes; others need to be set by 10-minute intervals.)

5. Once the loaf has reached 200°F (100°C), remove it from the pan immediately and let cool completely on a rack.

Raisin Bran Bread

Instead of a raisin bran muffin, enjoy a slice of raisin bran toast.

Tips

To ensure success, see page 14 for information on using your bread machine and page 18 for general tips on bread machine baking.

Warm up rice bran that has been stored in the refrigerator or freezer to room temperature.

1¼ cups	sorghum flour	300 mL
¾ cup	whole bean flour	175 mL
¼ cup	quinoa flour	60 mL
3 tbsp	rice bran	45 mL
⅓ cup	potato starch	75 mL
3 tbsp	tapioca starch	45 mL
1 tbsp	xanthan gum	15 mL
1½ tsp	bread machine or instant yeast	7 mL
1½ tsp	salt	7 mL
1 cup	raisins	250 mL
1½ cups	water	375 mL
3 tbsp	vegetable oil	45 mL
3 tbsp	light (fancy) molasses	45 mL
2 tbsp	liquid honey	30 mL
1 tsp	cider vinegar	5 mL
2	eggs, lightly beaten	2
2	egg whites, lightly beaten	2

1. In a large bowl, combine sorghum flour, whole bean flour, quinoa flour, rice bran, potato starch, tapioca starch, xanthan gum, yeast, salt and raisins; mix well and set aside.

2. Pour water, oil, molasses, honey and vinegar into the bread machine baking pan. Add eggs and egg whites.

3. Select the **Gluten-Free Cycle**. As the bread machine is mixing, gradually add the dry ingredients, scraping bottom and sides of pan with a rubber spatula. Try to incorporate all the dry ingredients within 1 to 2 minutes. When the mixing and kneading are complete, remove the kneading blade, leaving the bread pan in the bread machine. Quickly smooth the top of the loaf. Allow the cycle to finish.

4. At the end of the cycle, take the temperature of the loaf using an instant-read thermometer. It is baked at 200°F (100°C). If it's between 180°F (85°C) and 200°F (100°C), leave machine on the **Keep Warm Cycle** until baked. If it's below 180°F (85°C), turn on the **Bake Cycle** and check the internal temperature every 10 minutes. (Some bread machines are automatically set for 60 minutes; others need to be set by 10-minute intervals.)

5. Once the loaf has reached 200°F (100°C), remove it from the pan immediately and let cool completely on a rack.

NUTRITIONAL VALUES per serving	
Calories	196
Fat, total	5 g
Fat, saturated	0 g
Cholesterol	22 mg
Sodium	254 mg
Carbohydrate	34 g
Fiber	3 g
Protein	5 g
Calcium	27 mg
Iron	2 mg

Thoroughly mix the dry ingredients before adding them to the liquids — they are powder-fine and could clump together.

Slice this or any bread with an electric knife for thin, even sandwich slices.

Variation
Substitute GF oat bran for the rice bran.

Dough Cycle and Bake Cycle

If your bread machine does not have a Gluten-Free Cycle, use the Dough Cycle followed by the Bake Cycle.

1. In a large bowl, combine sorghum flour, whole bean flour, quinoa flour, rice bran, potato starch, tapioca starch, xanthan gum, yeast, salt and raisins; mix well and set aside.

2. Pour water, oil, molasses, honey and vinegar into the bread machine baking pan. Add eggs and egg whites.

3. Select the **Dough Cycle**. As the bread machine is mixing, gradually add the dry ingredients, scraping bottom and sides of pan with a rubber spatula. Try to incorporate all the dry ingredients within 1 to 2 minutes. When the mixing and kneading are complete, remove the kneading blade, leaving the bread pan in the bread machine. Quickly smooth the top of the loaf. Allow the cycle to finish. Turn off the bread machine.

4. Select the **Bake Cycle**. Set time to 60 minutes and temperature to 350°F (180°C). Allow the cycle to finish. Do not turn machine off before taking the internal temperature of the loaf with an instant-read thermometer. It should be 200°F (100°C). If it's between 180°F (85°C) and 200°F (100°C), leave machine on the **Keep Warm Cycle** until baked. If it's below 180°F (85°C), turn on the **Bake Cycle** and check the internal temperature every 10 minutes. (Some bread machines are automatically set for 60 minutes; others need to be set by 10-minute intervals.)

5. Once the loaf has reached 200°F (100°C), remove it from the pan immediately and let cool completely on a rack.

Buttermilk Buckwheat Bread

The buttermilk powder in this recipe results in a soft-textured loaf.

Tips

To ensure success, see page 14 for information on using your bread machine and page 18 for general tips on bread machine baking.

Make sure buckwheat is on your list of allowable foods before you try this recipe.

1¼ cups	whole bean flour	300 mL
½ cup	buckwheat flour	125 mL
½ cup	potato starch	125 mL
¼ cup	tapioca starch	60 mL
⅔ cup	buttermilk powder	150 mL
⅓ cup	packed brown sugar	75 mL
1 tbsp	xanthan gum	15 mL
1½ tsp	bread machine or instant yeast	7 mL
1¼ tsp	salt	6 mL
1 tsp	ground nutmeg	5 mL
1¾ cups	water	425 mL
¼ cup	vegetable oil	60 mL
1 tsp	cider vinegar	5 mL
2	eggs, lightly beaten	2

1. In a large bowl or plastic bag, combine whole bean flour, buckwheat flour, potato starch, tapioca starch, buttermilk powder, brown sugar, xanthan gum, yeast, salt and nutmeg; mix well and set aside.

2. Pour water, oil and vinegar into the bread machine baking pan. Add eggs.

3. Select the **Gluten-Free Cycle**. As the bread machine is mixing, gradually add the dry ingredients, scraping bottom and sides of pan with a rubber spatula. Try to incorporate all the dry ingredients within 1 to 2 minutes. When the mixing and kneading are complete, remove the kneading blade, leaving the bread pan in the bread machine. Quickly smooth the top of the loaf. Allow the cycle to finish.

4. At the end of the cycle, take the temperature of the loaf using an instant-read thermometer. It is baked at 200°F (100°C). If it's between 180°F (85°C) and 200°F (100°C), leave machine on the **Keep Warm Cycle** until baked. If it's below 180°F (85°C), turn on the **Bake Cycle** and check the internal temperature every 10 minutes. (Some bread machines are automatically set for 60 minutes; others need to be set by 10-minute intervals.)

5. Once the loaf has reached 200°F (100°C), remove it from the pan immediately and let cool completely on a rack.

NUTRITIONAL VALUES
per serving

Calories	174
Fat, total	6 g
Fat, saturated	1 g
Cholesterol	25 mg
Sodium	235 mg
Carbohydrate	26 g
Fiber	2 g
Protein	6 g
Calcium	89 mg
Iron	1 mg

Remember to thoroughly
mix the dry ingredients
before adding them to
the liquids — they are
powder-fine and could
clump together.

Variation
Substitute an equal amount
of ground cardamom for
the nutmeg.

Dough Cycle and Bake Cycle

If your bread machine does not have a Gluten-Free Cycle,
use the Dough Cycle followed by the Bake Cycle.

1. In a large bowl or plastic bag, combine whole bean
   flour, buckwheat flour, potato starch, tapioca starch,
   buttermilk powder, brown sugar, xanthan gum, yeast,
   salt and nutmeg; mix well and set aside.

2. Pour water, oil and vinegar into the bread machine
   baking pan. Add eggs.

3. Select the **Dough Cycle**. As the bread machine is
   mixing, gradually add the dry ingredients, scraping
   bottom and sides of pan with a rubber spatula. Try
   to incorporate all the dry ingredients within 1 to
   2 minutes. When the mixing and kneading are
   complete, remove the kneading blade, leaving the
   bread pan in the bread machine. Quickly smooth
   the top of the loaf. Allow the cycle to finish. Turn off
   the bread machine.

4. Select the **Bake Cycle**. Set time to 60 minutes and
   temperature to 350°F (180°C). Allow the cycle to
   finish. Do not turn machine off before taking the
   internal temperature of the loaf with an instant-read
   thermometer. It should be 200°F (100°C). If it's
   between 180°F (85°C) and 200°F (100°C), leave
   machine on the **Keep Warm Cycle** until baked. If
   it's below 180°F (85°C), turn on the **Bake Cycle** and
   check the internal temperature every 10 minutes. (Some
   bread machines are automatically set for 60 minutes;
   others need to be set by 10-minute intervals.)

5. Once the loaf has reached 200°F (100°C), remove it
   from the pan immediately and let cool completely on
   a rack.

Seedy Buckwheat Bread

A rich, dark brown exterior and a warm interior balance the strong flavor of this loaf.

Tips

To ensure success, see page 14 for information on using your bread machine and page 18 for general tips on bread machine baking.

Make sure buckwheat is on your list of allowable foods before you try this recipe.

1½ cups	sorghum flour	375 mL
½ cup	buckwheat flour	125 mL
½ cup	lentil flour	125 mL
½ cup	tapioca starch	125 mL
1 tbsp	xanthan gum	15 mL
1½ tsp	bread machine or instant yeast	7 mL
1¼ tsp	salt	6 mL
1 tbsp	caraway seeds	15 mL
1 tbsp	cumin seeds	15 mL
1 tbsp	fennel seeds	15 mL
1½ cups	water	375 mL
¼ cup	vegetable oil	60 mL
2 tbsp	liquid honey	30 mL
2 tbsp	light (fancy) molasses	30 mL
1 tsp	cider vinegar	5 mL
2	eggs, lightly beaten	2
2	egg whites, lightly beaten	2

1. In a large bowl or plastic bag, combine sorghum flour, buckwheat flour, lentil flour, tapioca starch, xanthan gum, yeast, salt, caraway seeds, cumin seeds and fennel seeds; mix well and set aside.

2. Pour water, oil, honey, molasses and vinegar into the bread machine baking pan. Add eggs and egg whites.

3. Select the **Gluten-Free Cycle**. As the bread machine is mixing, gradually add the dry ingredients, scraping bottom and sides of pan with a rubber spatula. Try to incorporate all the dry ingredients within 1 to 2 minutes. When the mixing and kneading are complete, remove the kneading blade, leaving the bread pan in the bread machine. Quickly smooth the top of the loaf. Allow the cycle to finish.

4. At the end of the cycle, take the temperature of the loaf using an instant-read thermometer. It is baked at 200°F (100°C). If it's between 180°F (85°C) and 200°F (100°C), leave machine on the **Keep Warm Cycle** until baked. If it's below 180°F (85°C), turn on the **Bake Cycle** and check the internal temperature every 10 minutes. (Some bread machines are automatically set for 60 minutes; others need to be set by 10-minute intervals.)

NUTRITIONAL VALUES
per serving

Calories	161
Fat, total	5 g
Fat, saturated	1 g
Cholesterol	22 mg
Sodium	213 mg
Carbohydrate	25 g
Fiber	3 g
Protein	5 g
Calcium	28 mg
Iron	2 mg

5. Once the loaf has reached 200°F (100°C), remove it from the pan immediately and let cool completely on a rack.

Dough Cycle and Bake Cycle

If your bread machine does not have a Gluten-Free Cycle, use the Dough Cycle followed by the Bake Cycle.

1. In a large bowl or plastic bag, combine sorghum flour, buckwheat flour, lentil flour, tapioca starch, xanthan gum, yeast, salt, caraway seeds, cumin seeds and fennel seeds; mix well and set aside.

2. Pour water, oil, honey, molasses and vinegar into the bread machine baking pan. Add eggs and egg whites.

3. Select the **Dough Cycle**. As the bread machine is mixing, gradually add the dry ingredients, scraping bottom and sides of pan with a rubber spatula. Try to incorporate all the dry ingredients within 1 to 2 minutes. When the mixing and kneading are complete, remove the kneading blade, leaving the bread pan in the bread machine. Quickly smooth the top of the loaf. Allow the cycle to finish. Turn off the bread machine.

4. Select the **Bake Cycle**. Set time to 60 minutes and temperature to 350°F (180°C). Allow the cycle to finish. Do not turn machine off before taking the internal temperature of the loaf with an instant-read thermometer. It should be 200°F (100°C). If it's between 180°F (85°C) and 200°F (100°C), leave machine on the **Keep Warm Cycle** until baked. If it's below 180°F (85°C), turn on the **Bake Cycle** and check the internal temperature every 10 minutes. (Some bread machines are automatically set for 60 minutes; others need to be set by 10-minute intervals.)

5. Once the loaf has reached 200°F (100°C), remove it from the pan immediately and let cool completely on a rack.

Blueberry Buckwheat Bread

Many folks don't realize that buckwheat is gluten-free. Blueberries and buckwheat are a great flavor combo.

Tips

To ensure success, see page 14 for information on using your bread machine and page 18 for general tips on bread machine baking.

Make sure buckwheat is on your list of allowable foods before you try this recipe.

1²/₃ cups	teff flour	400 mL
³/₄ cup	buckwheat flour	175 mL
¹/₃ cup	potato starch	75 mL
1 tbsp	xanthan gum	15 mL
1¹/₂ tsp	bread machine or instant yeast	7 mL
1¹/₄ tsp	salt	6 mL
³/₄ cup	dried blueberries	175 mL
1³/₄ cups	water	425 mL
¹/₄ cup	vegetable oil	60 mL
2 tbsp	liquid honey	30 mL
2 tbsp	light (fancy) molasses	30 mL
1 tsp	cider vinegar	5 mL
2	eggs, lightly beaten	2
2	egg whites, lightly beaten	2

1. In a large bowl or plastic bag, combine teff flour, buckwheat flour, potato starch, xanthan gum, yeast, salt and blueberries; mix well and set aside.

2. Pour water, oil, honey, molasses and vinegar into the bread machine baking pan. Add eggs and egg whites.

3. Select the **Gluten-Free Cycle**. As the bread machine is mixing, gradually add the dry ingredients, scraping bottom and sides of pan with a rubber spatula. Try to incorporate all the dry ingredients within 1 to 2 minutes. When the mixing and kneading are complete, remove the kneading blade, leaving the bread pan in the bread machine. Quickly smooth the top of the loaf. Allow the cycle to finish.

4. At the end of the cycle, take the temperature of the loaf using an instant-read thermometer. It is baked at 200°F (100°C). If it's between 180°F (85°C) and 200°F (100°C), leave machine on the **Keep Warm Cycle** until baked. If it's below 180°F (85°C), turn on the **Bake Cycle** and check the internal temperature every 10 minutes. (Some bread machines are automatically set for 60 minutes; others need to be set by 10-minute intervals.)

5. Once the loaf has reached 200°F (100°C), remove it from the pan immediately and let cool completely on a rack.

NUTRITIONAL VALUES
per serving

Calories	173
Fat, total	5 g
Fat, saturated	1 g
Cholesterol	23 mg
Sodium	216 mg
Carbohydrate	28 g
Fiber	4 g
Protein	4 g
Calcium	36 mg
Iron	2 mg

It is easier to measure honey and molasses if they are warmed in the microwave for a few seconds, or set in a pan of hot water for a few minutes.

Variation

Substitute brown rice flour for the buckwheat flour.

Dough Cycle and Bake Cycle

If your bread machine does not have a Gluten-Free Cycle, use the Dough Cycle followed by the Bake Cycle.

1. In a large bowl or plastic bag, combine teff flour, buckwheat flour, potato starch, xanthan gum, yeast, salt and blueberries; mix well and set aside.

2. Pour water, oil, honey, molasses and vinegar into the bread machine baking pan. Add eggs and egg whites.

3. Select the **Dough Cycle**. As the bread machine is mixing, gradually add the dry ingredients, scraping bottom and sides of pan with a rubber spatula. Try to incorporate all the dry ingredients within 1 to 2 minutes. When the mixing and kneading are complete, remove the kneading blade, leaving the bread pan in the bread machine. Quickly smooth the top of the loaf. Allow the cycle to finish. Turn off the bread machine.

4. Select the **Bake Cycle**. Set time to 60 minutes and temperature to 350°F (180°C). Allow the cycle to finish. Do not turn machine off before taking the internal temperature of the loaf with an instant-read thermometer. It should be 200°F (100°C). If it's between 180°F (85°C) and 200°F (100°C), leave machine on the **Keep Warm Cycle** until baked. If it's below 180°F (85°C), turn on the **Bake Cycle** and check the internal temperature every 10 minutes. (Some bread machines are automatically set for 60 minutes; others need to be set by 10-minute intervals.)

5. Once the loaf has reached 200°F (100°C), remove it from the pan immediately and let cool completely on a rack.

Banana Buckwheat Loaf

Sweet banana is a lovely complement to the assertive flavor of buckwheat. This loaf can have a very dark crust.

Tips

To ensure success, see page 14 for information on using your bread machine and page 18 for general tips on bread machine baking.

Make sure buckwheat is on your list of allowable foods before you try this recipe.

1¼ cups	whole bean flour	300 mL
½ cup	buckwheat flour	125 mL
⅓ cup	potato starch	75 mL
¼ cup	tapioca starch	60 mL
¼ cup	packed brown sugar	60 mL
1 tbsp	xanthan gum	15 mL
1½ tsp	bread machine or instant yeast	7 mL
1¼ tsp	salt	6 mL
1 tsp	ground cardamom	5 mL
1 cup	chopped pecans	250 mL
1 cup	mashed bananas	250 mL
¾ cup	water	175 mL
¼ cup	vegetable oil	60 mL
1 tsp	cider vinegar	5 mL
2	eggs, lightly beaten	2
2	egg whites, lightly beaten	2

1. In a large bowl or plastic bag, combine whole bean flour, buckwheat flour, potato starch, tapioca starch, brown sugar, xanthan gum, yeast, salt, cardamom and pecans; mix well and set aside.

2. Pour bananas, water, oil and vinegar into the bread machine baking pan. Add eggs and egg whites.

3. Select the **Gluten-Free Cycle**. As the bread machine is mixing, gradually add the dry ingredients, scraping bottom and sides of pan with a rubber spatula. Try to incorporate all the dry ingredients within 1 to 2 minutes. When the mixing and kneading are complete, remove the kneading blade, leaving the bread pan in the bread machine. Quickly smooth the top of the loaf. Allow the cycle to finish.

4. At the end of the cycle, take the temperature of the loaf using an instant-read thermometer. It is baked at 200°F (100°C). If it's between 180°F (85°C) and 200°F (100°C), leave machine on the **Keep Warm Cycle** until baked. If it's below 180°F (85°C), turn on the **Bake Cycle** and check the internal temperature every 10 minutes. (Some bread machines are automatically set for 60 minutes; others need to be set by 10-minute intervals.)

5. Once the loaf has reached 200°F (100°C), remove it from the pan immediately and let cool completely on a rack.

NUTRITIONAL VALUES
per serving

Calories	207
Fat, total	11 g
Fat, saturated	1 g
Cholesterol	22 mg
Sodium	212 mg
Carbohydrate	25 g
Fiber	3 g
Protein	6 g
Calcium	23 mg
Iron	1 mg

If you use thawed frozen bananas, don't use any thin, watery parts, just the thicker banana.

If possible, bake on a light crust setting.

Variation
Substitute brown rice flour for the buckwheat flour.

Dough Cycle and Bake Cycle

If your bread machine does not have a Gluten-Free Cycle, use the Dough Cycle followed by the Bake Cycle.

1. In a large bowl or plastic bag, combine whole bean flour, buckwheat flour, potato starch, tapioca starch, brown sugar, xanthan gum, yeast, salt, cardamom and pecans; mix well and set aside.

2. Pour bananas, water, oil and vinegar into the bread machine baking pan. Add eggs and egg whites.

3. Select the **Dough Cycle**. As the bread machine is mixing, gradually add the dry ingredients, scraping bottom and sides of pan with a rubber spatula. Try to incorporate all the dry ingredients within 1 to 2 minutes. When the mixing and kneading are complete, remove the kneading blade, leaving the bread pan in the bread machine. Quickly smooth the top of the loaf. Allow the cycle to finish. Turn off the bread machine.

4. Select the **Bake Cycle**. Set time to 60 minutes and temperature to 350°F (180°C). Allow the cycle to finish. Do not turn machine off before taking the internal temperature of the loaf with an instant-read thermometer. It should be 200°F (100°C). If it's between 180°F (85°C) and 200°F (100°C), leave machine on the **Keep Warm Cycle** until baked. If it's below 180°F (85°C), turn on the **Bake Cycle** and check the internal temperature every 10 minutes. (Some bread machines are automatically set for 60 minutes; others need to be set by 10-minute intervals.)

5. Once the loaf has reached 200°F (100°C), remove it from the pan immediately and let cool completely on a rack.

Banana Millet Bread

**MAKES 15 SLICES
(1 per serving)**

Dotted with light yellow millet seeds, this loaf is packed with the flavors of banana and spices.

Tips

To ensure success, see page 14 for information on using your bread machine and page 18 for general tips on bread machine baking.

If you use thawed frozen bananas, don't use any thin, watery parts, just the thicker banana.

1¼ cups	sorghum flour	300 mL
1 cup	whole bean flour	250 mL
¼ cup	millet flour	60 mL
⅓ cup	millet seeds	75 mL
⅓ cup	tapioca starch	75 mL
¼ cup	packed brown sugar	60 mL
2½ tsp	xanthan gum	12 mL
1½ tsp	bread machine or instant yeast	7 mL
1¼ tsp	salt	6 mL
1 tsp	ground cinnamon	5 mL
½ tsp	ground nutmeg	2 mL
¼ tsp	ground allspice	1 mL
1 cup	mashed bananas	250 mL
¾ cup	water	175 mL
¼ cup	vegetable oil	60 mL
1 tsp	cider vinegar	5 mL
2	eggs, lightly beaten	2
2	egg whites, lightly beaten	2

1. In a large bowl or plastic bag, combine sorghum flour, whole bean flour, millet flour, millet seeds, tapioca starch, brown sugar, xanthan gum, yeast, salt, cinnamon, nutmeg and allspice; mix well and set aside.

2. Pour bananas, water, oil and vinegar into the bread machine baking pan. Add eggs and egg whites.

3. Select the **Gluten-Free Cycle**. As the bread machine is mixing, gradually add the dry ingredients, scraping bottom and sides of pan with a rubber spatula. Try to incorporate all the dry ingredients within 1 to 2 minutes. When the mixing and kneading are complete, remove the kneading blade, leaving the bread pan in the bread machine. Quickly smooth the top of the loaf. Allow the cycle to finish.

4. At the end of the cycle, take the temperature of the loaf using an instant-read thermometer. It is baked at 200°F (100°C). If it's between 180°F (85°C) and 200°F (100°C), leave machine on the **Keep Warm Cycle** until baked. If it's below 180°F (85°C), turn on the **Bake Cycle** and check the internal temperature every 10 minutes. (Some bread machines are automatically set for 60 minutes; others need to be set by 10-minute intervals.)

NUTRITIONAL VALUES
per serving

Calories	186
Fat, total	6 g
Fat, saturated	1 g
Cholesterol	22 mg
Sodium	212 mg
Carbohydrate	29 g
Fiber	4 g
Protein	6 g
Calcium	17 mg
Iron	1 mg

Tips

Thoroughly mix the dry ingredients before adding them to the liquids — they are powder-fine and could clump together.

Slice this or any bread with an electric knife for thin, even sandwich slices.

Variation

Substitute either lentil flour or brown rice flour for the millet flour.

Dough Cycle and Bake Cycle

If your bread machine does not have a Gluten-Free Cycle, use the Dough Cycle followed by the Bake Cycle.

1. In a large bowl or plastic bag, combine sorghum flour, whole bean flour, millet flour, millet seeds, tapioca starch, brown sugar, xanthan gum, yeast, salt, cinnamon, nutmeg and allspice; mix well and set aside.

2. Pour bananas, water, oil and vinegar into the bread machine baking pan. Add eggs and egg whites.

3. Select the **Dough Cycle**. As the bread machine is mixing, gradually add the dry ingredients, scraping bottom and sides of pan with a rubber spatula. Try to incorporate all the dry ingredients within 1 to 2 minutes. When the mixing and kneading are complete, remove the kneading blade, leaving the bread pan in the bread machine. Quickly smooth the top of the loaf. Allow the cycle to finish. Turn off the bread machine.

4. Select the **Bake Cycle**. Set time to 60 minutes and temperature to 350°F (180°C). Allow the cycle to finish. Do not turn machine off before taking the internal temperature of the loaf with an instant-read thermometer. It should be 200°F (100°C). If it's between 180°F (85°C) and 200°F (100°C), leave machine on the **Keep Warm Cycle** until baked. If it's below 180°F (85°C), turn on the **Bake Cycle** and check the internal temperature every 10 minutes. (Some bread machines are automatically set for 60 minutes; others need to be set by 10-minute intervals.)

5. Once the loaf has reached 200°F (100°C), remove it from the pan immediately and let cool completely on a rack.

Rice-Free Millet Bread

A nutritionist recently asked us for a rice-free grainy bread she could recommend to her clients. We developed this recipe for her. We continue to be amazed by the number of people who need rice-free options.

Tips

To ensure success, see page 14 for information on using your bread machine and page 18 for general tips on bread machine baking.

No need to cook the millet seeds — they soften enough during baking to provide an interesting crunch.

NUTRITIONAL VALUES
per serving

Calories	175
Fat, total	4 g
Fat, saturated	1 g
Cholesterol	22 mg
Sodium	213 mg
Carbohydrate	31 g
Fiber	4 g
Protein	5 g
Calcium	18 mg
Iron	2 mg

1½ cups	sorghum flour	375 mL
1 cup	amaranth flour	250 mL
¼ cup	millet flour	60 mL
⅓ cup	tapioca starch	75 mL
½ cup	millet seeds	125 mL
1 tbsp	xanthan gum	15 mL
1 tbsp	bread machine or instant yeast	15 mL
1¼ tsp	salt	6 mL
2 tbsp	grated orange zest	30 mL
1 cup	water	250 mL
⅓ cup	freshly squeezed orange juice	75 mL
2 tbsp	vegetable oil	30 mL
¼ cup	liquid honey	60 mL
2	eggs, lightly beaten	2
2	egg whites, lightly beaten	2

1. In a large bowl or plastic bag, combine sorghum flour, amaranth flour, millet flour, tapioca starch, millet seeds, xanthan gum, yeast, salt and orange zest; mix well and set aside.

2. Pour water, orange juice, oil and honey into the bread machine baking pan. Add eggs and egg whites.

3. Select the **Gluten-Free Cycle**. As the bread machine is mixing, gradually add the dry ingredients, scraping bottom and sides of pan with a rubber spatula. Try to incorporate all the dry ingredients within 1 to 2 minutes. When the mixing and kneading are complete, remove the kneading blade, leaving the bread pan in the bread machine. Quickly smooth the top of the loaf. Allow the cycle to finish.

4. At the end of the cycle, take the temperature of the loaf using an instant-read thermometer. It is baked at 200°F (100°C). If it's between 180°F (85°C) and 200°F (100°C), leave machine on the **Keep Warm Cycle** until baked. If it's below 180°F (85°C), turn on the **Bake Cycle** and check the internal temperature every 10 minutes. (Some bread machines are automatically set for 60 minutes; others need to be set by 10-minute intervals.)

5. Once the loaf has reached 200°F (100°C), remove it from the pan immediately and let cool completely on a rack.

Tips

Use a zester to make long, thin strips of orange zest. Be sure to remove only the colored outer layer, avoiding the bitter white pith beneath.

Freshly squeezed orange juice enhances the flavor of this loaf. Roll the orange on the counter or between your hands to loosen the juice.

Keep an orange in the freezer. Zest while frozen, then juice after warming in the microwave.

Variation

Substitute lemon zest and juice for the orange.

Dough Cycle and Bake Cycle

If your bread machine does not have a Gluten-Free Cycle, use the Dough Cycle followed by the Bake Cycle.

1. In a large bowl or plastic bag, combine sorghum flour, amaranth flour, millet flour, tapioca starch, millet seeds, xanthan gum, yeast, salt and orange zest; mix well and set aside.

2. Pour water, orange juice, oil and honey into the bread machine baking pan. Add eggs and egg whites.

3. Select the **Dough Cycle**. As the bread machine is mixing, gradually add the dry ingredients, scraping bottom and sides of pan with a rubber spatula. Try to incorporate all the dry ingredients within 1 to 2 minutes. When the mixing and kneading are complete, remove the kneading blade, leaving the bread pan in the bread machine. Quickly smooth the top of the loaf. Allow the cycle to finish. Turn off the bread machine.

4. Select the **Bake Cycle**. Set time to 60 minutes and temperature to 350°F (180°C). Allow the cycle to finish. Do not turn machine off before taking the internal temperature of the loaf with an instant-read thermometer. It should be 200°F (100°C). If it's between 180°F (85°C) and 200°F (100°C), leave machine on the **Keep Warm Cycle** until baked. If it's below 180°F (85°C), turn on the **Bake Cycle** and check the internal temperature every 10 minutes. (Some bread machines are automatically set for 60 minutes; others need to be set by 10-minute intervals.)

5. Once the loaf has reached 200°F (100°C), remove it from the pan immediately and let cool completely on a rack.

Flaxseed Millet Bread

Here's a nutritious sandwich bread with the added crunch of flaxseed and millet.

Tips

To ensure success, see page 14 for information on using your bread machine and page 18 for general tips on bread machine baking.

For information on cracking flaxseed, see the Technique Glossary, page 307.

1¼ cups	brown rice flour	300 mL
⅓ cup	flax flour	75 mL
⅓ cup	millet flour	75 mL
⅓ cup	potato starch	75 mL
¼ cup	cracked flaxseed	60 mL
¼ cup	millet seeds	60 mL
2½ tsp	xanthan gum	12 mL
1¼ tsp	bread machine or instant yeast	6 mL
1½ tsp	salt	7 mL
1¼ cups	water	300 mL
¼ cup	vegetable oil	60 mL
¼ cup	liquid honey	60 mL
2 tsp	cider vinegar	10 mL
2	eggs, lightly beaten	2
2	egg whites, lightly beaten	2

1. In a large bowl or plastic bag, combine brown rice flour, flax flour, millet flour, potato starch, flaxseed, millet seeds, xanthan gum, yeast and salt; mix well and set aside.

2. Pour water, oil, honey and vinegar into the bread machine baking pan. Add eggs and egg whites.

3. Select the **Gluten-Free Cycle**. As the bread machine is mixing, gradually add the dry ingredients, scraping bottom and sides of pan with a rubber spatula. Try to incorporate all the dry ingredients within 1 to 2 minutes. When the mixing and kneading are complete, remove the kneading blade, leaving the bread pan in the bread machine. Quickly smooth the top of the loaf. Allow the cycle to finish.

4. At the end of the cycle, take the temperature of the loaf using an instant-read thermometer. It is baked at 200°F (100°C). If it's between 180°F (85°C) and 200°F (100°C), leave machine on the **Keep Warm Cycle** until baked. If it's below 180°F (85°C), turn on the **Bake Cycle** and check the internal temperature every 10 minutes. (Some bread machines are automatically set for 60 minutes; others need to be set by 10-minute intervals.)

5. Once the loaf has reached 200°F (100°C), remove it from the pan immediately and let cool completely on a rack.

NUTRITIONAL VALUES per serving	
Calories	168
Fat, total	7 g
Fat, saturated	1 g
Cholesterol	22 mg
Sodium	252 mg
Carbohydrate	25 g
Fiber	3 g
Protein	4 g
Calcium	19 mg
Iron	1 mg

Tip
We tried this bread with sprouted flax powder, flax meal and ground flaxseed in place of the flax flour. All yielded acceptable loaves.

Variation
Replace the honey with an equal amount of packed brown sugar, adding it to the dry ingredients in step 1.

Dough Cycle and Bake Cycle

If your bread machine does not have a Gluten-Free Cycle, use the Dough Cycle followed by the Bake Cycle.

1. In a large bowl or plastic bag, combine brown rice flour, flax flour, millet flour, potato starch, flaxseed, millet seeds, xanthan gum, yeast and salt; mix well and set aside.

2. Pour water, oil, honey and vinegar into the bread machine baking pan. Add eggs and egg whites.

3. Select the **Dough Cycle**. As the bread machine is mixing, gradually add the dry ingredients, scraping bottom and sides of pan with a rubber spatula. Try to incorporate all the dry ingredients within 1 to 2 minutes. When the mixing and kneading are complete, remove the kneading blade, leaving the bread pan in the bread machine. Quickly smooth the top of the loaf. Allow the cycle to finish. Turn off the bread machine.

4. Select the **Bake Cycle**. Set time to 60 minutes and temperature to 350°F (180°C). Allow the cycle to finish. Do not turn machine off before taking the internal temperature of the loaf with an instant-read thermometer. It should be 200°F (100°C). If it's between 180°F (85°C) and 200°F (100°C), leave machine on the **Keep Warm Cycle** until baked. If it's below 180°F (85°C), turn on the **Bake Cycle** and check the internal temperature every 10 minutes. (Some bread machines are automatically set for 60 minutes; others need to be set by 10-minute intervals.)

5. Once the loaf has reached 200°F (100°C), remove it from the pan immediately and let cool completely on a rack.

Maple Oat Loaf

This sweet loaf reminds us of springtime in New England and eastern Canada.

Tips

To ensure success, see page 14 for information on using your bread machine and page 18 for general tips on bread machine baking.

Don't omit the maple flavoring — it intensifies the maple flavor.

1¾ cups	sorghum flour	425 mL
⅔ cup	GF oats	150 mL
½ cup	GF oat flour	125 mL
½ cup	tapioca starch	125 mL
1 tbsp	xanthan gum	15 mL
2 tsp	bread machine or instant yeast	10 mL
1¼ tsp	salt	6 mL
1 tsp	ground ginger	5 mL
1¼ cups	water	300 mL
¼ cup	vegetable oil	60 mL
¼ cup	pure maple syrup	60 mL
2 tsp	maple flavoring	10 mL
2 tsp	cider vinegar	10 mL
2	eggs, lightly beaten	2
2	egg whites, lightly beaten	2

1. In a large bowl or plastic bag, combine sorghum flour, oats, oat flour, tapioca starch, xanthan gum, yeast, salt and ginger; mix well and set aside.

2. Pour water, oil, maple syrup, maple flavoring and vinegar into the bread machine baking pan. Add eggs and egg whites.

3. Select the **Gluten-Free Cycle**. As the bread machine is mixing, gradually add the dry ingredients, scraping bottom and sides of pan with a rubber spatula. Try to incorporate all the dry ingredients within 1 to 2 minutes. When the mixing and kneading are complete, remove the kneading blade, leaving the bread pan in the bread machine. Quickly smooth the top of the loaf. Allow the cycle to finish.

4. At the end of the cycle, take the temperature of the loaf using an instant-read thermometer. It is baked at 200°F (100°C). If it's between 180°F (85°C) and 200°F (100°C), leave machine on the **Keep Warm Cycle** until baked. If it's below 180°F (85°C), turn on the **Bake Cycle** and check the internal temperature every 10 minutes. (Some bread machines are automatically set for 60 minutes; others need to be set by 10-minute intervals.)

5. Once the loaf has reached 200°F (100°C), remove it from the pan immediately and let cool completely on a rack.

NUTRITIONAL VALUES
per serving

Calories	157
Fat, total	5 g
Fat, saturated	1 g
Cholesterol	22 mg
Sodium	211 mg
Carbohydrate	25 g
Fiber	3 g
Protein	4 g
Calcium	13 mg
Iron	1 mg

Tip

Always store bread at room temperature or wrapped airtight in the freezer. The refrigerator accelerates the staling process.

Variation

Add ¾ cup (175 mL) toasted chopped walnuts with the dry ingredients.

Dough Cycle and Bake Cycle

If your bread machine does not have a Gluten-Free Cycle, use the Dough Cycle followed by the Bake Cycle.

1. In a large bowl or plastic bag, combine sorghum flour, oats, oat flour, tapioca starch, xanthan gum, yeast, salt and ginger; mix well and set aside.

2. Pour water, oil, maple syrup, maple flavoring and vinegar into the bread machine baking pan. Add eggs and egg whites.

3. Select the **Dough Cycle**. As the bread machine is mixing, gradually add the dry ingredients, scraping bottom and sides of pan with a rubber spatula. Try to incorporate all the dry ingredients within 1 to 2 minutes. When the mixing and kneading are complete, remove the kneading blade, leaving the bread pan in the bread machine. Quickly smooth the top of the loaf. Allow the cycle to finish. Turn off the bread machine.

4. Select the **Bake Cycle**. Set time to 60 minutes and temperature to 350°F (180°C). Allow the cycle to finish. Do not turn machine off before taking the internal temperature of the loaf with an instant-read thermometer. It should be 200°F (100°C). If it's between 180°F (85°C) and 200°F (100°C), leave machine on the **Keep Warm Cycle** until baked. If it's below 180°F (85°C), turn on the **Bake Cycle** and check the internal temperature every 10 minutes. (Some bread machines are automatically set for 60 minutes; others need to be set by 10-minute intervals.)

5. Once the loaf has reached 200°F (100°C), remove it from the pan immediately and let cool completely on a rack.

Oatmeal Teff Bread

The brown color of each slice is speckled with lighter flecks of oats, making this loaf beautiful as well as tasty.

Tips

To ensure success, see page 14 for information on using your bread machine and page 18 for general tips on bread machine baking.

Use a zester to make long, thin strips of orange zest. Be sure to remove only the colored outer layer, avoiding the bitter white pith beneath.

1 cup	teff flour	250 mL
¾ cup	brown rice flour	175 mL
½ cup	GF oat flour	125 mL
½ cup	potato starch	125 mL
½ cup	GF oats	125 mL
¼ cup	teff grain	60 mL
1 tbsp	xanthan gum	15 mL
2 tsp	bread machine or instant yeast	10 mL
1½ tsp	salt	7 mL
2 tbsp	grated orange zest	30 mL
1¼ cups	water	300 mL
¼ cup	vegetable oil	60 mL
¼ cup	liquid honey	60 mL
2 tsp	cider vinegar	10 mL
2	eggs, lightly beaten	2
2	egg whites, lightly beaten	2

1. In a large bowl or plastic bag, combine teff flour, brown rice flour, oat flour, potato starch, oats, teff grain, xanthan gum, yeast, salt and orange zest; mix well and set aside.

2. Pour water, oil, honey and vinegar into the bread machine baking pan. Add eggs and egg whites.

3. Select the **Gluten-Free Cycle**. As the bread machine is mixing, gradually add the dry ingredients, scraping bottom and sides of pan with a rubber spatula. Try to incorporate all the dry ingredients within 1 to 2 minutes. When the mixing and kneading are complete, remove the kneading blade, leaving the bread pan in the bread machine. Quickly smooth the top of the loaf. Allow the cycle to finish.

4. At the end of the cycle, take the temperature of the loaf using an instant-read thermometer. It is baked at 200°F (100°C). If it's between 180°F (85°C) and 200°F (100°C), leave machine on the **Keep Warm Cycle** until baked. If it's below 180°F (85°C), turn on the **Bake Cycle** and check the internal temperature every 10 minutes. (Some bread machines are automatically set for 60 minutes; others need to be set by 10-minute intervals.)

5. Once the loaf has reached 200°F (100°C), remove it from the pan immediately and let cool completely on a rack.

NUTRITIONAL VALUES
per serving

Calories	177
Fat, total	5 g
Fat, saturated	1 g
Cholesterol	22 mg
Sodium	253 mg
Carbohydrate	29 g
Fiber	3 g
Protein	4 g
Calcium	26 mg
Iron	1 mg

Tip

It is easier to measure honey if it is warmed in the microwave for a few seconds, or set in a pan of hot water for a few minutes. Measure the oil first, then measure the honey; it will slide out of the measuring cup more easily that way.

Variation

If you can't find teff grain, substitute ¼ cup (60 mL) poppy seeds or amaranth grain.

Dough Cycle and Bake Cycle

If your bread machine does not have a Gluten-Free Cycle, use the Dough Cycle followed by the Bake Cycle.

1. In a large bowl or plastic bag, combine teff flour, brown rice flour, oat flour, potato starch, oats, teff grain, xanthan gum, yeast, salt and orange zest; mix well and set aside.

2. Pour water, oil, honey and vinegar into the bread machine baking pan. Add eggs and egg whites.

3. Select the **Dough Cycle**. As the bread machine is mixing, gradually add the dry ingredients, scraping bottom and sides of pan with a rubber spatula. Try to incorporate all the dry ingredients within 1 to 2 minutes. When the mixing and kneading are complete, remove the kneading blade, leaving the bread pan in the bread machine. Quickly smooth the top of the loaf. Allow the cycle to finish. Turn off the bread machine.

4. Select the **Bake Cycle**. Set time to 60 minutes and temperature to 350°F (180°C). Allow the cycle to finish. Do not turn machine off before taking the internal temperature of the loaf with an instant-read thermometer. It should be 200°F (100°C). If it's between 180°F (85°C) and 200°F (100°C), leave machine on the **Keep Warm Cycle** until baked. If it's below 180°F (85°C), turn on the **Bake Cycle** and check the internal temperature every 10 minutes. (Some bread machines are automatically set for 60 minutes; others need to be set by 10-minute intervals.)

5. Once the loaf has reached 200°F (100°C), remove it from the pan immediately and let cool completely on a rack.

Quinoa Bread

MAKES 15 SLICES
(1 per serving)

Vegetarians looking for complete plant protein will be happy to see this recipe. Black quinoa gives the bread a more interesting appearance and a stronger flavor than white quinoa would.

Tips

To ensure success, see page 14 for information on using your bread machine and page 18 for general tips on bread machine baking.

Be sure to soak the quinoa the night before you plan to make this bread. See the Technique Glossary, page 309, for information on soaking quinoa.

1¼ cups	sorghum flour	300 mL
⅔ cup	whole bean flour	150 mL
¼ cup	quinoa flour	60 mL
½ cup	tapioca starch	125 mL
1 tbsp	xanthan gum	15 mL
1 tbsp	bread machine or instant yeast	15 mL
1¼ tsp	salt	6 mL
1 cup	drained soaked black quinoa (see tip, at left), at room temperature	250 mL
1¼ cups	water	300 mL
2 tbsp	vegetable oil	30 mL
¼ cup	liquid honey	60 mL
2 tsp	cider vinegar	10 mL
2	eggs, lightly beaten	2
2	egg whites, lightly beaten	2

1. In a large bowl or plastic bag, combine sorghum flour, whole bean flour, quinoa flour, tapioca starch, xanthan gum, yeast, salt and quinoa; mix well and set aside.

2. Pour water, oil, honey and vinegar into the bread machine baking pan. Add eggs and egg whites.

3. Select the **Gluten-Free Cycle**. As the bread machine is mixing, gradually add the dry ingredients, scraping bottom and sides of pan with a rubber spatula. Try to incorporate all the dry ingredients within 1 to 2 minutes. When the mixing and kneading are complete, remove the kneading blade, leaving the bread pan in the bread machine. Quickly smooth the top of the loaf. Allow the cycle to finish.

4. At the end of the cycle, take the temperature of the loaf using an instant-read thermometer. It is baked at 200°F (100°C). If it's between 180°F (85°C) and 200°F (100°C), leave machine on the **Keep Warm Cycle** until baked. If it's below 180°F (85°C), turn on the **Bake Cycle** and check the internal temperature every 10 minutes. (Some bread machines are automatically set for 60 minutes; others need to be set by 10-minute intervals.)

5. Once the loaf has reached 200°F (100°C), remove it from the pan immediately and let cool completely on a rack.

NUTRITIONAL VALUES
per serving

Calories	203
Fat, total	4 g
Fat, saturated	0 g
Cholesterol	22 mg
Sodium	410 mg
Carbohydrate	36 g
Fiber	4 g
Protein	7 g
Calcium	16 mg
Iron	2 mg

Thoroughly mix the dry ingredients before adding them to the liquids — they are powder-fine and could clump together.

Slice this or any bread with an electric knife for thin, even sandwich slices.

Dough Cycle and Bake Cycle

If your bread machine does not have a Gluten-Free Cycle, use the Dough Cycle followed by the Bake Cycle.

1. In a large bowl or plastic bag, combine sorghum flour, whole bean flour, quinoa flour, tapioca starch, xanthan gum, yeast, salt and quinoa; mix well and set aside.

2. Pour water, oil, honey and vinegar into the bread machine baking pan. Add eggs and egg whites.

3. Select the **Dough Cycle**. As the bread machine is mixing, gradually add the dry ingredients, scraping bottom and sides of pan with a rubber spatula. Try to incorporate all the dry ingredients within 1 to 2 minutes. When the mixing and kneading are complete, remove the kneading blade, leaving the bread pan in the bread machine. Quickly smooth the top of the loaf. Allow the cycle to finish. Turn off the bread machine.

4. Select the **Bake Cycle**. Set time to 60 minutes and temperature to 350°F (180°C). Allow the cycle to finish. Do not turn machine off before taking the internal temperature of the loaf with an instant-read thermometer. It should be 200°F (100°C). If it's between 180°F (85°C) and 200°F (100°C), leave machine on the **Keep Warm Cycle** until baked. If it's below 180°F (85°C), turn on the **Bake Cycle** and check the internal temperature every 10 minutes. (Some bread machines are automatically set for 60 minutes; others need to be set by 10-minute intervals.)

5. Once the loaf has reached 200°F (100°C), remove it from the pan immediately and let cool completely on a rack.

Quinoa Molasses Bread

Rich, dark molasses color and flavor make this the perfect bread to serve with baked beans.

Tips

To ensure success, see page 14 for information on using your bread machine and page 18 for general tips on bread machine baking.

If the molasses is really thick or is straight out of the refrigerator, warm it slightly in the microwave before measuring.

2 cups	sorghum flour	500 mL
⅔ cup	quinoa flour	150 mL
⅓ cup	tapioca starch	75 mL
1 tbsp	xanthan gum	15 mL
2 tsp	bread machine or instant yeast	10 mL
1¼ tsp	salt	6 mL
1¼ cups	water	300 mL
2 tbsp	vegetable oil	30 mL
¼ cup	light (fancy) molasses	60 mL
1 tsp	cider vinegar	5 mL
2	eggs, lightly beaten	2
2	egg whites, lightly beaten	2
1 cup	cooked quinoa, at room temperature	250 mL

1. In a large bowl or plastic bag, combine sorghum flour, quinoa flour, tapioca starch, xanthan gum, yeast and salt; mix well and set aside.

2. Pour water, oil, molasses and vinegar into the bread machine baking pan. Add eggs, egg whites and quinoa.

3. Select the **Gluten-Free Cycle**. As the bread machine is mixing, gradually add the dry ingredients, scraping bottom and sides of pan with a rubber spatula. Try to incorporate all the dry ingredients within 1 to 2 minutes. When the mixing and kneading are complete, remove the kneading blade, leaving the bread pan in the bread machine. Quickly smooth the top of the loaf. Allow the cycle to finish.

4. At the end of the cycle, take the temperature of the loaf using an instant-read thermometer. It is baked at 200°F (100°C). If it's between 180°F (85°C) and 200°F (100°C), leave machine on the **Keep Warm Cycle** until baked. If it's below 180°F (85°C), turn on the **Bake Cycle** and check the internal temperature every 10 minutes. (Some bread machines are automatically set for 60 minutes; others need to be set by 10-minute intervals.)

5. Once the loaf has reached 200°F (100°C), remove it from the pan immediately and let cool completely on a rack.

NUTRITIONAL VALUES
per serving

Calories	182
Fat, total	4 g
Fat, saturated	0 g
Cholesterol	22 mg
Sodium	217 mg
Carbohydrate	32 g
Fiber	4 g
Protein	6 g
Calcium	27 mg
Iron	2 mg

When cooking quinoa for
dinner, make extra for
this recipe.

Dough Cycle and Bake Cycle

If your bread machine does not have a Gluten-Free Cycle,
use the Dough Cycle followed by the Bake Cycle.

1. In a large bowl or plastic bag, combine sorghum flour,
quinoa flour, tapioca starch, xanthan gum, yeast and
salt; mix well and set aside.

2. Pour water, oil, molasses and vinegar into the bread
machine baking pan. Add eggs, egg whites and quinoa.

3. Select the **Dough Cycle**. As the bread machine is
mixing, gradually add the dry ingredients, scraping
bottom and sides of pan with a rubber spatula. Try
to incorporate all the dry ingredients within 1 to
2 minutes. When the mixing and kneading are
complete, remove the kneading blade, leaving the
bread pan in the bread machine. Quickly smooth
the top of the loaf. Allow the cycle to finish. Turn off
the bread machine.

4. Select the **Bake Cycle**. Set time to 60 minutes and
temperature to 350°F (180°C). Allow the cycle to
finish. Do not turn machine off before taking the
internal temperature of the loaf with an instant-read
thermometer. It should be 200°F (100°C). If it's
between 180°F (85°C) and 200°F (100°C), leave
machine on the **Keep Warm Cycle** until baked. If
it's below 180°F (85°C), turn on the **Bake Cycle** and
check the internal temperature every 10 minutes. (Some
bread machines are automatically set for 60 minutes;
others need to be set by 10-minute intervals.)

5. Once the loaf has reached 200°F (100°C), remove it
from the pan immediately and let cool completely on
a rack.

Wild Rice Loaf

MAKES 15 SLICES
(1 per serving)

This delicious loaf brought rave reviews from our taste tasters.

Tips

To ensure success, see page 14 for information on using your bread machine and page 18 for general tips on bread machine baking.

See the Technique Glossary, page 309, for instructions on cooking wild rice.

1 cup	almond flour	250 mL
1 cup	brown rice flour	250 mL
2/3 cup	tapioca starch	150 mL
1/3 cup	potato starch	75 mL
1/4 cup	granulated sugar	60 mL
2 1/2 tsp	xanthan gum	12 mL
1 tbsp	bread machine or instant yeast	15 mL
1 1/2 tsp	salt	7 mL
1 tbsp	grated orange zest	15 mL
1 cup	cooked wild rice	250 mL
1 1/4 cups	freshly squeezed orange juice	300 mL
1/4 cup	vegetable oil	60 mL
2	eggs, lightly beaten	2
2	egg whites, lightly beaten	2

1. In a large bowl or plastic bag, combine almond flour, brown rice flour, tapioca starch, potato starch, sugar, xanthan gum, yeast, salt, orange zest and wild rice; mix well and set aside.

2. Pour orange juice and oil into the bread machine baking pan. Add eggs and egg whites.

3. Select the **Gluten-Free Cycle**. As the bread machine is mixing, gradually add the dry ingredients, scraping bottom and sides of pan with a rubber spatula. Try to incorporate all the dry ingredients within 1 to 2 minutes. When the mixing and kneading are complete, remove the kneading blade, leaving the bread pan in the bread machine. Quickly smooth the top of the loaf. Allow the cycle to finish.

4. At the end of the cycle, take the temperature of the loaf using an instant-read thermometer. It is baked at 200°F (100°C). If it's between 180°F (85°C) and 200°F (100°C), leave machine on the **Keep Warm Cycle** until baked. If it's below 180°F (85°C), turn on the **Bake Cycle** and check the internal temperature every 10 minutes. (Some bread machines are automatically set for 60 minutes; others need to be set by 10-minute intervals.)

5. Once the loaf has reached 200°F (100°C), remove it from the pan immediately and let cool completely on a rack.

NUTRITIONAL VALUES
per serving

Calories	199
Fat, total	8 g
Fat, saturated	1 g
Cholesterol	22 mg
Sodium	254 mg
Carbohydrate	28 g
Fiber	2 g
Protein	5 g
Calcium	24 mg
Iron	1 mg

Tips

Use a zester to make long, thin strips of orange zest. Be sure to remove only the colored outer layer, avoiding the bitter white pith beneath.

Freshly squeezed orange juice enhances the flavor of this loaf. Roll the orange on the counter or between your hands to loosen the juice.

Keep an orange in the freezer. Zest while frozen, then juice after warming in the microwave.

Dough Cycle and Bake Cycle

If your bread machine does not have a Gluten-Free Cycle, use the Dough Cycle followed by the Bake Cycle.

1. In a large bowl or plastic bag, combine almond flour, brown rice flour, tapioca starch, potato starch, sugar, xanthan gum, yeast, salt, orange zest and wild rice; mix well and set aside.

2. Pour orange juice and oil into the bread machine baking pan. Add eggs and egg whites.

3. Select the **Dough Cycle**. As the bread machine is mixing, gradually add the dry ingredients, scraping bottom and sides of pan with a rubber spatula. Try to incorporate all the dry ingredients within 1 to 2 minutes. When the mixing and kneading are complete, remove the kneading blade, leaving the bread pan in the bread machine. Quickly smooth the top of the loaf. Allow the cycle to finish. Turn off the bread machine.

4. Select the **Bake Cycle**. Set time to 60 minutes and temperature to 350°F (180°C). Allow the cycle to finish. Do not turn machine off before taking the internal temperature of the loaf with an instant-read thermometer. It should be 200°F (100°C). If it's between 180°F (85°C) and 200°F (100°C), leave machine on the **Keep Warm Cycle** until baked. If it's below 180°F (85°C), turn on the **Bake Cycle** and check the internal temperature every 10 minutes. (Some bread machines are automatically set for 60 minutes; others need to be set by 10-minute intervals.)

5. Once the loaf has reached 200°F (100°C), remove it from the pan immediately and let cool completely on a rack.

Wild Rice Teff Loaf

This flavorful loaf is also extra-nutritious.

Tips

To ensure success, see page 14 for information on using your bread machine and page 18 for general tips on bread machine baking.

See the Technique Glossary, page 309, for instructions on cooking wild rice.

1¾ cups	teff flour	425 mL
⅔ cup	tapioca starch	150 mL
2 tbsp	granulated sugar	30 mL
2½ tsp	xanthan gum	12 mL
1½ tsp	bread machine or instant yeast	7 mL
1½ tsp	salt	7 mL
1 tbsp	fennel seeds	15 mL
1 tbsp	teff grain	15 mL
1⅓ cups	cooked wild rice, at room temperature	325 mL
1¼ cups	water	300 mL
¼ cup	extra virgin olive oil	60 mL
2	eggs, lightly beaten	2
2	egg whites, lightly beaten	2

1. In a large bowl or plastic bag, combine teff flour, tapioca starch, sugar, xanthan gum, yeast, salt, fennel seeds, teff grain and wild rice; mix well and set aside.

2. Pour water and oil into the bread machine baking pan. Add eggs and egg whites.

3. Select the **Gluten-Free Cycle**. As the bread machine is mixing, gradually add the dry ingredients, scraping bottom and sides of pan with a rubber spatula. Try to incorporate all the dry ingredients within 1 to 2 minutes. When the mixing and kneading are complete, remove the kneading blade, leaving the bread pan in the bread machine. Quickly smooth the top of the loaf. Allow the cycle to finish.

4. At the end of the cycle, take the temperature of the loaf using an instant-read thermometer. It is baked at 200°F (100°C). If it's between 180°F (85°C) and 200°F (100°C), leave machine on the **Keep Warm Cycle** until baked. If it's below 180°F (85°C), turn on the **Bake Cycle** and check the internal temperature every 10 minutes. (Some bread machines are automatically set for 60 minutes; others need to be set by 10-minute intervals.)

5. Once the loaf has reached 200°F (100°C), remove it from the pan immediately and let cool completely on a rack.

NUTRITIONAL VALUES
per serving

Calories	153
Fat, total	5 g
Fat, saturated	1 g
Cholesterol	22 mg
Sodium	253 mg
Carbohydrate	24 g
Fiber	3 g
Protein	5 g
Calcium	35 mg
Iron	2 mg

Thoroughly mix the dry ingredients before adding them to the liquids — they are powder-fine and could clump together.

Slice this or any bread with an electric knife for thin, even sandwich slices.

Dough Cycle and Bake Cycle

If your bread machine does not have a Gluten-Free Cycle, use the Dough Cycle followed by the Bake Cycle.

1. In a large bowl or plastic bag, combine teff flour, tapioca starch, sugar, xanthan gum, yeast, salt, fennel seeds, teff grain and wild rice; mix well and set aside.

2. Pour water and oil into the bread machine baking pan. Add eggs and egg whites.

3. Select the **Dough Cycle**. As the bread machine is mixing, gradually add the dry ingredients, scraping bottom and sides of pan with a rubber spatula. Try to incorporate all the dry ingredients within 1 to 2 minutes. When the mixing and kneading are complete, remove the kneading blade, leaving the bread pan in the bread machine. Quickly smooth the top of the loaf. Allow the cycle to finish. Turn off the bread machine.

4. Select the **Bake Cycle**. Set time to 60 minutes and temperature to 350°F (180°C). Allow the cycle to finish. Do not turn machine off before taking the internal temperature of the loaf with an instant-read thermometer. It should be 200°F (100°C). If it's between 180°F (85°C) and 200°F (100°C), leave machine on the **Keep Warm Cycle** until baked. If it's below 180°F (85°C), turn on the **Bake Cycle** and check the internal temperature every 10 minutes. (Some bread machines are automatically set for 60 minutes; others need to be set by 10-minute intervals.)

5. Once the loaf has reached 200°F (100°C), remove it from the pan immediately and let cool completely on a rack.

Sun-Dried Tomato Bread

A smaller loaf than some, this is just the size to accompany an Italian dinner!

Tips

To ensure success, see page 14 for information on using your bread machine and page 18 for general tips on bread machine baking.

The tomato vegetable juice should be at room temperature. If using cold from the refrigerator, microwave it on High for 1 minute.

Use dry (not oil-packed) sun-dried tomatoes.

1 cup	sorghum flour	250 mL
½ cup	whole bean flour	125 mL
½ cup	cornstarch	125 mL
¼ cup	granulated sugar	60 mL
1 tbsp	xanthan gum	15 mL
1 tbsp	bread machine or instant yeast	15 mL
½ tsp	salt	2 mL
2 tbsp	snipped fresh rosemary	30 mL
½ cup	snipped dry-packed sun-dried tomatoes	125 mL
1¼ cups	tomato vegetable juice, warmed to room temperature	300 mL
¼ cup	vegetable oil	60 mL
1	egg, lightly beaten	1
2	egg whites, lightly beaten	2

1. In a large bowl or plastic bag, combine sorghum flour, whole bean flour, cornstarch, sugar, xanthan gum, yeast, salt, rosemary and tomatoes. Mix well and set aside.

2. Pour tomato vegetable juice and oil into the bread machine baking pan. Add egg and egg whites.

3. Select the **Gluten-Free Cycle**. As the bread machine is mixing, gradually add the dry ingredients, scraping bottom and sides of pan with a rubber spatula. Try to incorporate all the dry ingredients within 1 to 2 minutes. When the mixing and kneading are complete, remove the kneading blade, leaving the bread pan in the bread machine. Quickly smooth the top of the loaf. Allow the cycle to finish.

4. At the end of the cycle, take the temperature of the loaf using an instant-read thermometer. It is baked at 200°F (100°C). If it's between 180°F (85°C) and 200°F (100°C), leave machine on the **Keep Warm Cycle** until baked. If it's below 180°F (85°C), turn on the **Bake Cycle** and check the internal temperature every 10 minutes. (Some bread machines are automatically set for 60 minutes; others need to be set by 10-minute intervals.)

5. Once the loaf has reached 200°F (100°C), remove it from the pan immediately and let cool completely on a rack.

NUTRITIONAL VALUES
per serving

Calories	132
Fat, total	5 g
Fat, saturated	0 g
Cholesterol	11 mg
Sodium	143 mg
Carbohydrate	20 g
Fiber	2 g
Protein	4 g
Calcium	11 mg
Iron	1 mg

Tip

Always store bread at room temperature or wrapped airtight in the freezer. The refrigerator accelerates the staling process.

Variation

Substitute ¼ cup (60 mL) of a tomato-friendly fresh herb, such as oregano, basil or thyme, for the rosemary.

Dough Cycle and Bake Cycle

If your bread machine does not have a Gluten-Free Cycle, use the Dough Cycle followed by the Bake Cycle.

1. In a large bowl or plastic bag, combine sorghum flour, whole bean flour, cornstarch, sugar, xanthan gum, yeast, salt, rosemary and tomatoes. Mix well and set aside.

2. Pour tomato vegetable juice and oil into the bread machine baking pan. Add egg and egg whites.

3. Select the **Dough Cycle**. As the bread machine is mixing, gradually add the dry ingredients, scraping bottom and sides of pan with a rubber spatula. Try to incorporate all the dry ingredients within 1 to 2 minutes. When the mixing and kneading are complete, remove the kneading blade, leaving the bread pan in the bread machine. Quickly smooth the top of the loaf. Allow the cycle to finish. Turn off the bread machine.

4. Select the **Bake Cycle**. Set time to 60 minutes and temperature to 350°F (180°C). Allow the cycle to finish. Do not turn machine off before taking the internal temperature of the loaf with an instant-read thermometer. It should be 200°F (100°C). If it's between 180°F (85°C) and 200°F (100°C), leave machine on the **Keep Warm Cycle** until baked. If it's below 180°F (85°C), turn on the **Bake Cycle** and check the internal temperature every 10 minutes. (Some bread machines are automatically set for 60 minutes; others need to be set by 10-minute intervals.)

5. Once the loaf has reached 200°F (100°C), remove it from the pan immediately and let cool completely on a rack.

Carrot Poppy Loaf

*In this attractive loaf,
the bright orange carrots
contrast beautifully with
dark poppy seeds.*

Tips

To ensure success, see
page 14 for information on
using your bread machine
and page 18 for general tips
on bread machine baking.

For a moist loaf, select
young, tender carrots.

Use a dry measuring cup to
measure the carrots, and
be sure to only lightly pack
them.

1 cup	amaranth flour	250 mL
1 cup	brown rice flour	250 mL
½ cup	quinoa flour	125 mL
¼ cup	tapioca starch	60 mL
1 tbsp	xanthan gum	15 mL
1¼ tsp	bread machine or instant yeast	6 mL
1¼ tsp	salt	6 mL
¼ cup	poppy seeds	60 mL
¼ cup	snipped fresh tarragon	60 mL
1 tbsp	grated orange zest	15 mL
1 cup	water	250 mL
1 cup	lightly packed grated carrots	250 mL
2 tbsp	vegetable oil	30 mL
3 tbsp	liquid honey	45 mL
1 tsp	cider vinegar	5 mL
2	eggs, lightly beaten	2

1. In a large bowl or plastic bag, combine amaranth flour, brown rice flour, quinoa flour, tapioca starch, xanthan gum, yeast, salt, poppy seeds, tarragon and orange zest; mix well and set aside.

2. Pour water, carrots, oil, honey and vinegar into the bread machine baking pan. Add eggs.

3. Select the **Gluten-Free Cycle**. As the bread machine is mixing, gradually add the dry ingredients, scraping bottom and sides of pan with a rubber spatula. Try to incorporate all the dry ingredients within 1 to 2 minutes. When the mixing and kneading are complete, remove the kneading blade, leaving the bread pan in the bread machine. Quickly smooth the top of the loaf. Allow the cycle to finish.

4. At the end of the cycle, take the temperature of the loaf using an instant-read thermometer. It is baked at 200°F (100°C). If it's between 180°F (85°C) and 200°F (100°C), leave machine on the **Keep Warm Cycle** until baked. If it's below 180°F (85°C), turn on the **Bake Cycle** and check the internal temperature every 10 minutes. (Some bread machines are automatically set for 60 minutes; others need to be set by 10-minute intervals.)

5. Once the loaf has reached 200°F (100°C), remove it from the pan immediately and let cool completely on a rack.

NUTRITIONAL VALUES per serving	
Calories	148
Fat, total	5 g
Fat, saturated	1 g
Cholesterol	22 mg
Sodium	212 mg
Carbohydrate	24 g
Fiber	3 g
Protein	4 g
Calcium	57 mg
Iron	1 mg

Tip

It is easier to measure honey if it is warmed in the microwave for a few seconds, or set in a pan of hot water for a few minutes. Measure the oil first, then measure the honey; it will slide off the measuring spoon more easily that way.

Variation

Substitute ¼ cup (60 mL) toasted chopped walnuts for the poppy seeds.

Dough Cycle and Bake Cycle

If your bread machine does not have a Gluten-Free Cycle, use the Dough Cycle followed by the Bake Cycle.

1. In a large bowl or plastic bag, combine amaranth flour, brown rice flour, quinoa flour, tapioca starch, xanthan gum, yeast, salt, poppy seeds, tarragon and orange zest; mix well and set aside.

2. Pour water, carrots, oil, honey and vinegar into the bread machine baking pan. Add eggs.

3. Select the **Dough Cycle**. As the bread machine is mixing, gradually add the dry ingredients, scraping bottom and sides of pan with a rubber spatula. Try to incorporate all the dry ingredients within 1 to 2 minutes. When the mixing and kneading are complete, remove the kneading blade, leaving the bread pan in the bread machine. Quickly smooth the top of the loaf. Allow the cycle to finish. Turn off the bread machine.

4. Select the **Bake Cycle**. Set time to 60 minutes and temperature to 350°F (180°C). Allow the cycle to finish. Do not turn machine off before taking the internal temperature of the loaf with an instant-read thermometer. It should be 200°F (100°C). If it's between 180°F (85°C) and 200°F (100°C), leave machine on the **Keep Warm Cycle** until baked. If it's below 180°F (85°C), turn on the **Bake Cycle** and check the internal temperature every 10 minutes. (Some bread machines are automatically set for 60 minutes; others need to be set by 10-minute intervals.)

5. Once the loaf has reached 200°F (100°C), remove it from the pan immediately and let cool completely on a rack.

Spicy Peach Spread

Slather this delightful spread — a favorite among our readers — over any of the breads in this chapter for a tasty treat at breakfast.

Tips

To quickly and easily remove peels from peaches, see the Technique Glossary, page 306, for information on blanching.

Be sure to purchase freestone peaches.

Variation

Substitute pears for all or some of the peaches.

6	large peaches, peeled, pitted and cut into eighths	6
2 cups	peach nectar	500 mL
1/4 cup	packed brown sugar	50 mL
1/2 tsp	ground ginger	2 mL

1. In a large saucepan, combine peaches and peach nectar. Bring to a boil over high heat. Reduce heat to medium and boil gently for 30 minutes, or until soft.

2. Transfer to a food processor fitted with a metal blade and purée until smooth.

3. Return purée to saucepan and add brown sugar and ginger. Bring to a boil over medium-low heat and cook, stirring occasionally, for 10 minutes, or until desired thickness. (Keep in mind that it will thicken more as it cools.) Store in the refrigerator for up to 2 weeks or freeze for up to 3 months.

NUTRITIONAL VALUES
per serving

Calories	24
Fat, total	0 g
Fat, saturated	0 g
Cholesterol	0 mg
Sodium	3 mg
Carbohydrate	6 g
Fiber	1 g
Protein	0 g
Calcium	3 mg
Iron	0 mg

Challah (page 56)

Chocolate Almond Bread (page 80)
and Hazelnut Buckwheat Loaf (page 78)

Hawaiian Mini Loaves (page 84)

Whole-Grain Hamburger Buns (page 88)

Grainy Cinnamon Raisin Bread (page 94)

Oatmeal Teff Bread (page 114) and
Blueberry Buckwheat Bread (page 102)

Wild Rice Loaf (page 120)

Clockwise from bottom left: Flatbread (page 268) with Sun-Dried
Tomato Topping (page 271), Asiago Herb Pan Rolls (page 89),
Golden Harvest Loaf (page 176) and Harvest Seed Bread (page 140)

Seed, Nut and Fruit Breads

High-fiber multigrain breads have become the top choice of today's health-conscious baker. Breads made from grains, seeds, nuts and fruits are excellent choices.

Seedy Sandwich Loaf

Pumpkin, sunflower and sesame seeds add crunch to this loaf. Toast each slice for a nuttier flavor.

Tips

To ensure success, see page 14 for information on using your bread machine and page 18 for general tips on bread machine baking.

To make this loaf rice-free, substitute GF oat bran for the rice bran.

For a milder-tasting loaf, increase the honey to 3 tbsp (45 mL) and decrease the molasses to 1 tbsp (15 mL).

¾ cup	sorghum flour	175 mL
¾ cup	whole bean flour	175 mL
¼ cup	potato starch	60 mL
¼ cup	rice bran	60 mL
2½ tsp	xanthan gum	12 mL
2 tsp	bread machine or instant yeast	10 mL
1¼ tsp	salt	6 mL
½ cup	unsalted green pumpkin seeds	125 mL
½ cup	unsalted raw sunflower seeds	125 mL
½ cup	sesame seeds	125 mL
1¼ cups	water	300 mL
¼ cup	vegetable oil	60 mL
2 tbsp	liquid honey	30 mL
2 tbsp	light (fancy) molasses	30 mL
1 tsp	cider vinegar	5 mL
2	eggs, lightly beaten	2

1. In a large bowl or plastic bag, combine sorghum flour, whole bean flour, potato starch, rice bran, xanthan gum, yeast, salt, pumpkin seeds, sunflower seeds and sesame seeds; mix well and set aside.

2. Pour water, oil, honey, molasses and vinegar into the bread machine baking pan. Add eggs.

3. Select the **Gluten-Free Cycle**. As the bread machine is mixing, gradually add the dry ingredients, scraping bottom and sides of pan with a rubber spatula. Try to incorporate all the dry ingredients within 1 to 2 minutes. When the mixing and kneading are complete, remove the kneading blade, leaving the bread pan in the bread machine. Quickly smooth the top of the loaf. Allow the cycle to finish.

4. At the end of the cycle, take the temperature of the loaf using an instant-read thermometer. It is baked at 200°F (100°C). If it's between 180°F (85°C) and 200°F (100°C), leave machine on the **Keep Warm Cycle** until baked. If it's below 180°F (85°C), turn on the **Bake Cycle** and check the internal temperature every 10 minutes. (Some bread machines are automatically set for 60 minutes; others need to be set by 10-minute intervals.)

5. Once the loaf has reached 200°F (100°C), remove it from the pan immediately and let cool completely on a rack.

NUTRITIONAL VALUES
per serving

Calories	207
Fat, total	12 g
Fat, saturated	1 g
Cholesterol	22 mg
Sodium	214 mg
Carbohydrate	21 g
Fiber	3 g
Protein	7 g
Calcium	37 mg
Iron	2 mg

Thoroughly mix the dry ingredients before adding them to the liquids — they are powder-fine and could clump together.

Slice this or any bread with an electric knife for thin, even sandwich slices.

Dough Cycle and Bake Cycle

If your bread machine does not have a Gluten-Free Cycle, use the Dough Cycle followed by the Bake Cycle.

1. In a large bowl or plastic bag, combine sorghum flour, whole bean flour, potato starch, rice bran, xanthan gum, yeast, salt, pumpkin seeds, sunflower seeds and sesame seeds; mix well and set aside.

2. Pour water, oil, honey, molasses and vinegar into the bread machine baking pan. Add eggs.

3. Select the **Dough Cycle**. As the bread machine is mixing, gradually add the dry ingredients, scraping bottom and sides of pan with a rubber spatula. Try to incorporate all the dry ingredients within 1 to 2 minutes. When the mixing and kneading are complete, remove the kneading blade, leaving the bread pan in the bread machine. Quickly smooth the top of the loaf. Allow the cycle to finish. Turn off the bread machine.

4. Select the **Bake Cycle**. Set time to 60 minutes and temperature to 350°F (180°C). Allow the cycle to finish. Do not turn machine off before taking the internal temperature of the loaf with an instant-read thermometer. It should be 200°F (100°C). If it's between 180°F (85°C) and 200°F (100°C), leave machine on the **Keep Warm Cycle** until baked. If it's below 180°F (85°C), turn on the **Bake Cycle** and check the internal temperature every 10 minutes. (Some bread machines are automatically set for 60 minutes; others need to be set by 10-minute intervals.)

5. Once the loaf has reached 200°F (100°C), remove it from the pan immediately and let cool completely on a rack.

Corn-Free Flax Loaf

MAKES 15 SLICES
(1 per serving)

Corn is one of the top 10 food allergens, and anyone who cannot eat it is sure to enjoy this loaf, developed just for them.

Tips

To ensure success, see page 14 for information on using your bread machine and page 18 for general tips on bread machine baking.

For information on cracking flaxseed, see the Technique Glossary, page 307.

¾ cup	amaranth flour	175 mL
⅔ cup	sorghum flour	150 mL
⅓ cup	flax flour	75 mL
⅔ cup	potato starch	150 mL
⅓ cup	arrowroot starch	75 mL
2½ tsp	xanthan gum	12 mL
2 tsp	bread machine or instant yeast	10 mL
1½ tsp	salt	7 mL
½ cup	cracked flaxseed	125 mL
1¼ cups	water	300 mL
3 tbsp	vegetable oil	45 mL
¼ cup	liquid honey	60 mL
2 tsp	cider vinegar	10 mL
2	eggs, lightly beaten	2
2	egg whites, lightly beaten	2

1. In a large bowl or plastic bag, combine amaranth flour, sorghum flour, flax flour, potato starch, arrowroot starch, xanthan gum, yeast, salt and flaxseed; mix well and set aside.

2. Pour water, oil, honey and vinegar into the bread machine baking pan. Add eggs and egg whites.

3. Select the **Gluten-Free Cycle**. As the bread machine is mixing, gradually add the dry ingredients, scraping bottom and sides of pan with a rubber spatula. Try to incorporate all the dry ingredients within 1 to 2 minutes. When the mixing and kneading are complete, remove the kneading blade, leaving the bread pan in the bread machine. Quickly smooth the top of the loaf. Allow the cycle to finish.

4. At the end of the cycle, take the temperature of the loaf using an instant-read thermometer. It is baked at 200°F (100°C). If it's between 180°F (85°C) and 200°F (100°C), leave machine on the **Keep Warm Cycle** until baked. If it's below 180°F (85°C), turn on the **Bake Cycle** and check the internal temperature every 10 minutes. (Some bread machines are automatically set for 60 minutes; others need to be set by 10-minute intervals.)

5. Once the loaf has reached 200°F (100°C), remove it from the pan immediately and let cool completely on a rack.

NUTRITIONAL VALUES
per serving

Calories	174
Fat, total	7 g
Fat, saturated	1 g
Cholesterol	22 mg
Sodium	252 mg
Carbohydrate	26 g
Fiber	4 g
Protein	5 g
Calcium	26 mg
Iron	1 mg

Dough Cycle and Bake Cycle

If your bread machine does not have a Gluten-Free Cycle, use the Dough Cycle followed by the Bake Cycle.

1. In a large bowl or plastic bag, combine amaranth flour, sorghum flour, flax flour, potato starch, arrowroot starch, xanthan gum, yeast, salt and flaxseed; mix well and set aside.

2. Pour water, oil, honey and vinegar into the bread machine baking pan. Add eggs and egg whites.

3. Select the **Dough Cycle**. As the bread machine is mixing, gradually add the dry ingredients, scraping bottom and sides of pan with a rubber spatula. Try to incorporate all the dry ingredients within 1 to 2 minutes. When the mixing and kneading are complete, remove the kneading blade, leaving the bread pan in the bread machine. Quickly smooth the top of the loaf. Allow the cycle to finish. Turn off the bread machine.

4. Select the **Bake Cycle**. Set time to 60 minutes and temperature to 350°F (180°C). Allow the cycle to finish. Do not turn machine off before taking the internal temperature of the loaf with an instant-read thermometer. It should be 200°F (100°C). If it's between 180°F (85°C) and 200°F (100°C), leave machine on the **Keep Warm Cycle** until baked. If it's below 180°F (85°C), turn on the **Bake Cycle** and check the internal temperature every 10 minutes. (Some bread machines are automatically set for 60 minutes; others need to be set by 10-minute intervals.)

5. Once the loaf has reached 200°F (100°C), remove it from the pan immediately and let cool completely on a rack.

Millet Multigrain Bread

Our good friend Sheila Williams suggested this combination of grains, as it accommodates her food intolerances.

Tips

To ensure success, see page 14 for information on using your bread machine and page 18 for general tips on bread machine baking.

For information on making your own almond flour (aka almond meal), see the Technique Glossary, page 308.

1¼ cups	brown rice flour	300 mL
½ cup	almond flour	125 mL
½ cup	quinoa flour	125 mL
¼ cup	millet flour	60 mL
¼ cup	sorghum flour	60 mL
½ cup	arrowroot starch	125 mL
1 tbsp	xanthan gum	15 mL
1¼ tsp	bread machine or instant yeast	6 mL
1¼ tsp	salt	6 mL
¼ cup	millet seeds	60 mL
1¼ cups	water	300 mL
2 tbsp	vegetable oil	30 mL
2 tbsp	liquid honey	30 mL
1 tsp	cider vinegar	5 mL
2	eggs, lightly beaten	2
2	egg whites, lightly beaten	2

1. In a large bowl or plastic bag, combine brown rice flour, almond flour, quinoa flour, millet flour, sorghum flour, arrowroot starch, xanthan gum, yeast, salt and millet seeds; mix well and set aside.

2. Pour water, oil, honey and vinegar into the bread machine baking pan. Add eggs and egg whites.

3. Select the **Gluten-Free Cycle**. As the bread machine is mixing, gradually add the dry ingredients, scraping bottom and sides of pan with a rubber spatula. Try to incorporate all the dry ingredients within 1 to 2 minutes. When the mixing and kneading are complete, remove the kneading blade, leaving the bread pan in the bread machine. Quickly smooth the top of the loaf. Allow the cycle to finish.

4. At the end of the cycle, take the temperature of the loaf using an instant-read thermometer. It is baked at 200°F (100°C). If it's between 180°F (85°C) and 200°F (100°C), leave machine on the **Keep Warm Cycle** until baked. If it's below 180°F (85°C), turn on the **Bake Cycle** and check the internal temperature every 10 minutes. (Some bread machines are automatically set for 60 minutes; others need to be set by 10-minute intervals.)

5. Once the loaf has reached 200°F (100°C), remove it from the pan immediately and let cool completely on a rack.

NUTRITIONAL VALUES
per serving

Calories	164
Fat, total	5 g
Fat, saturated	1 g
Cholesterol	22 mg
Sodium	215 mg
Carbohydrate	26 g
Fiber	3 g
Protein	5 g
Calcium	14 mg
Iron	1 mg

Dough Cycle and Bake Cycle

If your bread machine does not have a Gluten-Free Cycle, use the Dough Cycle followed by the Bake Cycle.

1. In a large bowl or plastic bag, combine brown rice flour, almond flour, quinoa flour, millet flour, sorghum flour, arrowroot starch, xanthan gum, yeast, salt and millet seeds; mix well and set aside.

2. Pour water, oil, honey and vinegar into the bread machine baking pan. Add eggs and egg whites.

3. Select the **Dough Cycle**. As the bread machine is mixing, gradually add the dry ingredients, scraping bottom and sides of pan with a rubber spatula. Try to incorporate all the dry ingredients within 1 to 2 minutes. When the mixing and kneading are complete, remove the kneading blade, leaving the bread pan in the bread machine. Quickly smooth the top of the loaf. Allow the cycle to finish. Turn off the bread machine.

4. Select the **Bake Cycle**. Set time to 60 minutes and temperature to 350°F (180°C). Allow the cycle to finish. Do not turn machine off before taking the internal temperature of the loaf with an instant-read thermometer. It should be 200°F (100°C). If it's between 180°F (85°C) and 200°F (100°C), leave machine on the **Keep Warm Cycle** until baked. If it's below 180°F (85°C), turn on the **Bake Cycle** and check the internal temperature every 10 minutes. (Some bread machines are automatically set for 60 minutes; others need to be set by 10-minute intervals.)

5. Once the loaf has reached 200°F (100°C), remove it from the pan immediately and let cool completely on a rack.

Poppy Thyme Bread

Dots of black stand out against the white background in this savory loaf.

Tip
To ensure success, see page 14 for information on using your bread machine and page 18 for general tips on bread machine baking.

1¾ cups	brown rice flour	425 mL
½ cup	quinoa flour	125 mL
⅓ cup	arrowroot starch	75 mL
¼ cup	tapioca starch	60 mL
⅓ cup	granulated sugar	75 mL
1 tbsp	xanthan gum	15 mL
1½ tsp	bread machine or instant yeast	7 mL
1¼ tsp	salt	6 mL
⅓ cup	poppy seeds	75 mL
3 tbsp	fresh thyme leaves	45 mL
¾ cup	water	175 mL
½ cup	plain yogurt	125 mL
¼ cup	vegetable oil	60 mL
2	eggs, lightly beaten	2
2	egg whites, lightly beaten	2

1. In a large bowl or plastic bag, combine brown rice flour, quinoa flour, arrowroot starch, tapioca starch, sugar, xanthan gum, yeast, salt, poppy seeds and thyme; mix well and set aside.

2. Pour water, yogurt and oil into the bread machine baking pan. Add eggs and egg whites.

3. Select the **Gluten-Free Cycle**. As the bread machine is mixing, gradually add the dry ingredients, scraping bottom and sides of pan with a rubber spatula. Try to incorporate all the dry ingredients within 1 to 2 minutes. When the mixing and kneading are complete, remove the kneading blade, leaving the bread pan in the bread machine. Quickly smooth the top of the loaf. Allow the cycle to finish.

4. At the end of the cycle, take the temperature of the loaf using an instant-read thermometer. It is baked at 200°F (100°C). If it's between 180°F (85°C) and 200°F (100°C), leave machine on the **Keep Warm Cycle** until baked. If it's below 180°F (85°C), turn on the **Bake Cycle** and check the internal temperature every 10 minutes. (Some bread machines are automatically set for 60 minutes; others need to be set by 10-minute intervals.)

5. Once the loaf has reached 200°F (100°C), remove it from the pan immediately and let cool completely on a rack.

NUTRITIONAL VALUES
per serving

Calories	185
Fat, total	7 g
Fat, saturated	1 g
Cholesterol	22 mg
Sodium	220 mg
Carbohydrate	28 g
Fiber	2 g
Protein	5 g
Calcium	70 mg
Iron	1 mg

Vanilla-flavored yogurt or GF sour cream can replace the plain yogurt. Read the label carefully, because some yogurts and sour creams contain wheat starch.

Dough Cycle and Bake Cycle

If your bread machine does not have a Gluten-Free Cycle, use the Dough Cycle followed by the Bake Cycle.

1. In a large bowl or plastic bag, combine brown rice flour, quinoa flour, arrowroot starch, tapioca starch, sugar, xanthan gum, yeast, salt, poppy seeds and thyme; mix well and set aside.

2. Pour water, yogurt and oil into the bread machine baking pan. Add eggs and egg whites.

3. Select the **Dough Cycle**. As the bread machine is mixing, gradually add the dry ingredients, scraping bottom and sides of pan with a rubber spatula. Try to incorporate all the dry ingredients within 1 to 2 minutes. When the mixing and kneading are complete, remove the kneading blade, leaving the bread pan in the bread machine. Quickly smooth the top of the loaf. Allow the cycle to finish. Turn off the bread machine.

4. Select the **Bake Cycle**. Set time to 60 minutes and temperature to 350°F (180°C). Allow the cycle to finish. Do not turn machine off before taking the internal temperature of the loaf with an instant-read thermometer. It should be 200°F (100°C). If it's between 180°F (85°C) and 200°F (100°C), leave machine on the **Keep Warm Cycle** until baked. If it's below 180°F (85°C), turn on the **Bake Cycle** and check the internal temperature every 10 minutes. (Some bread machines are automatically set for 60 minutes; others need to be set by 10-minute intervals.)

5. Once the loaf has reached 200°F (100°C), remove it from the pan immediately and let cool completely on a rack.

Five-Seed Brown Bread

If you love strong-flavored brown bread, be sure to try this one!

Tips

To ensure success, see page 14 for information on using your bread machine and page 18 for general tips on bread machine baking.

You can substitute other seeds for the ones called for here, but make sure the total volume remains the same. Use smaller amounts of the stronger-tasting seeds.

1 cup	sorghum flour	250 mL
¾ cup	whole bean flour	175 mL
⅔ cup	quinoa flour	150 mL
⅓ cup	tapioca starch	75 mL
¼ cup	packed brown sugar	60 mL
1 tbsp	xanthan gum	15 mL
2 tsp	bread machine or instant yeast	10 mL
1¼ tsp	salt	6 mL
1 tbsp	anise seeds	15 mL
1 tbsp	caraway seeds	15 mL
1 tbsp	cumin seeds	15 mL
1 tbsp	fennel seeds	15 mL
1 tbsp	poppy seeds	15 mL
1¼ cups	water	300 mL
2 tbsp	vegetable oil	30 mL
1 tsp	cider vinegar	5 mL
2	eggs, lightly beaten	2
2	egg whites, lightly beaten	2

1. In a large bowl or plastic bag, combine sorghum flour, whole bean flour, quinoa flour, tapioca starch, brown sugar, xanthan gum, yeast, salt, anise seeds, caraway seeds, cumin seeds, fennel seeds and poppy seeds; mix well and set aside.

2. Pour water, oil and vinegar into the bread machine baking pan. Add eggs and egg whites.

3. Select the **Gluten-Free Cycle**. As the bread machine is mixing, gradually add the dry ingredients, scraping bottom and sides of pan with a rubber spatula. Try to incorporate all the dry ingredients within 1 to 2 minutes. When the mixing and kneading are complete, remove the kneading blade, leaving the bread pan in the bread machine. Quickly smooth the top of the loaf. Allow the cycle to finish.

4. At the end of the cycle, take the temperature of the loaf using an instant-read thermometer. It is baked at 200°F (100°C). If it's between 180°F (85°C) and 200°F (100°C), leave machine on the **Keep Warm Cycle** until baked. If it's below 180°F (85°C), turn on the **Bake Cycle** and check the internal temperature every 10 minutes. (Some bread machines are automatically set for 60 minutes; others need to be set by 10-minute intervals.)

NUTRITIONAL VALUES
per serving

Calories	148
Fat, total	5 g
Fat, saturated	0 g
Cholesterol	22 mg
Sodium	214 mg
Carbohydrate	23 g
Fiber	3 g
Protein	6 g
Calcium	46 mg
Iron	2 mg

Thoroughly mix the dry ingredients before adding them to the liquids — they are powder-fine and could clump together.

Slice this or any bread with an electric knife for thin, even sandwich slices.

5. Once the loaf has reached 200°F (100°C), remove it from the pan immediately and let cool completely on a rack.

Dough Cycle and Bake Cycle

If your bread machine does not have a Gluten-Free Cycle, use the Dough Cycle followed by the Bake Cycle.

1. In a large bowl or plastic bag, combine sorghum flour, whole bean flour, quinoa flour, tapioca starch, brown sugar, xanthan gum, yeast, salt, anise seeds, caraway seeds, cumin seeds, fennel seeds and poppy seeds; mix well and set aside.

2. Pour water, oil and vinegar into the bread machine baking pan. Add eggs and egg whites.

3. Select the **Dough Cycle**. As the bread machine is mixing, gradually add the dry ingredients, scraping bottom and sides of pan with a rubber spatula. Try to incorporate all the dry ingredients within 1 to 2 minutes. When the mixing and kneading are complete, remove the kneading blade, leaving the bread pan in the bread machine. Quickly smooth the top of the loaf. Allow the cycle to finish. Turn off the bread machine.

4. Select the **Bake Cycle**. Set time to 60 minutes and temperature to 350°F (180°C). Allow the cycle to finish. Do not turn machine off before taking the internal temperature of the loaf with an instant-read thermometer. It should be 200°F (100°C). If it's between 180°F (85°C) and 200°F (100°C), leave machine on the **Keep Warm Cycle** until baked. If it's below 180°F (85°C), turn on the **Bake Cycle** and check the internal temperature every 10 minutes. (Some bread machines are automatically set for 60 minutes; others need to be set by 10-minute intervals.)

5. Once the loaf has reached 200°F (100°C), remove it from the pan immediately and let cool completely on a rack.

Harvest Seed Bread

Enjoy this colorful loaf in the fall — it's perfect for Thanksgiving and the holidays.

Tips

To ensure success, see page 14 for information on using your bread machine and page 18 for general tips on bread machine baking.

Be sure to use unsweetened pumpkin purée; pumpkin pie filling is too sweet.

1½ cups	sorghum flour	375 mL
⅓ cup	teff flour	75 mL
½ cup	tapioca starch	125 mL
¼ cup	packed brown sugar	60 mL
2½ tsp	xanthan gum	12 mL
2 tsp	bread machine or instant yeast	10 mL
1½ tsp	salt	7 mL
½ cup	dried cranberries	125 mL
½ cup	unsalted green pumpkin seeds	125 mL
⅓ cup	unsalted raw sunflower seeds	75 mL
1¼ cups	pumpkin purée (not pie filling)	300 mL
⅓ cup	water	75 mL
¼ cup	vegetable oil	60 mL
2 tsp	cider vinegar	10 mL
2	eggs, lightly beaten	2
2	egg whites, lightly beaten	2

1. In a large bowl or plastic bag, combine sorghum flour, teff flour, tapioca starch, brown sugar, xanthan gum, yeast, salt, cranberries, pumpkin seeds and sunflower seeds; mix well and set aside.

2. Pour pumpkin purée, water, oil and vinegar into the bread machine baking pan. Add eggs and egg whites.

3. Select the **Gluten-Free Cycle**. As the bread machine is mixing, gradually add the dry ingredients, scraping bottom and sides of pan with a rubber spatula. Try to incorporate all the dry ingredients within 1 to 2 minutes. When the mixing and kneading are complete, remove the kneading blade, leaving the bread pan in the bread machine. Quickly smooth the top of the loaf. Allow the cycle to finish.

4. At the end of the cycle, take the temperature of the loaf using an instant-read thermometer. It is baked at 200°F (100°C). If it's between 180°F (85°C) and 200°F (100°C), leave machine on the **Keep Warm Cycle** until baked. If it's below 180°F (85°C), turn on the **Bake Cycle** and check the internal temperature every 10 minutes. (Some bread machines are automatically set for 60 minutes; others need to be set by 10-minute intervals.)

5. Once the loaf has reached 200°F (100°C), remove it from the pan immediately and let cool completely on a rack.

NUTRITIONAL VALUES
per serving

Calories	166
Fat, total	6 g
Fat, saturated	1 g
Cholesterol	22 mg
Sodium	251 mg
Carbohydrate	25 g
Fiber	3 g
Protein	4 g
Calcium	19 mg
Iron	1 mg

To prevent seeds from becoming rancid, store them in an airtight container in the refrigerator.

Variations

Substitute halved dried cherries for the cranberries.

Substitute chopped pecans for the pumpkin seeds.

Dough Cycle and Bake Cycle

If your bread machine does not have a Gluten-Free Cycle, use the Dough Cycle followed by the Bake Cycle.

1. In a large bowl or plastic bag, combine sorghum flour, teff flour, tapioca starch, brown sugar, xanthan gum, yeast, salt, cranberries, pumpkin seeds and sunflower seeds; mix well and set aside.

2. Pour pumpkin purée, water, oil and vinegar into the bread machine baking pan. Add eggs and egg whites.

3. Select the **Dough Cycle**. As the bread machine is mixing, gradually add the dry ingredients, scraping bottom and sides of pan with a rubber spatula. Try to incorporate all the dry ingredients within 1 to 2 minutes. When the mixing and kneading are complete, remove the kneading blade, leaving the bread pan in the bread machine. Quickly smooth the top of the loaf. Allow the cycle to finish. Turn off the bread machine.

4. Select the **Bake Cycle**. Set time to 60 minutes and temperature to 350°F (180°C). Allow the cycle to finish. Do not turn machine off before taking the internal temperature of the loaf with an instant-read thermometer. It should be 200°F (100°C). If it's between 180°F (85°C) and 200°F (100°C), leave machine on the **Keep Warm Cycle** until baked. If it's below 180°F (85°C), turn on the **Bake Cycle** and check the internal temperature every 10 minutes. (Some bread machines are automatically set for 60 minutes; others need to be set by 10-minute intervals.)

5. Once the loaf has reached 200°F (100°C), remove it from the pan immediately and let cool completely on a rack.

Seed and Soy Loaf

With its dark gold, shiny crust studded with seeds, this loaf is so attractive, you'll forget it is healthy.

Tips

To ensure success, see page 14 for information on using your bread machine and page 18 for general tips on bread machine baking.

It is easier to measure honey and molasses if they are warmed in the microwave for a few seconds, or set in a pan of hot water for a few minutes.

1¼ cups	brown rice flour	300 mL
½ cup	low-fat soy flour	125 mL
½ cup	potato starch	125 mL
⅓ cup	cornstarch	75 mL
2½ tsp	xanthan gum	12 mL
2 tsp	bread machine or instant yeast	10 mL
1½ tsp	salt	7 mL
¼ cup	unsalted raw sunflower seeds	60 mL
2 tbsp	sesame seeds	30 mL
1 tbsp	caraway seeds	15 mL
1¼ cups	water	300 mL
¼ cup	vegetable oil	60 mL
2 tbsp	liquid honey	30 mL
1 tbsp	light (fancy) molasses	15 mL
2 tsp	cider vinegar	10 mL
2	eggs, lightly beaten	2
2	egg whites, lightly beaten	2

1. In a large bowl or plastic bag, combine brown rice flour, soy flour, potato starch, cornstarch, xanthan gum, yeast, salt, sunflower seeds, sesame seeds and caraway seeds; mix well and set aside.

2. Pour water, oil, honey, molasses and vinegar into the bread machine baking pan. Add eggs and egg whites.

3. Select the **Gluten-Free Cycle**. As the bread machine is mixing, gradually add the dry ingredients, scraping bottom and sides of pan with a rubber spatula. Try to incorporate all the dry ingredients within 1 to 2 minutes. When the mixing and kneading are complete, remove the kneading blade, leaving the bread pan in the bread machine. Quickly smooth the top of the loaf. Allow the cycle to finish.

4. At the end of the cycle, take the temperature of the loaf using an instant-read thermometer. It is baked at 200°F (100°C). If it's between 180°F (85°C) and 200°F (100°C), leave machine on the **Keep Warm Cycle** until baked. If it's below 180°F (85°C), turn on the **Bake Cycle** and check the internal temperature every 10 minutes. (Some bread machines are automatically set for 60 minutes; others need to be set by 10-minute intervals.)

NUTRITIONAL VALUES
per serving

Calories	172
Fat, total	7 g
Fat, saturated	1 g
Cholesterol	22 mg
Sodium	254 mg
Carbohydrate	24 g
Fiber	2 g
Protein	5 g
Calcium	24 mg
Iron	1 mg

Replace the honey with an equal amount of packed brown sugar, adding it to the dry ingredients in step 1.

Substitute anise or fennel seeds for the caraway seeds and/or millet seeds for the sesame seeds.

5. Once the loaf has reached 200°F (100°C), remove it from the pan immediately and let cool completely on a rack.

Dough Cycle and Bake Cycle

If your bread machine does not have a Gluten-Free Cycle, use the Dough Cycle followed by the Bake Cycle.

1. In a large bowl or plastic bag, combine brown rice flour, soy flour, potato starch, cornstarch, xanthan gum, yeast, salt, sunflower seeds, sesame seeds and caraway seeds; mix well and set aside.

2. Pour water, oil, honey, molasses and vinegar into the bread machine baking pan. Add eggs and egg whites.

3. Select the **Dough Cycle**. As the bread machine is mixing, gradually add the dry ingredients, scraping bottom and sides of pan with a rubber spatula. Try to incorporate all the dry ingredients within 1 to 2 minutes. When the mixing and kneading are complete, remove the kneading blade, leaving the bread pan in the bread machine. Quickly smooth the top of the loaf. Allow the cycle to finish. Turn off the bread machine.

4. Select the **Bake Cycle**. Set time to 60 minutes and temperature to 350°F (180°C). Allow the cycle to finish. Do not turn machine off before taking the internal temperature of the loaf with an instant-read thermometer. It should be 200°F (100°C). If it's between 180°F (85°C) and 200°F (100°C), leave machine on the **Keep Warm Cycle** until baked. If it's below 180°F (85°C), turn on the **Bake Cycle** and check the internal temperature every 10 minutes. (Some bread machines are automatically set for 60 minutes; others need to be set by 10-minute intervals.)

5. Once the loaf has reached 200°F (100°C), remove it from the pan immediately and let cool completely on a rack.

Chunky Pecan Bread

Coarsely chopping the pecans results in a nicely crunchy bread. Toasting the pecans accentuates their flavor.

Tips

To ensure success, see page 14 for information on using your bread machine and page 18 for general tips on bread machine baking.

See the Technique Glossary, page 308, for information on toasting nuts.

1⅓ cups	amaranth flour	325 mL
1 cup	brown rice flour	250 mL
½ cup	pecan flour	125 mL
⅓ cup	tapioca starch	75 mL
1 tbsp	xanthan gum	15 mL
2 tsp	bread machine or instant yeast	10 mL
1¼ tsp	salt	6 mL
½ cup	toasted coarsely chopped pecans	125 mL
1¼ cups	water	300 mL
2 tbsp	pecan oil or vegetable oil	30 mL
⅓ cup	liquid honey	75 mL
2 tsp	cider vinegar	10 mL
2	eggs, lightly beaten	2
2	egg whites, lightly beaten	2

1. In a large bowl or plastic bag, combine amaranth flour, brown rice flour, pecan flour, tapioca starch, xanthan gum, yeast, salt and pecans; mix well and set aside.

2. Pour water, oil, honey and vinegar into the bread machine baking pan. Add eggs and egg whites.

3. Select the **Gluten-Free Cycle**. As the bread machine is mixing, gradually add the dry ingredients, scraping bottom and sides of pan with a rubber spatula. Try to incorporate all the dry ingredients within 1 to 2 minutes. When the mixing and kneading are complete, remove the kneading blade, leaving the bread pan in the bread machine. Quickly smooth the top of the loaf. Allow the cycle to finish.

4. At the end of the cycle, take the temperature of the loaf using an instant-read thermometer. It is baked at 200°F (100°C). If it's between 180°F (85°C) and 200°F (100°C), leave machine on the **Keep Warm Cycle** until baked. If it's below 180°F (85°C), turn on the **Bake Cycle** and check the internal temperature every 10 minutes. (Some bread machines are automatically set for 60 minutes; others need to be set by 10-minute intervals.)

5. Once the loaf has reached 200°F (100°C), remove it from the pan immediately and let cool completely on a rack.

NUTRITIONAL VALUES
per serving

Calories	185
Fat, total	8 g
Fat, saturated	1 g
Cholesterol	22 mg
Sodium	215 mg
Carbohydrate	26 g
Fiber	3 g
Protein	5 g
Calcium	29 mg
Iron	1 mg

Tip

For information on making your own pecan flour, see the Technique Glossary, page 308.

Variation

Use hazelnut flour and hazelnuts in place of the pecan flour and pecans.

Dough Cycle and Bake Cycle

If your bread machine does not have a Gluten-Free Cycle, use the Dough Cycle followed by the Bake Cycle.

1. In a large bowl or plastic bag, combine amaranth flour, brown rice flour, pecan flour, tapioca starch, xanthan gum, yeast, salt and pecans; mix well and set aside.

2. Pour water, oil, honey and vinegar into the bread machine baking pan. Add eggs and egg whites.

3. Select the **Dough Cycle**. As the bread machine is mixing, gradually add the dry ingredients, scraping bottom and sides of pan with a rubber spatula. Try to incorporate all the dry ingredients within 1 to 2 minutes. When the mixing and kneading are complete, remove the kneading blade, leaving the bread pan in the bread machine. Quickly smooth the top of the loaf. Allow the cycle to finish. Turn off the bread machine.

4. Select the **Bake Cycle**. Set time to 60 minutes and temperature to 350°F (180°C). Allow the cycle to finish. Do not turn machine off before taking the internal temperature of the loaf with an instant-read thermometer. It should be 200°F (100°C). If it's between 180°F (85°C) and 200°F (100°C), leave machine on the **Keep Warm Cycle** until baked. If it's below 180°F (85°C), turn on the **Bake Cycle** and check the internal temperature every 10 minutes. (Some bread machines are automatically set for 60 minutes; others need to be set by 10-minute intervals.)

5. Once the loaf has reached 200°F (100°C), remove it from the pan immediately and let cool completely on a rack.

Maple Walnut Loaf

Pure maple syrup intensifies the flavor in this classic combination of maple and walnuts.

Tips

To ensure success, see page 14 for information on using your bread machine and page 18 for general tips on bread machine baking.

It's worth the time to toast the walnuts (for instructions, see the Technique Glossary, page 308). No need to let them cool; just add them to the dry ingredients. Toast more walnuts than you need for this recipe. Cool and store the extra in a sealable plastic bag in the refrigerator.

1½ cups	sorghum flour	375 mL
¾ cup	low-fat soy flour	175 mL
½ cup	walnut flour (walnut meal)	125 mL
½ cup	cornstarch	125 mL
1 tbsp	xanthan gum	15 mL
1½ tsp	bread machine or instant yeast	7 mL
1½ tsp	salt	7 mL
1 cup	toasted coarsely chopped walnuts	250 mL
1¼ cups	water	300 mL
2 tbsp	walnut oil or vegetable oil	30 mL
⅓ cup	pure maple syrup	75 mL
2 tsp	maple flavoring	10 mL
1 tsp	cider vinegar	5 mL
2	eggs, lightly beaten	2
2	egg whites, lightly beaten	2

1. In a large bowl or plastic bag, combine sorghum flour, soy flour, walnut flour, cornstarch, xanthan gum, yeast, salt and walnuts; mix well and set aside.

2. Pour water, oil, maple syrup, maple flavoring and vinegar into the bread machine baking pan. Add eggs and egg whites.

3. Select the **Gluten-Free Cycle**. As the bread machine is mixing, gradually add the dry ingredients, scraping bottom and sides of pan with a rubber spatula. Try to incorporate all the dry ingredients within 1 to 2 minutes. When the mixing and kneading are complete, remove the kneading blade, leaving the bread pan in the bread machine. Quickly smooth the top of the loaf. Allow the cycle to finish.

4. At the end of the cycle, take the temperature of the loaf using an instant-read thermometer. It is baked at 200°F (100°C). If it's between 180°F (85°C) and 200°F (100°C), leave machine on the **Keep Warm Cycle** until baked. If it's below 180°F (85°C), turn on the **Bake Cycle** and check the internal temperature every 10 minutes. (Some bread machines are automatically set for 60 minutes; others need to be set by 10-minute intervals.)

5. Once the loaf has reached 200°F (100°C), remove it from the pan immediately and let cool completely on a rack.

NUTRITIONAL VALUES
per serving

Calories	203
Fat, total	10 g
Fat, saturated	1 g
Cholesterol	22 mg
Sodium	251 mg
Carbohydrate	22 g
Fiber	3 g
Protein	8 g
Calcium	30 mg
Iron	2 mg

Tips
For information on making your own walnut flour, see the Technique Glossary, page 308.

You can use ½ cup (125 mL) liquid whole eggs and ¼ cup (60 mL) liquid egg whites, if you prefer.

Dough Cycle and Bake Cycle

If your bread machine does not have a Gluten-Free Cycle, use the Dough Cycle followed by the Bake Cycle.

1. In a large bowl or plastic bag, combine sorghum flour, soy flour, walnut flour, cornstarch, xanthan gum, yeast, salt and walnuts; mix well and set aside.

2. Pour water, oil, maple syrup, maple flavoring and vinegar into the bread machine baking pan. Add eggs and egg whites.

3. Select the **Dough Cycle**. As the bread machine is mixing, gradually add the dry ingredients, scraping bottom and sides of pan with a rubber spatula. Try to incorporate all the dry ingredients within 1 to 2 minutes. When the mixing and kneading are complete, remove the kneading blade, leaving the bread pan in the bread machine. Quickly smooth the top of the loaf. Allow the cycle to finish. Turn off the bread machine.

4. Select the **Bake Cycle**. Set time to 60 minutes and temperature to 350°F (180°C). Allow the cycle to finish. Do not turn machine off before taking the internal temperature of the loaf with an instant-read thermometer. It should be 200°F (100°C). If it's between 180°F (85°C) and 200°F (100°C), leave machine on the **Keep Warm Cycle** until baked. If it's below 180°F (85°C), turn on the **Bake Cycle** and check the internal temperature every 10 minutes. (Some bread machines are automatically set for 60 minutes; others need to be set by 10-minute intervals.)

5. Once the loaf has reached 200°F (100°C), remove it from the pan immediately and let cool completely on a rack.

Almond Apricot Loaf

Serve this sweet almond apricot loaf for dessert, paired with an extra-sharp Cheddar.

Tips

To ensure success, see page 14 for information on using your bread machine and page 18 for general tips on bread machine baking.

Instead of chopping dried apricots with a knife, snip them with kitchen shears. Dip the blades in hot water when they become sticky.

1½ cups	sorghum flour	375 mL
½ cup	amaranth flour	125 mL
½ cup	almond flour	125 mL
½ cup	tapioca starch	125 mL
1 tbsp	xanthan gum	15 mL
2 tsp	bread machine or instant yeast	10 mL
1¼ tsp	salt	6 mL
¾ cup	toasted slivered almonds	175 mL
½ cup	snipped dried apricots	125 mL
1¼ cups	water	300 mL
¼ cup	vegetable oil	60 mL
⅓ cup	liquid honey	75 mL
2 tsp	cider vinegar	10 mL
2 tsp	almond extract	10 mL
2	eggs, lightly beaten	2
2	egg whites, lightly beaten	2

1. In a large bowl or plastic bag, combine sorghum flour, amaranth flour, almond flour, tapioca starch, xanthan gum, yeast, salt, almonds and apricots; mix well and set aside.

2. Pour water, oil, honey, vinegar and almond extract into the bread machine baking pan. Add eggs and egg whites.

3. Select the **Gluten-Free Cycle**. As the bread machine is mixing, gradually add the dry ingredients, scraping bottom and sides of pan with a rubber spatula. Try to incorporate all the dry ingredients within 1 to 2 minutes. When the mixing and kneading are complete, remove the kneading blade, leaving the bread pan in the bread machine. Quickly smooth the top of the loaf. Allow the cycle to finish.

4. At the end of the cycle, take the temperature of the loaf using an instant-read thermometer. It is baked at 200°F (100°C). If it's between 180°F (85°C) and 200°F (100°C), leave machine on the **Keep Warm Cycle** until baked. If it's below 180°F (85°C), turn on the **Bake Cycle** and check the internal temperature every 10 minutes. (Some bread machines are automatically set for 60 minutes; others need to be set by 10-minute intervals.)

5. Once the loaf has reached 200°F (100°C), remove it from the pan immediately and let cool completely on a rack.

NUTRITIONAL VALUES per serving	
Calories	210
Fat, total	10 g
Fat, saturated	1 g
Cholesterol	22 mg
Sodium	216 mg
Carbohydrate	28 g
Fiber	4 g
Protein	6 g
Calcium	36 mg
Iron	2 mg

Tip

For information on toasting nuts, see the Technique Glossary, page 308.

Variation

Replace half the apricots with quartered dried figs.

Dough Cycle and Bake Cycle

If your bread machine does not have a Gluten-Free Cycle, use the Dough Cycle followed by the Bake Cycle.

1. In a large bowl or plastic bag, combine sorghum flour, amaranth flour, almond flour, tapioca starch, xanthan gum, yeast, salt, almonds and apricots; mix well and set aside.

2. Pour water, oil, honey, vinegar and almond extract into the bread machine baking pan. Add eggs and egg whites.

3. Select the **Dough Cycle**. As the bread machine is mixing, gradually add the dry ingredients, scraping bottom and sides of pan with a rubber spatula. Try to incorporate all the dry ingredients within 1 to 2 minutes. When the mixing and kneading are complete, remove the kneading blade, leaving the bread pan in the bread machine. Quickly smooth the top of the loaf. Allow the cycle to finish. Turn off the bread machine.

4. Select the **Bake Cycle**. Set time to 60 minutes and temperature to 350°F (180°C). Allow the cycle to finish. Do not turn machine off before taking the internal temperature of the loaf with an instant-read thermometer. It should be 200°F (100°C). If it's between 180°F (85°C) and 200°F (100°C), leave machine on the **Keep Warm Cycle** until baked. If it's below 180°F (85°C), turn on the **Bake Cycle** and check the internal temperature every 10 minutes. (Some bread machines are automatically set for 60 minutes; others need to be set by 10-minute intervals.)

5. Once the loaf has reached 200°F (100°C), remove it from the pan immediately and let cool completely on a rack.

Figgy Apricot Bread

Want to increase your fiber in a delicious way? Enjoy this loaf.

Tips

To ensure success, see page 14 for information on using your bread machine and page 18 for general tips on bread machine baking.

Warm up rice bran that has been stored in the refrigerator or freezer to room temperature.

Snip the apricots and figs with kitchen shears. Dip the blades in hot water when they become sticky.

1¼ cups	sorghum flour	300 mL
1 cup	whole bean flour	250 mL
¼ cup	rice bran	60 mL
½ cup	potato starch	125 mL
1 tbsp	xanthan gum	15 mL
1½ tsp	bread machine or instant yeast	7 mL
1½ tsp	salt	7 mL
¾ cup	dried apricots, cut in thirds	175 mL
½ cup	dried whole figs, cut in half	125 mL
1½ cups	water	375 mL
3 tbsp	vegetable oil	45 mL
3 tbsp	liquid honey	45 mL
1 tbsp	light (fancy) molasses	15 mL
1 tsp	cider vinegar	5 mL
2	eggs, lightly beaten	2
2	egg whites, lightly beaten	2

1. In a large bowl, combine sorghum flour, whole bean flour, rice bran, potato starch, xanthan gum, yeast, salt, apricots and figs; mix well and set aside.

2. Pour water, oil, honey, molasses and vinegar into the bread machine baking pan. Add eggs and egg whites.

3. Select the **Gluten-Free Cycle**. As the bread machine is mixing, gradually add the dry ingredients, scraping bottom and sides of pan with a rubber spatula. Try to incorporate all the dry ingredients within 1 to 2 minutes. When the mixing and kneading are complete, remove the kneading blade, leaving the bread pan in the bread machine. Quickly smooth the top of the loaf. Allow the cycle to finish.

4. At the end of the cycle, take the temperature of the loaf using an instant-read thermometer. It is baked at 200°F (100°C). If it's between 180°F (85°C) and 200°F (100°C), leave machine on the **Keep Warm Cycle** until baked. If it's below 180°F (85°C), turn on the **Bake Cycle** and check the internal temperature every 10 minutes. (Some bread machines are automatically set for 60 minutes; others need to be set by 10-minute intervals.)

5. Once the loaf has reached 200°F (100°C), remove it from the pan immediately and let cool completely on a rack.

NUTRITIONAL VALUES
per serving

Calories	193
Fat, total	5 g
Fat, saturated	1 g
Cholesterol	22 mg
Sodium	255 mg
Carbohydrate	34 g
Fiber	4 g
Protein	6 g
Calcium	29 mg
Iron	2 mg

It is easier to measure honey and molasses if they are warmed in the microwave for a few seconds, or set in a pan of hot water for a few minutes. Measure the oil first, then measure the honey and molasses; they will slide off the measuring spoon more easily that way.

Variation

Substitute GF oat bran for the rice bran.

Dough Cycle and Bake Cycle

If your bread machine does not have a Gluten-Free Cycle, use the Dough Cycle followed by the Bake Cycle.

1. In a large bowl, combine sorghum flour, whole bean flour, rice bran, potato starch, xanthan gum, yeast, salt, apricots and figs; mix well and set aside.

2. Pour water, oil, honey, molasses and vinegar into the bread machine baking pan. Add eggs and egg whites.

3. Select the **Dough Cycle**. As the bread machine is mixing, gradually add the dry ingredients, scraping bottom and sides of pan with a rubber spatula. Try to incorporate all the dry ingredients within 1 to 2 minutes. When the mixing and kneading are complete, remove the kneading blade, leaving the bread pan in the bread machine. Quickly smooth the top of the loaf. Allow the cycle to finish. Turn off the bread machine.

4. Select the **Bake Cycle**. Set time to 60 minutes and temperature to 350°F (180°C). Allow the cycle to finish. Do not turn machine off before taking the internal temperature of the loaf with an instant-read thermometer. It should be 200°F (100°C). If it's between 180°F (85°C) and 200°F (100°C), leave machine on the **Keep Warm Cycle** until baked. If it's below 180°F (85°C), turn on the **Bake Cycle** and check the internal temperature every 10 minutes. (Some bread machines are automatically set for 60 minutes; others need to be set by 10-minute intervals.)

5. Once the loaf has reached 200°F (100°C), remove it from the pan immediately and let cool completely on a rack.

Blueberry Flaxseed Loaf

MAKES 15 SLICES
(1 per serving)

This loaf is so attractive, with blue and gold flecks and a warm beige background!

Tips

To ensure success, see page 14 for information on using your bread machine and page 18 for general tips on bread machine baking.

For information on cracking flaxseed, see the Technique Glossary, page 307.

¾ cup	sorghum flour	175 mL
⅔ cup	amaranth flour	150 mL
⅓ cup	flax flour	75 mL
⅔ cup	tapioca starch	150 mL
⅓ cup	cornstarch	75 mL
¼ cup	packed brown sugar	60 mL
2½ tsp	xanthan gum	12 mL
2 tsp	bread machine or instant yeast	10 mL
1½ tsp	salt	7 mL
½ cup	cracked golden flaxseed	125 mL
½ cup	dried blueberries	125 mL
1¼ cups	water	300 mL
2 tbsp	grated orange zest	30 mL
3 tbsp	vegetable oil	45 mL
2 tsp	cider vinegar	10 mL
2	eggs, lightly beaten	2
2	egg whites, lightly beaten	2

1. In a large bowl or plastic bag, combine sorghum flour, amaranth flour, flax flour, tapioca starch, cornstarch, brown sugar, xanthan gum, yeast, salt, flaxseed and blueberries; mix well and set aside.

2. Pour water, orange zest, oil and vinegar into the bread machine baking pan. Add eggs and egg whites.

3. Select the **Gluten-Free Cycle**. As the bread machine is mixing, gradually add the dry ingredients, scraping bottom and sides of pan with a rubber spatula. Try to incorporate all the dry ingredients within 1 to 2 minutes. When the mixing and kneading are complete, remove the kneading blade, leaving the bread pan in the bread machine. Quickly smooth the top of the loaf. Allow the cycle to finish.

4. At the end of the cycle, take the temperature of the loaf using an instant-read thermometer. It is baked at 200°F (100°C). If it's between 180°F (85°C) and 200°F (100°C), leave machine on the **Keep Warm Cycle** until baked. If it's below 180°F (85°C), turn on the **Bake Cycle** and check the internal temperature every 10 minutes. (Some bread machines are automatically set for 60 minutes; others need to be set by 10-minute intervals.)

NUTRITIONAL VALUES
per serving

Calories	181
Fat, total	7 g
Fat, saturated	1 g
Cholesterol	22 mg
Sodium	255 mg
Carbohydrate	26 g
Fiber	5 g
Protein	5 g
Calcium	30 mg
Iron	1 mg

Use a zester to make long, thin strips of orange zest. Be sure to remove only the colored outer layer, avoiding the bitter white pith beneath.

Keep an orange in the freezer. Zest while frozen, then juice after warming in the microwave.

Variation

Substitute an equal amount of dried cranberries for the blueberries.

5. Once the loaf has reached 200°F (100°C), remove it from the pan immediately and let cool completely on a rack.

Dough Cycle and Bake Cycle

If your bread machine does not have a Gluten-Free Cycle, use the Dough Cycle followed by the Bake Cycle.

1. In a large bowl or plastic bag, combine sorghum flour, amaranth flour, flax flour, tapioca starch, cornstarch, brown sugar, xanthan gum, yeast, salt, flaxseed and blueberries; mix well and set aside.

2. Pour water, orange zest, oil and vinegar into the bread machine baking pan. Add eggs and egg whites.

3. Select the **Dough Cycle**. As the bread machine is mixing, gradually add the dry ingredients, scraping bottom and sides of pan with a rubber spatula. Try to incorporate all the dry ingredients within 1 to 2 minutes. When the mixing and kneading are complete, remove the kneading blade, leaving the bread pan in the bread machine. Quickly smooth the top of the loaf. Allow the cycle to finish. Turn off the bread machine.

4. Select the **Bake Cycle**. Set time to 60 minutes and temperature to 350°F (180°C). Allow the cycle to finish. Do not turn machine off before taking the internal temperature of the loaf with an instant-read thermometer. It should be 200°F (100°C). If it's between 180°F (85°C) and 200°F (100°C), leave machine on the **Keep Warm Cycle** until baked. If it's below 180°F (85°C), turn on the **Bake Cycle** and check the internal temperature every 10 minutes. (Some bread machines are automatically set for 60 minutes; others need to be set by 10-minute intervals.)

5. Once the loaf has reached 200°F (100°C), remove it from the pan immediately and let cool completely on a rack.

Quinoa and Seed Bread

You're sure to enjoy this delightful combination of honey, quinoa, sesame and sunflower seeds.

Tips

To ensure success, see page 14 for information on using your bread machine and page 18 for general tips on bread machine baking.

To prevent seeds from becoming rancid, store them in an airtight container in the refrigerator.

1 cup	sorghum flour	250 mL
1/2 cup	whole bean flour	125 mL
1/4 cup	quinoa flour	60 mL
1/2 cup	tapioca starch	125 mL
1 tbsp	xanthan gum	15 mL
2 tsp	bread machine or instant yeast	10 mL
1 1/4 tsp	salt	6 mL
1/3 cup	unsalted raw sunflower seeds	75 mL
2 tbsp	sesame seeds	30 mL
1 1/4 cups	water	300 mL
2 tbsp	vegetable oil	30 mL
1/4 cup	liquid honey	60 mL
1 tsp	cider vinegar	5 mL
2	eggs, lightly beaten	2
2	egg whites, lightly beaten	2
1/2 cup	cooked quinoa, at room temperature	125 mL

1. In a large bowl or plastic bag, combine sorghum flour, whole bean flour, quinoa flour, tapioca starch, xanthan gum, yeast, salt, sunflower seeds and sesame seeds; mix well and set aside.

2. Pour water, oil, honey and vinegar into the bread machine baking pan. Add eggs, egg whites and quinoa.

3. Select the **Gluten-Free Cycle**. As the bread machine is mixing, gradually add the dry ingredients, scraping bottom and sides of pan with a rubber spatula. Try to incorporate all the dry ingredients within 1 to 2 minutes. When the mixing and kneading are complete, remove the kneading blade, leaving the bread pan in the bread machine. Quickly smooth the top of the loaf. Allow the cycle to finish.

4. At the end of the cycle, take the temperature of the loaf using an instant-read thermometer. It is baked at 200°F (100°C). If it's between 180°F (85°C) and 200°F (100°C), leave machine on the **Keep Warm Cycle** until baked. If it's below 180°F (85°C), turn on the **Bake Cycle** and check the internal temperature every 10 minutes. (Some bread machines are automatically set for 60 minutes; others need to be set by 10-minute intervals.)

5. Once the loaf has reached 200°F (100°C), remove it from the pan immediately and let cool completely on a rack.

NUTRITIONAL VALUES per serving	
Calories	151
Fat, total	5 g
Fat, saturated	1 g
Cholesterol	22 mg
Sodium	214 mg
Carbohydrate	22 g
Fiber	3 g
Protein	5 g
Calcium	15 mg
Iron	1 mg

See the Technique Glossary, page 309, for information on cooking quinoa.

Variation

Try different types of seeds, such as poppy seeds or unsalted green pumpkin seeds, but keep the total amount the same.

Dough Cycle and Bake Cycle

If your bread machine does not have a Gluten-Free Cycle, use the Dough Cycle followed by the Bake Cycle.

1. In a large bowl or plastic bag, combine sorghum flour, whole bean flour, quinoa flour, tapioca starch, xanthan gum, yeast, salt, sunflower seeds and sesame seeds; mix well and set aside.

2. Pour water, oil, honey and vinegar into the bread machine baking pan. Add eggs, egg whites and quinoa.

3. Select the **Dough Cycle**. As the bread machine is mixing, gradually add the dry ingredients, scraping bottom and sides of pan with a rubber spatula. Try to incorporate all the dry ingredients within 1 to 2 minutes. When the mixing and kneading are complete, remove the kneading blade, leaving the bread pan in the bread machine. Quickly smooth the top of the loaf. Allow the cycle to finish. Turn off the bread machine.

4. Select the **Bake Cycle**. Set time to 60 minutes and temperature to 350°F (180°C). Allow the cycle to finish. Do not turn machine off before taking the internal temperature of the loaf with an instant-read thermometer. It should be 200°F (100°C). If it's between 180°F (85°C) and 200°F (100°C), leave machine on the **Keep Warm Cycle** until baked. If it's below 180°F (85°C), turn on the **Bake Cycle** and check the internal temperature every 10 minutes. (Some bread machines are automatically set for 60 minutes; others need to be set by 10-minute intervals.)

5. Once the loaf has reached 200°F (100°C), remove it from the pan immediately and let cool completely on a rack.

Orange Poppy Seed Loaf

This moist, soft, tall loaf is picture perfect — and it tastes good too!

Tips

To ensure success, see page 14 for information on using your bread machine and page 18 for general tips on bread machine baking.

Use a zester to make long, thin strips of orange zest. Be sure to remove only the colored outer layer, avoiding the bitter white pith beneath.

1⅓ cups	brown rice flour	325 mL
⅔ cup	amaranth flour	150 mL
⅔ cup	potato starch	150 mL
⅓ cup	arrowroot starch	75 mL
⅓ cup	granulated sugar	75 mL
1 tbsp	xanthan gum	15 mL
1¼ tsp	bread machine or instant yeast	6 mL
1¼ tsp	salt	6 mL
⅓ cup	poppy seeds	75 mL
1 cup	water	250 mL
1 tbsp	grated orange zest	15 mL
½ cup	freshly squeezed orange juice	125 mL
¼ cup	vegetable oil	60 mL
2	eggs, lightly beaten	2
2	egg whites, lightly beaten	2

1. In a large bowl or plastic bag, combine brown rice flour, amaranth flour, potato starch, arrowroot starch, sugar, xanthan gum, yeast, salt and poppy seeds; mix well and set aside.

2. Pour water, orange zest, orange juice and oil into the bread machine baking pan. Add eggs and egg whites.

3. Select the **Gluten-Free Cycle**. As the bread machine is mixing, gradually add the dry ingredients, scraping bottom and sides of pan with a rubber spatula. Try to incorporate all the dry ingredients within 1 to 2 minutes. When the mixing and kneading are complete, remove the kneading blade, leaving the bread pan in the bread machine. Quickly smooth the top of the loaf. Allow the cycle to finish.

4. At the end of the cycle, take the temperature of the loaf using an instant-read thermometer. It is baked at 200°F (100°C). If it's between 180°F (85°C) and 200°F (100°C), leave machine on the **Keep Warm Cycle** until baked. If it's below 180°F (85°C), turn on the **Bake Cycle** and check the internal temperature every 10 minutes. (Some bread machines are automatically set for 60 minutes; others need to be set by 10-minute intervals.)

5. Once the loaf has reached 200°F (100°C), remove it from the pan immediately and let cool completely on a rack.

NUTRITIONAL VALUES
per serving

Calories	193
Fat, total	7 g
Fat, saturated	1 g
Cholesterol	22 mg
Sodium	213 mg
Carbohydrate	31 g
Fiber	2 g
Protein	4 g
Calcium	60 mg
Iron	1 mg

Tips

Freshly squeezed orange juice enhances the flavor of this loaf. Roll the orange on the counter or between your hands to loosen the juice.

Keep an orange in the freezer. Zest while frozen, then juice after warming in the microwave.

Dough Cycle and Bake Cycle

If your bread machine does not have a Gluten-Free Cycle, use the Dough Cycle followed by the Bake Cycle.

1. In a large bowl or plastic bag, combine brown rice flour, amaranth flour, potato starch, arrowroot starch, sugar, xanthan gum, yeast, salt and poppy seeds; mix well and set aside.

2. Pour water, orange zest, orange juice and oil into the bread machine baking pan. Add eggs and egg whites.

3. Select the **Dough Cycle**. As the bread machine is mixing, gradually add the dry ingredients, scraping bottom and sides of pan with a rubber spatula. Try to incorporate all the dry ingredients within 1 to 2 minutes. When the mixing and kneading are complete, remove the kneading blade, leaving the bread pan in the bread machine. Quickly smooth the top of the loaf. Allow the cycle to finish. Turn off the bread machine.

4. Select the **Bake Cycle**. Set time to 60 minutes and temperature to 350°F (180°C). Allow the cycle to finish. Do not turn machine off before taking the internal temperature of the loaf with an instant-read thermometer. It should be 200°F (100°C). If it's between 180°F (85°C) and 200°F (100°C), leave machine on the **Keep Warm Cycle** until baked. If it's below 180°F (85°C), turn on the **Bake Cycle** and check the internal temperature every 10 minutes. (Some bread machines are automatically set for 60 minutes; others need to be set by 10-minute intervals.)

5. Once the loaf has reached 200°F (100°C), remove it from the pan immediately and let cool completely on a rack.

Banana Teff Bread

This loaf looks like pumpernickel, but offers the slight sweetness of banana.

Tip

To ensure success, see page 14 for information on using your bread machine and page 18 for general tips on bread machine baking.

2¼ cups	brown teff flour	550 mL
⅓ cup	tapioca starch	75 mL
¼ cup	packed brown sugar	60 mL
2½ tsp	xanthan gum	12 mL
1½ tsp	bread machine or instant yeast	7 mL
1¼ tsp	salt	6 mL
1 cup	mashed bananas	250 mL
¾ cup	water	175 mL
¼ cup	vegetable oil	60 mL
1 tsp	cider vinegar	5 mL
2	eggs, lightly beaten	2

1. In a large bowl or plastic bag, combine teff flour, tapioca starch, brown sugar, xanthan gum, yeast and salt; mix well and set aside.

2. Pour bananas, water, oil and vinegar into the bread machine baking pan. Add eggs.

3. Select the **Gluten-Free Cycle**. As the bread machine is mixing, gradually add the dry ingredients, scraping bottom and sides of pan with a rubber spatula. Try to incorporate all the dry ingredients within 1 to 2 minutes. When the mixing and kneading are complete, remove the kneading blade, leaving the bread pan in the bread machine. Quickly smooth the top of the loaf. Allow the cycle to finish.

4. At the end of the cycle, take the temperature of the loaf using an instant-read thermometer. It is baked at 200°F (100°C). If it's between 180°F (85°C) and 200°F (100°C), leave machine on the **Keep Warm Cycle** until baked. If it's below 180°F (85°C), turn on the **Bake Cycle** and check the internal temperature every 10 minutes. (Some bread machines are automatically set for 60 minutes; others need to be set by 10-minute intervals.)

5. Once the loaf has reached 200°F (100°C), remove it from the pan immediately and let cool completely on a rack.

NUTRITIONAL VALUES
per serving

Calories	146
Fat, total	5 g
Fat, saturated	1 g
Cholesterol	22 mg
Sodium	52 mg
Carbohydrate	23 g
Fiber	3 g
Protein	4 g
Calcium	37 mg
Iron	2 mg

Dough Cycle and Bake Cycle

If your bread machine does not have a Gluten-Free Cycle, use the Dough Cycle followed by the Bake Cycle.

1. In a large bowl or plastic bag, combine teff flour, tapioca starch, brown sugar, xanthan gum, yeast and salt; mix well and set aside.

2. Pour bananas, water, oil and vinegar into the bread machine baking pan. Add eggs.

3. Select the **Dough Cycle**. As the bread machine is mixing, gradually add the dry ingredients, scraping bottom and sides of pan with a rubber spatula. Try to incorporate all the dry ingredients within 1 to 2 minutes. When the mixing and kneading are complete, remove the kneading blade, leaving the bread pan in the bread machine. Quickly smooth the top of the loaf. Allow the cycle to finish. Turn off the bread machine.

4. Select the **Bake Cycle**. Set time to 60 minutes and temperature to 350°F (180°C). Allow the cycle to finish. Do not turn machine off before taking the internal temperature of the loaf with an instant-read thermometer. It should be 200°F (100°C). If it's between 180°F (85°C) and 200°F (100°C), leave machine on the **Keep Warm Cycle** until baked. If it's below 180°F (85°C), turn on the **Bake Cycle** and check the internal temperature every 10 minutes. (Some bread machines are automatically set for 60 minutes; others need to be set by 10-minute intervals.)

5. Once the loaf has reached 200°F (100°C), remove it from the pan immediately and let cool completely on a rack.

Banana Raisin Bread

Really like your raisin toast on Sunday mornings? We've made it more kid-friendly by adding bananas.

Tips

To ensure success, see page 14 for information on using your bread machine and page 18 for general tips on bread machine baking.

If you use thawed frozen bananas, don't use any thin, watery parts, just the thicker banana.

1 cup	sorghum flour	250 mL
1 cup	whole bean flour	250 mL
¼ cup	tapioca starch	60 mL
2½ tsp	xanthan gum	12 mL
1 tbsp	bread machine or instant yeast	15 mL
1¼ tsp	salt	6 mL
2 tsp	ground cinnamon	10 mL
1 cup	raisins	250 mL
1 cup	mashed bananas	250 mL
¾ cup	water	175 mL
¼ cup	vegetable oil	60 mL
¼ cup	liquid honey	60 mL
2 tsp	cider vinegar	10 mL
2	eggs, lightly beaten	2

1. In a large bowl or plastic bag, combine sorghum flour, whole bean flour, tapioca starch, xanthan gum, yeast, salt, cinnamon and raisins; mix well and set aside.

2. Pour bananas, water, oil, honey and vinegar into the bread machine baking pan. Add eggs.

3. Select the **Gluten-Free Cycle**. As the bread machine is mixing, gradually add the dry ingredients, scraping bottom and sides of pan with a rubber spatula. Try to incorporate all the dry ingredients within 1 to 2 minutes. When the mixing and kneading are complete, remove the kneading blade, leaving the bread pan in the bread machine. Quickly smooth the top of the loaf. Allow the cycle to finish.

4. At the end of the cycle, take the temperature of the loaf using an instant-read thermometer. It is baked at 200°F (100°C). If it's between 180°F (85°C) and 200°F (100°C), leave machine on the **Keep Warm Cycle** until baked. If it's below 180°F (85°C), turn on the **Bake Cycle** and check the internal temperature every 10 minutes. (Some bread machines are automatically set for 60 minutes; others need to be set by 10-minute intervals.)

5. Once the loaf has reached 200°F (100°C), remove it from the pan immediately and let cool completely on a rack.

NUTRITIONAL VALUES per serving	
Calories	189
Fat, total	5 g
Fat, saturated	1 g
Cholesterol	22 mg
Sodium	206 mg
Carbohydrate	32 g
Fiber	3 g
Protein	5 g
Calcium	20 mg
Iron	1 mg

Tip

It is easier to measure honey if it is warmed in the microwave for a few seconds, or set in a pan of hot water for a few minutes. Measure the oil first, then measure the honey; it will slide out of the measuring cup more easily that way.

Dough Cycle and Bake Cycle

If your bread machine does not have a Gluten-Free Cycle, use the Dough Cycle followed by the Bake Cycle.

1. In a large bowl or plastic bag, combine sorghum flour, whole bean flour, tapioca starch, xanthan gum, yeast, salt, cinnamon and raisins; mix well and set aside.

2. Pour bananas, water, oil, honey and vinegar into the bread machine baking pan. Add eggs.

3. Select the **Dough Cycle**. As the bread machine is mixing, gradually add the dry ingredients, scraping bottom and sides of pan with a rubber spatula. Try to incorporate all the dry ingredients within 1 to 2 minutes. When the mixing and kneading are complete, remove the kneading blade, leaving the bread pan in the bread machine. Quickly smooth the top of the loaf. Allow the cycle to finish. Turn off the bread machine.

4. Select the **Bake Cycle**. Set time to 60 minutes and temperature to 350°F (180°C). Allow the cycle to finish. Do not turn machine off before taking the internal temperature of the loaf with an instant-read thermometer. It should be 200°F (100°C). If it's between 180°F (85°C) and 200°F (100°C), leave machine on the **Keep Warm Cycle** until baked. If it's below 180°F (85°C), turn on the **Bake Cycle** and check the internal temperature every 10 minutes. (Some bread machines are automatically set for 60 minutes; others need to be set by 10-minute intervals.)

5. Once the loaf has reached 200°F (100°C), remove it from the pan immediately and let cool completely on a rack.

Black Forest Loaf

Love the cake? Try our yeast bread version!

Tips

To ensure success, see page 14 for information on using your bread machine and page 18 for general tips on bread machine baking.

See the Technique Glossary, page 308, for instructions on warming milk.

1¼ cups	sorghum flour	300 mL
¾ cup	amaranth flour	175 mL
½ cup	almond flour	125 mL
½ cup	tapioca starch	125 mL
2½ tsp	xanthan gum	12 mL
1½ tsp	bread machine or instant yeast	7 mL
1½ tsp	salt	7 mL
½ cup	semisweet chocolate chips	125 mL
½ cup	dried cherries, cut in half	125 mL
1¼ cups	milk, at room temperature	300 mL
¼ cup	vegetable oil	60 mL
3 tbsp	liquid honey	45 mL
2 tbsp	brandy	30 mL
2	eggs, lightly beaten	2
2	egg whites, lightly beaten	2

1. In a large bowl or plastic bag, combine sorghum flour, amaranth flour, almond flour, tapioca starch, xanthan gum, yeast, salt, chocolate chips and cherries; mix well and set aside.

2. Pour milk, oil, honey and brandy into the bread machine baking pan. Add eggs and egg whites.

3. Select the **Gluten-Free Cycle**. As the bread machine is mixing, gradually add the dry ingredients, scraping bottom and sides of pan with a rubber spatula. Try to incorporate all the dry ingredients within 1 to 2 minutes. When the mixing and kneading are complete, remove the kneading blade, leaving the bread pan in the bread machine. Quickly smooth the top of the loaf. Allow the cycle to finish.

4. At the end of the cycle, take the temperature of the loaf using an instant-read thermometer. It is baked at 200°F (100°C). If it's between 180°F (85°C) and 200°F (100°C), leave machine on the **Keep Warm Cycle** until baked. If it's below 180°F (85°C), turn on the **Bake Cycle** and check the internal temperature every 10 minutes. (Some bread machines are automatically set for 60 minutes; others need to be set by 10-minute intervals.)

5. Once the loaf has reached 200°F (100°C), remove it from the pan immediately and let cool completely on a rack.

NUTRITIONAL VALUES
per serving

Calories	221
Fat, total	9 g
Fat, saturated	2 g
Cholesterol	23 mg
Sodium	263 mg
Carbohydrate	30 g
Fiber	4 g
Protein	6 g
Calcium	50 mg
Iron	2 mg

Tips
Thoroughly mix the dry ingredients before adding them to the liquids — they are powder-fine and could clump together.

Slice this or any bread with an electric knife for thin, even sandwich slices.

Variation
Substitute unsweetened apple juice for the brandy.

Dough Cycle and Bake Cycle

If your bread machine does not have a Gluten-Free Cycle, use the Dough Cycle followed by the Bake Cycle.

1. In a large bowl or plastic bag, combine sorghum flour, amaranth flour, almond flour, tapioca starch, xanthan gum, yeast, salt, chocolate chips and cherries; mix well and set aside.

2. Pour milk, oil, honey and brandy into the bread machine baking pan. Add eggs and egg whites.

3. Select the **Dough Cycle**. As the bread machine is mixing, gradually add the dry ingredients, scraping bottom and sides of pan with a rubber spatula. Try to incorporate all the dry ingredients within 1 to 2 minutes. When the mixing and kneading are complete, remove the kneading blade, leaving the bread pan in the bread machine. Quickly smooth the top of the loaf. Allow the cycle to finish. Turn off the bread machine.

4. Select the **Bake Cycle**. Set time to 60 minutes and temperature to 350°F (180°C). Allow the cycle to finish. Do not turn machine off before taking the internal temperature of the loaf with an instant-read thermometer. It should be 200°F (100°C). If it's between 180°F (85°C) and 200°F (100°C), leave machine on the **Keep Warm Cycle** until baked. If it's below 180°F (85°C), turn on the **Bake Cycle** and check the internal temperature every 10 minutes. (Some bread machines are automatically set for 60 minutes; others need to be set by 10-minute intervals.)

5. Once the loaf has reached 200°F (100°C), remove it from the pan immediately and let cool completely on a rack.

Chocolate Banana Bread

MAKES 15 SLICES
(1 per serving)

Here's a bread with dark, rich color, deep flavor, and a moist texture. Enjoy it warm for dessert.

Tips

To ensure success, see page 14 for information on using your bread machine and page 18 for general tips on bread machine baking.

Sift cocoa just before using, as it lumps easily.

You can use mini or jumbo chocolate chips, or just stick with the regular size.

If you use thawed frozen bananas, don't use any thin, watery parts, just the thicker banana.

1½ cups	sorghum flour	375 mL
¾ cup	quinoa flour	175 mL
½ cup	tapioca starch	125 mL
¼ cup	granulated sugar	60 mL
1 tbsp	xanthan gum	15 mL
2½ tsp	bread machine or instant yeast	12 mL
1¼ tsp	salt	6 mL
¼ cup	unsweetened cocoa powder, sifted	60 mL
½ cup	semisweet or bittersweet (dark) chocolate chips	125 mL
¾ cup	dried banana chips	175 mL
1 cup	mashed bananas	250 mL
¾ cup	milk, warmed to room temperature	175 mL
¼ cup	vegetable oil	60 mL
2 tsp	cider vinegar	10 mL
2	eggs, lightly beaten	2
2	egg whites, lightly beaten	2

1. In a large bowl or plastic bag, combine sorghum flour, quinoa flour, tapioca starch, sugar, xanthan gum, yeast, salt, cocoa, chocolate chips and banana chips; mix well and set aside.

2. Pour bananas, milk, oil and vinegar into the bread machine baking pan. Add eggs and egg whites.

3. Select the **Gluten-Free Cycle**. As the bread machine is mixing, gradually add the dry ingredients, scraping bottom and sides of pan with a rubber spatula. Try to incorporate all the dry ingredients within 1 to 2 minutes. When the mixing and kneading are complete, remove the kneading blade, leaving the bread pan in the bread machine. Quickly smooth the top of the loaf. Allow the cycle to finish.

4. At the end of the cycle, take the temperature of the loaf using an instant-read thermometer. It is baked at 200°F (100°C). If it's between 180°F (85°C) and 200°F (100°C), leave machine on the **Keep Warm Cycle** until baked. If it's below 180°F (85°C), turn on the **Bake Cycle** and check the internal temperature every 10 minutes. (Some bread machines are automatically set for 60 minutes; others need to be set by 10-minute intervals.)

NUTRITIONAL VALUES	
per serving	
Calories	250
Fat, total	10 g
Fat, saturated	4 g
Cholesterol	23 mg
Sodium	220 mg
Carbohydrate	37 g
Fiber	5 g
Protein	5 g
Calcium	26 mg
Iron	2 mg

Tip
For instructions on warming milk, see the Technique Glossary, page 308.

Variation
For a stronger chocolate flavor, increase the unsweetened cocoa powder to 1/3 cup (75 mL).

5. Once the loaf has reached 200°F (100°C), remove it from the pan immediately and let cool completely on a rack.

Dough Cycle and Bake Cycle

If your bread machine does not have a Gluten-Free Cycle, use the Dough Cycle followed by the Bake Cycle.

1. In a large bowl or plastic bag, combine sorghum flour, quinoa flour, tapioca starch, sugar, xanthan gum, yeast, salt, cocoa, chocolate chips and banana chips; mix well and set aside.

2. Pour bananas, milk, oil and vinegar into the bread machine baking pan. Add eggs and egg whites.

3. Select the **Dough Cycle**. As the bread machine is mixing, gradually add the dry ingredients, scraping bottom and sides of pan with a rubber spatula. Try to incorporate all the dry ingredients within 1 to 2 minutes. When the mixing and kneading are complete, remove the kneading blade, leaving the bread pan in the bread machine. Quickly smooth the top of the loaf. Allow the cycle to finish. Turn off the bread machine.

4. Select the **Bake Cycle**. Set time to 60 minutes and temperature to 350°F (180°C). Allow the cycle to finish. Do not turn machine off before taking the internal temperature of the loaf with an instant-read thermometer. It should be 200°F (100°C). If it's between 180°F (85°C) and 200°F (100°C), leave machine on the **Keep Warm Cycle** until baked. If it's below 180°F (85°C), turn on the **Bake Cycle** and check the internal temperature every 10 minutes. (Some bread machines are automatically set for 60 minutes; others need to be set by 10-minute intervals.)

5. Once the loaf has reached 200°F (100°C), remove it from the pan immediately and let cool completely on a rack.

Coconut Banana Bread

This Caribbean-inspired loaf is creamy in color and delightfully sweet.

Tips

To ensure success, see page 14 for information on using your bread machine and page 18 for general tips on bread machine baking.

Remember to thoroughly mix the dry ingredients before adding them to the liquids — they are powder-fine and could clump together.

1¼ cups	sorghum flour	300 mL
¾ cup	coconut flour	175 mL
¼ cup	tapioca starch	60 mL
¼ cup	nonfat dry milk or skim milk powder	60 mL
¼ cup	granulated sugar	60 mL
2½ tsp	xanthan gum	12 mL
1 tbsp	bread machine or instant yeast	15 mL
1¾ tsp	salt	8 mL
⅔ cup	sweetened shredded coconut	150 mL
½ cup	dried banana chips	125 mL
1¼ cups	water	300 mL
¾ cup	mashed bananas	175 mL
¼ cup	coconut oil or vegetable oil	60 mL
2 tsp	cider vinegar	10 mL
2	eggs, lightly beaten	2
2	egg whites, lightly beaten	2

1. In a large bowl or plastic bag, combine sorghum flour, coconut flour, tapioca starch, dry milk, sugar, xanthan gum, yeast, salt, coconut and banana chips; mix well and set aside.

2. Pour water, bananas, coconut oil and vinegar into the bread machine baking pan. Add eggs and egg whites.

3. Select the **Gluten-Free Cycle**. As the bread machine is mixing, gradually add the dry ingredients, scraping bottom and sides of pan with a rubber spatula. Try to incorporate all the dry ingredients within 1 to 2 minutes. When the mixing and kneading are complete, remove the kneading blade, leaving the bread pan in the bread machine. Quickly smooth the top of the loaf. Allow the cycle to finish.

4. At the end of the cycle, take the temperature of the loaf using an instant-read thermometer. It is baked at 200°F (100°C). If it's between 180°F (85°C) and 200°F (100°C), leave machine on the **Keep Warm Cycle** until baked. If it's below 180°F (85°C), turn on the **Bake Cycle** and check the internal temperature every 10 minutes. (Some bread machines are automatically set for 60 minutes; others need to be set by 10-minute intervals.)

5. Once the loaf has reached 200°F (100°C), remove it from the pan immediately and let cool completely on a rack.

NUTRITIONAL VALUES per serving	
Calories	195
Fat, total	10 g
Fat, saturated	6 g
Cholesterol	22 mg
Sodium	307 mg
Carbohydrate	23 g
Fiber	3 g
Protein	4 g
Calcium	20 mg
Iron	1 mg

Dough Cycle and Bake Cycle

If your bread machine does not have a Gluten-Free Cycle, use the Dough Cycle followed by the Bake Cycle.

1. In a large bowl or plastic bag, combine sorghum flour, coconut flour, tapioca starch, dry milk, sugar, xanthan gum, yeast, salt, coconut and banana chips; mix well and set aside.

2. Pour water, bananas, coconut oil and vinegar into the bread machine baking pan. Add eggs and egg whites.

3. Select the **Dough Cycle**. As the bread machine is mixing, gradually add the dry ingredients, scraping bottom and sides of pan with a rubber spatula. Try to incorporate all the dry ingredients within 1 to 2 minutes. When the mixing and kneading are complete, remove the kneading blade, leaving the bread pan in the bread machine. Quickly smooth the top of the loaf. Allow the cycle to finish. Turn off the bread machine.

4. Select the **Bake Cycle**. Set time to 60 minutes and temperature to 350°F (180°C). Allow the cycle to finish. Do not turn machine off before taking the internal temperature of the loaf with an instant-read thermometer. It should be 200°F (100°C). If it's between 180°F (85°C) and 200°F (100°C), leave machine on the **Keep Warm Cycle** until baked. If it's below 180°F (85°C), turn on the **Bake Cycle** and check the internal temperature every 10 minutes. (Some bread machines are automatically set for 60 minutes; others need to be set by 10-minute intervals.)

5. Once the loaf has reached 200°F (100°C), remove it from the pan immediately and let cool completely on a rack.

Coconut Bread

Dotted with flecks of coconut, this sweet white bread is delightful served with fresh pineapple.

Tips

To ensure success, see page 14 for information on using your bread machine and page 18 for general tips on bread machine baking.

Remember to thoroughly mix the dry ingredients before adding them to the liquids — they are powder-fine and could clump together.

1 cup	brown rice flour	250 mL
¾ cup	coconut flour	175 mL
½ cup	potato starch	125 mL
¼ cup	tapioca starch	60 mL
¼ cup	nonfat dry milk or skim milk powder	60 mL
¼ cup	granulated sugar	60 mL
2½ tsp	xanthan gum	12 mL
1¼ tsp	bread machine or instant yeast	6 mL
1¾ tsp	salt	8 mL
½ cup	unsweetened shredded coconut	125 mL
1½ cups	water	375 mL
¼ cup	coconut oil or vegetable oil	60 mL
1 tsp	cider vinegar	5 mL
2	eggs, lightly beaten	2
2	egg whites, lightly beaten	2

1. In a large bowl or plastic bag, combine brown rice flour, coconut flour, potato starch, tapioca starch, dry milk, sugar, xanthan gum, yeast, salt and coconut; mix well and set aside.

2. Pour water, coconut oil and vinegar into the bread machine baking pan. Add eggs and egg whites.

3. Select the **Gluten-Free Cycle**. As the bread machine is mixing, gradually add the dry ingredients, scraping bottom and sides of pan with a rubber spatula. Try to incorporate all the dry ingredients within 1 to 2 minutes. When the mixing and kneading are complete, remove the kneading blade, leaving the bread pan in the bread machine. Quickly smooth the top of the loaf. Allow the cycle to finish.

4. At the end of the cycle, take the temperature of the loaf using an instant-read thermometer. It is baked at 200°F (100°C). If it's between 180°F (85°C) and 200°F (100°C), leave machine on the **Keep Warm Cycle** until baked. If it's below 180°F (85°C), turn on the **Bake Cycle** and check the internal temperature every 10 minutes. (Some bread machines are automatically set for 60 minutes; others need to be set by 10-minute intervals.)

5. Once the loaf has reached 200°F (100°C), remove it from the pan immediately and let cool completely on a rack.

NUTRITIONAL VALUES
per serving

Calories	179
Fat, total	9 g
Fat, saturated	8 g
Cholesterol	22 mg
Sodium	298 mg
Carbohydrate	22 g
Fiber	2 g
Protein	3 g
Calcium	18 mg
Iron	1 mg

Tip
Always store bread at room temperature or wrapped airtight in the freezer. The refrigerator accelerates the staling process.

Variation
Add 1½ cups (375 mL) milk instead of the water and nonfat dry milk or skim milk powder.

Dough Cycle and Bake Cycle

If your bread machine does not have a Gluten-Free Cycle, use the Dough Cycle followed by the Bake Cycle.

1. In a large bowl or plastic bag, combine brown rice flour, coconut flour, potato starch, tapioca starch, dry milk, sugar, xanthan gum, yeast, salt and coconut; mix well and set aside.

2. Pour water, coconut oil and vinegar into the bread machine baking pan. Add eggs and egg whites.

3. Select the **Dough Cycle**. As the bread machine is mixing, gradually add the dry ingredients, scraping bottom and sides of pan with a rubber spatula. Try to incorporate all the dry ingredients within 1 to 2 minutes. When the mixing and kneading are complete, remove the kneading blade, leaving the bread pan in the bread machine. Quickly smooth the top of the loaf. Allow the cycle to finish. Turn off the bread machine.

4. Select the **Bake Cycle**. Set time to 60 minutes and temperature to 350°F (180°C). Allow the cycle to finish. Do not turn machine off before taking the internal temperature of the loaf with an instant-read thermometer. It should be 200°F (100°C). If it's between 180°F (85°C) and 200°F (100°C), leave machine on the **Keep Warm Cycle** until baked. If it's below 180°F (85°C), turn on the **Bake Cycle** and check the internal temperature every 10 minutes. (Some bread machines are automatically set for 60 minutes; others need to be set by 10-minute intervals.)

5. Once the loaf has reached 200°F (100°C), remove it from the pan immediately and let cool completely on a rack.

Coffee Raisin Loaf

Enjoy this rich, dark and delicious breakfast bread on a Sunday morning with a second cup of coffee.

Tips

To ensure success, see page 14 for information on using your bread machine and page 18 for general tips on bread machine baking.

Be sure the coffee is cooled to room temperature, as hot liquid could inactivate the yeast.

1 cup	sorghum flour	250 mL
¾ cup	whole bean flour	175 mL
½ cup	quinoa flour	125 mL
½ cup	tapioca starch	125 mL
¼ cup	packed brown sugar	60 mL
1 tbsp	xanthan gum	15 mL
1¼ tsp	bread machine or instant yeast	6 mL
1¼ tsp	salt	6 mL
1½ tsp	ground cinnamon	7 mL
½ tsp	ground allspice	2 mL
¼ tsp	ground cloves	1 mL
1 cup	raisins	250 mL
1¼ cups	freshly brewed strong coffee, at room temperature	300 mL
2 tbsp	vegetable oil	30 mL
1 tsp	cider vinegar	5 mL
2	eggs, lightly beaten	2
2	egg whites, lightly beaten	2

1. In a large bowl or plastic bag, combine sorghum flour, whole bean flour, quinoa flour, tapioca starch, brown sugar, xanthan gum, yeast, salt, cinnamon, allspice, cloves and raisins; mix well and set aside.

2. Pour coffee, oil and vinegar into the bread machine baking pan. Add eggs and egg whites.

3. Select the **Gluten-Free Cycle**. As the bread machine is mixing, gradually add the dry ingredients, scraping bottom and sides of pan with a rubber spatula. Try to incorporate all the dry ingredients within 1 to 2 minutes. When the mixing and kneading are complete, remove the kneading blade, leaving the bread pan in the bread machine. Quickly smooth the top of the loaf. Allow the cycle to finish.

4. At the end of the cycle, take the temperature of the loaf using an instant-read thermometer. It is baked at 200°F (100°C). If it's between 180°F (85°C) and 200°F (100°C), leave machine on the **Keep Warm Cycle** until baked. If it's below 180°F (85°C), turn on the **Bake Cycle** and check the internal temperature every 10 minutes. (Some bread machines are automatically set for 60 minutes; others need to be set by 10-minute intervals.)

NUTRITIONAL VALUES per serving	
Calories	170
Fat, total	4 g
Fat, saturated	0 g
Cholesterol	22 mg
Sodium	216 mg
Carbohydrate	30 g
Fiber	3 g
Protein	5 g
Calcium	23 mg
Iron	2 mg

Tips

Thoroughly mix the dry ingredients before adding them to the liquids — they are powder-fine and could clump together.

Slice this or any bread with an electric knife for thin, even sandwich slices.

Dough Cycle and Bake Cycle

If your bread machine does not have a Gluten-Free Cycle, use the Dough Cycle followed by the Bake Cycle.

1. In a large bowl or plastic bag, combine sorghum flour, whole bean flour, quinoa flour, tapioca starch, brown sugar, xanthan gum, yeast, salt, cinnamon, allspice, cloves and raisins; mix well and set aside.

2. Pour coffee, oil and vinegar into the bread machine baking pan. Add eggs and egg whites.

3. Select the **Dough Cycle**. As the bread machine is mixing, gradually add the dry ingredients, scraping bottom and sides of pan with a rubber spatula. Try to incorporate all the dry ingredients within 1 to 2 minutes. When the mixing and kneading are complete, remove the kneading blade, leaving the bread pan in the bread machine. Quickly smooth the top of the loaf. Allow the cycle to finish. Turn off the bread machine.

4. Select the **Bake Cycle**. Set time to 60 minutes and temperature to 350°F (180°C). Allow the cycle to finish. Do not turn machine off before taking the internal temperature of the loaf with an instant-read thermometer. It should be 200°F (100°C). If it's between 180°F (85°C) and 200°F (100°C), leave machine on the **Keep Warm Cycle** until baked. If it's below 180°F (85°C), turn on the **Bake Cycle** and check the internal temperature every 10 minutes. (Some bread machines are automatically set for 60 minutes; others need to be set by 10-minute intervals.)

5. Once the loaf has reached 200°F (100°C), remove it from the pan immediately and let cool completely on a rack.

Date Bran Bread

The moist, dark, sweet slices of this loaf are delicious spread with cream cheese.

Tips

To ensure success, see page 14 for information on using your bread machine and page 18 for general tips on bread machine baking.

Warm up rice bran that has been stored in the refrigerator or freezer to room temperature.

Snip the dates with kitchen shears. Dip the blades in hot water when they become sticky.

1¼ cups	sorghum flour	300 mL
1 cup	whole bean flour	250 mL
¼ cup	rice bran	60 mL
½ cup	potato starch	125 mL
1 tbsp	xanthan gum	15 mL
1½ tsp	bread machine or instant yeast	7 mL
1½ tsp	salt	7 mL
1¼ cups	whole dates, cut in half	300 mL
1½ cups	water	375 mL
3 tbsp	vegetable oil	45 mL
3 tbsp	liquid honey	45 mL
1 tbsp	light (fancy) molasses	15 mL
1 tsp	cider vinegar	5 mL
2	eggs, lightly beaten	2
2	egg whites, lightly beaten	2

1. In a large bowl, combine sorghum flour, whole bean flour, rice bran, potato starch, xanthan gum, yeast, salt and dates; mix well and set aside.

2. Pour water, oil, honey, molasses and vinegar into the bread machine baking pan. Add eggs and egg whites.

3. Select the **Gluten-Free Cycle**. As the bread machine is mixing, gradually add the dry ingredients, scraping bottom and sides of pan with a rubber spatula. Try to incorporate all the dry ingredients within 1 to 2 minutes. When the mixing and kneading are complete, remove the kneading blade, leaving the bread pan in the bread machine. Quickly smooth the top of the loaf. Allow the cycle to finish.

4. At the end of the cycle, take the temperature of the loaf using an instant-read thermometer. It is baked at 200°F (100°C). If it's between 180°F (85°C) and 200°F (100°C), leave machine on the **Keep Warm Cycle** until baked. If it's below 180°F (85°C), turn on the **Bake Cycle** and check the internal temperature every 10 minutes. (Some bread machines are automatically set for 60 minutes; others need to be set by 10-minute intervals.)

5. Once the loaf has reached 200°F (100°C), remove it from the pan immediately and let cool completely on a rack.

NUTRITIONAL VALUES per serving	
Calories	204
Fat, total	5 g
Fat, saturated	1 g
Cholesterol	22 mg
Sodium	250 mg
Carbohydrate	37 g
Fiber	4 g
Protein	6 g
Calcium	22 mg
Iron	2 mg

It is easier to measure honey and molasses if they are warmed in the microwave for a few seconds, or set in a pan of hot water for a few minutes. Measure the oil first, then measure the honey and molasses; they will slide off the measuring spoon more easily that way.

Variation
Substitute GF oat bran for the rice bran.

Dough Cycle and Bake Cycle

If your bread machine does not have a Gluten-Free Cycle, use the Dough Cycle followed by the Bake Cycle.

1. In a large bowl, combine sorghum flour, whole bean flour, rice bran, potato starch, xanthan gum, yeast, salt and dates; mix well and set aside.

2. Pour water, oil, honey, molasses and vinegar into the bread machine baking pan. Add eggs and egg whites.

3. Select the **Dough Cycle**. As the bread machine is mixing, gradually add the dry ingredients, scraping bottom and sides of pan with a rubber spatula. Try to incorporate all the dry ingredients within 1 to 2 minutes. When the mixing and kneading are complete, remove the kneading blade, leaving the bread pan in the bread machine. Quickly smooth the top of the loaf. Allow the cycle to finish. Turn off the bread machine.

4. Select the **Bake Cycle**. Set time to 60 minutes and temperature to 350°F (180°C). Allow the cycle to finish. Do not turn machine off before taking the internal temperature of the loaf with an instant-read thermometer. It should be 200°F (100°C). If it's between 180°F (85°C) and 200°F (100°C), leave machine on the **Keep Warm Cycle** until baked. If it's below 180°F (85°C), turn on the **Bake Cycle** and check the internal temperature every 10 minutes. (Some bread machines are automatically set for 60 minutes; others need to be set by 10-minute intervals.)

5. Once the loaf has reached 200°F (100°C), remove it from the pan immediately and let cool completely on a rack.

Triple-Oat Fig Bread

Oatmeal lends a distinct color and flavor to bread. The three oat ingredients here add extra flavor and nutrition. Figs are a good source of fiber.

Tips

To ensure success, see page 14 for information on using your bread machine and page 18 for general tips on bread machine baking.

Instead of chopping with a knife, snip figs with kitchen shears. Dip the blades in hot water when they become sticky.

Use a zester to make long, thin strips of orange zest. Be sure to remove only the colored outer layer, avoiding the bitter white pith beneath.

1²/₃ cups	sorghum flour	400 mL
½ cup	GF oats	125 mL
½ cup	GF oat flour	125 mL
2 tbsp	GF oat bran	30 mL
½ cup	tapioca starch	125 mL
3 tbsp	packed brown sugar	45 mL
1 tbsp	xanthan gum	15 mL
2 tsp	bread machine or instant yeast	10 mL
1¼ tsp	salt	6 mL
1 cup	dried figs, snipped	250 mL
¾ cup	water	175 mL
2 tbsp	grated orange zest	30 mL
½ cup	freshly squeezed orange juice	125 mL
¼ cup	vegetable oil	60 mL
2	eggs, lightly beaten	2
2	egg whites, lightly beaten	2

1. In a large bowl or plastic bag, combine sorghum flour, oats, oat flour, oat bran, tapioca starch, brown sugar, xanthan gum, yeast, salt and figs; mix well and set aside.

2. Pour water, orange zest, orange juice and oil into the bread machine baking pan. Add eggs and egg whites.

3. Select the **Gluten-Free Cycle**. As the bread machine is mixing, gradually add the dry ingredients, scraping bottom and sides of pan with a rubber spatula. Try to incorporate all the dry ingredients within 1 to 2 minutes. When the mixing and kneading are complete, remove the kneading blade, leaving the bread pan in the bread machine. Quickly smooth the top of the loaf. Allow the cycle to finish.

4. At the end of the cycle, take the temperature of the loaf using an instant-read thermometer. It is baked at 200°F (100°C). If it's between 180°F (85°C) and 200°F (100°C), leave machine on the **Keep Warm Cycle** until baked. If it's below 180°F (85°C), turn on the **Bake Cycle** and check the internal temperature every 10 minutes. (Some bread machines are automatically set for 60 minutes; others need to be set by 10-minute intervals.)

5. Once the loaf has reached 200°F (100°C), remove it from the pan immediately and let cool completely on a rack.

NUTRITIONAL VALUES
per serving

Calories	175
Fat, total	5 g
Fat, saturated	1 g
Cholesterol	22 mg
Sodium	213 mg
Carbohydrate	30 g
Fiber	4 g
Protein	4 g
Calcium	27 mg
Iron	1 mg

Freshly squeezed orange juice enhances the flavor of this loaf. Roll the orange on the counter or between your hands to loosen the juice.

Keep an orange in the freezer. Zest while frozen, then juice after warming in the microwave.

Dough Cycle and Bake Cycle

If your bread machine does not have a Gluten-Free Cycle, use the Dough Cycle followed by the Bake Cycle.

1. In a large bowl or plastic bag, combine sorghum flour, oats, oat flour, oat bran, tapioca starch, brown sugar, xanthan gum, yeast, salt and figs; mix well and set aside.

2. Pour water, orange zest, orange juice and oil into the bread machine baking pan. Add eggs and egg whites.

3. Select the **Dough Cycle**. As the bread machine is mixing, gradually add the dry ingredients, scraping bottom and sides of pan with a rubber spatula. Try to incorporate all the dry ingredients within 1 to 2 minutes. When the mixing and kneading are complete, remove the kneading blade, leaving the bread pan in the bread machine. Quickly smooth the top of the loaf. Allow the cycle to finish. Turn off the bread machine.

4. Select the **Bake Cycle**. Set time to 60 minutes and temperature to 350°F (180°C). Allow the cycle to finish. Do not turn machine off before taking the internal temperature of the loaf with an instant-read thermometer. It should be 200°F (100°C). If it's between 180°F (85°C) and 200°F (100°C), leave machine on the **Keep Warm Cycle** until baked. If it's below 180°F (85°C), turn on the **Bake Cycle** and check the internal temperature every 10 minutes. (Some bread machines are automatically set for 60 minutes; others need to be set by 10-minute intervals.)

5. Once the loaf has reached 200°F (100°C), remove it from the pan immediately and let cool completely on a rack.

Golden Harvest Loaf

The warm golden color of this loaf reminds us of an autumn field ready for harvest.

Tips

To ensure success, see page 14 for information on using your bread machine and page 18 for general tips on bread machine baking.

Microwave the sweet potato as you would a regular baked potato, until fork-tender. (Cooking time will depend on size of potato.) Peel, then mash when cool enough to handle.

Wet pea flour has a strong odor that disappears when it is baked.

NUTRITIONAL VALUES per serving	
Calories	163
Fat, total	5 g
Fat, saturated	1 g
Cholesterol	22 mg
Sodium	269 mg
Carbohydrate	26 g
Fiber	4 g
Protein	5 g
Calcium	26 mg
Iron	2 mg

1 cup	amaranth flour	250 mL
2/3 cup	yellow pea flour	150 mL
1/3 cup	cornmeal	75 mL
1/2 cup	tapioca starch	125 mL
1/4 cup	packed brown sugar	60 mL
2 1/2 tsp	xanthan gum	12 mL
2 1/2 tsp	bread machine or instant yeast	12 mL
1 1/2 tsp	salt	7 mL
1 1/4 cups	mashed cooked sweet potato (see tip, at left), at room temperature	300 mL
1 tbsp	grated orange zest	15 mL
1/3 cup	freshly squeezed orange juice	75 mL
1/4 cup	vegetable oil	60 mL
2 tsp	cider vinegar	10 mL
2	eggs, lightly beaten	2
2	egg whites, lightly beaten	2

1. In a large bowl or plastic bag, combine amaranth flour, pea flour, cornmeal, tapioca starch, brown sugar, xanthan gum, yeast and salt; mix well and set aside.

2. Pour sweet potato, orange zest, orange juice, oil and vinegar into the bread machine baking pan. Add eggs and egg whites.

3. Select the **Gluten-Free Cycle**. As the bread machine is mixing, gradually add the dry ingredients, scraping bottom and sides of pan with a rubber spatula. Try to incorporate all the dry ingredients within 1 to 2 minutes. When the mixing and kneading are complete, remove the kneading blade, leaving the bread pan in the bread machine. Quickly smooth the top of the loaf. Allow the cycle to finish.

4. At the end of the cycle, take the temperature of the loaf using an instant-read thermometer. It is baked at 200°F (100°C). If it's between 180°F (85°C) and 200°F (100°C), leave machine on the **Keep Warm Cycle** until baked. If it's below 180°F (85°C), turn on the **Bake Cycle** and check the internal temperature every 10 minutes. (Some bread machines are automatically set for 60 minutes; others need to be set by 10-minute intervals.)

5. Once the loaf has reached 200°F (100°C), remove it from the pan immediately and let cool completely on a rack.

Tips

Use a zester to make long, thin strips of orange zest. Be sure to remove only the colored outer layer, avoiding the bitter white pith beneath.

Freshly squeezed orange juice enhances the flavor. Roll the orange on the counter or between your hands to loosen the juice.

Keep an orange in the freezer. Zest while frozen, then juice after warming in the microwave.

Variation

Substitute canned sweet potatoes or yams, well drained, for the fresh.

Dough Cycle and Bake Cycle

If your bread machine does not have a Gluten-Free Cycle, use the Dough Cycle followed by the Bake Cycle.

1. In a large bowl or plastic bag, combine amaranth flour, pea flour, cornmeal, tapioca starch, brown sugar, xanthan gum, yeast and salt; mix well and set aside.

2. Pour sweet potato, orange zest, orange juice, oil and vinegar into the bread machine baking pan. Add eggs and egg whites.

3. Select the **Dough Cycle**. As the bread machine is mixing, gradually add the dry ingredients, scraping bottom and sides of pan with a rubber spatula. Try to incorporate all the dry ingredients within 1 to 2 minutes. When the mixing and kneading are complete, remove the kneading blade, leaving the bread pan in the bread machine. Quickly smooth the top of the loaf. Allow the cycle to finish. Turn off the bread machine.

4. Select the **Bake Cycle**. Set time to 60 minutes and temperature to 350°F (180°C). Allow the cycle to finish. Do not turn machine off before taking the internal temperature of the loaf with an instant-read thermometer. It should be 200°F (100°C). If it's between 180°F (85°C) and 200°F (100°C), leave machine on the **Keep Warm Cycle** until baked. If it's below 180°F (85°C), turn on the **Bake Cycle** and check the internal temperature every 10 minutes. (Some bread machines are automatically set for 60 minutes; others need to be set by 10-minute intervals.)

5. Once the loaf has reached 200°F (100°C), remove it from the pan immediately and let cool completely on a rack.

Autumn Squash Bread

Warm slices of this golden bread make the perfect complement to your autumn Sunday supper.

Tips

To ensure success, see page 14 for information on using your bread machine and page 18 for general tips on bread machine baking.

Use butternut or Hubbard squash for this recipe. Scoop out seeds from one-half squash and microwave on High for 3 to 4 minutes per pound (500 g), or until tender. Mash without adding butter or sugar.

1½ cups	sorghum flour	375 mL
⅓ cup	amaranth flour	75 mL
¼ cup	quinoa flour	60 mL
½ cup	tapioca starch	125 mL
¼ cup	packed brown sugar	60 mL
2½ tsp	xanthan gum	12 mL
2 tsp	bread machine or instant yeast	10 mL
1½ tsp	salt	7 mL
1 tsp	ground nutmeg	5 mL
1¼ cups	mashed cooked squash, at room temperature	300 mL
¼ cup	water	60 mL
¼ cup	vegetable oil	60 mL
2 tsp	cider vinegar	10 mL
2	eggs, lightly beaten	2
2	egg whites, lightly beaten	2

1. In a large bowl or plastic bag, combine sorghum flour, amaranth flour, quinoa flour, tapioca starch, brown sugar, xanthan gum, yeast, salt and nutmeg; mix well and set aside.

2. Pour squash, water, oil and vinegar into the bread machine baking pan. Add eggs and egg whites.

3. Select the **Gluten-Free Cycle**. As the bread machine is mixing, gradually add the dry ingredients, scraping bottom and sides of pan with a rubber spatula. Try to incorporate all the dry ingredients within 1 to 2 minutes. When the mixing and kneading are complete, remove the kneading blade, leaving the bread pan in the bread machine. Quickly smooth the top of the loaf. Allow the cycle to finish.

4. At the end of the cycle, take the temperature of the loaf using an instant-read thermometer. It is baked at 200°F (100°C). If it's between 180°F (85°C) and 200°F (100°C), leave machine on the **Keep Warm Cycle** until baked. If it's below 180°F (85°C), turn on the **Bake Cycle** and check the internal temperature every 10 minutes. (Some bread machines are automatically set for 60 minutes; others need to be set by 10-minute intervals.)

5. Once the loaf has reached 200°F (100°C), remove it from the pan immediately and let cool completely on a rack.

NUTRITIONAL VALUES per serving	
Calories	141
Fat, total	5 g
Fat, saturated	1 g
Cholesterol	22 mg
Sodium	252 mg
Carbohydrate	22 g
Fiber	3 g
Protein	4 g
Calcium	14 mg
Iron	1 mg

Thoroughly mix the dry ingredients before adding them to the liquids — they are powder-fine and could clump together.

Slice this or any bread with an electric knife for thin, even sandwich slices.

Dough Cycle and Bake Cycle

If your bread machine does not have a Gluten-Free Cycle, use the Dough Cycle followed by the Bake Cycle.

1. In a large bowl or plastic bag, combine sorghum flour, amaranth flour, quinoa flour, tapioca starch, brown sugar, xanthan gum, yeast, salt and nutmeg; mix well and set aside.

2. Pour squash, water, oil and vinegar into the bread machine baking pan. Add eggs and egg whites.

3. Select the **Dough Cycle**. As the bread machine is mixing, gradually add the dry ingredients, scraping bottom and sides of pan with a rubber spatula. Try to incorporate all the dry ingredients within 1 to 2 minutes. When the mixing and kneading are complete, remove the kneading blade, leaving the bread pan in the bread machine. Quickly smooth the top of the loaf. Allow the cycle to finish. Turn off the bread machine.

4. Select the **Bake Cycle**. Set time to 60 minutes and temperature to 350°F (180°C). Allow the cycle to finish. Do not turn machine off before taking the internal temperature of the loaf with an instant-read thermometer. It should be 200°F (100°C). If it's between 180°F (85°C) and 200°F (100°C), leave machine on the **Keep Warm Cycle** until baked. If it's below 180°F (85°C), turn on the **Bake Cycle** and check the internal temperature every 10 minutes. (Some bread machines are automatically set for 60 minutes; others need to be set by 10-minute intervals.)

5. Once the loaf has reached 200°F (100°C), remove it from the pan immediately and let cool completely on a rack.

Pumpkin Pie Bread

MAKES 15 SLICES
(1 per serving)

This attractive loaf is sure to bring compliments and memories of autumn and Thanksgiving.

Tips

To ensure success, see page 14 for information on using your bread machine and page 18 for general tips on bread machine baking.

Be sure to use unsweetened pumpkin purée; pumpkin pie filling is too sweet.

1½ cups	sorghum flour	375 mL
½ cup	pea flour	125 mL
½ cup	tapioca starch	125 mL
½ cup	buttermilk powder	125 mL
¼ cup	granulated sugar	60 mL
2½ tsp	xanthan gum	12 mL
1 tbsp	bread machine or instant yeast	15 mL
1½ tsp	salt	7 mL
2 tsp	ground cinnamon	10 mL
1 tsp	ground cloves	5 mL
½ tsp	ground nutmeg	2 mL
1¼ cups	pumpkin purée (not pie filling)	300 mL
¼ cup	water	60 mL
¼ cup	vegetable oil	60 mL
2 tsp	cider vinegar	10 mL
2	eggs, lightly beaten	2
2	egg whites, lightly beaten	2

1. In a large bowl or plastic bag, combine sorghum flour, pea flour, tapioca starch, buttermilk powder, sugar, xanthan gum, yeast, salt, cinnamon, cloves and nutmeg; mix well and set aside.

2. Pour pumpkin purée, water, oil and vinegar into the bread machine baking pan. Add eggs and egg whites.

3. Select the **Gluten-Free Cycle**. As the bread machine is mixing, gradually add the dry ingredients, scraping bottom and sides of pan with a rubber spatula. Try to incorporate all the dry ingredients within 1 to 2 minutes. When the mixing and kneading are complete, remove the kneading blade, leaving the bread pan in the bread machine. Quickly smooth the top of the loaf. Allow the cycle to finish.

4. At the end of the cycle, take the temperature of the loaf using an instant-read thermometer. It is baked at 200°F (100°C). If it's between 180°F (85°C) and 200°F (100°C), leave machine on the **Keep Warm Cycle** until baked. If it's below 180°F (85°C), turn on the **Bake Cycle** and check the internal temperature every 10 minutes. (Some bread machines are automatically set for 60 minutes; others need to be set by 10-minute intervals.)

NUTRITIONAL VALUES
per serving

Calories	160
Fat, total	5 g
Fat, saturated	1 g
Cholesterol	25 mg
Sodium	274 mg
Carbohydrate	24 g
Fiber	4 g
Protein	6 g
Calcium	65 mg
Iron	1 mg

Tips

Thoroughly mix the dry ingredients before adding them to the liquids — they are powder-fine and could clump together.

Slice this or any bread with an electric knife for thin, even sandwich slices.

Dough Cycle and Bake Cycle

If your bread machine does not have a Gluten-Free Cycle, use the Dough Cycle followed by the Bake Cycle.

1. In a large bowl or plastic bag, combine sorghum flour, pea flour, tapioca starch, buttermilk powder, sugar, xanthan gum, yeast, salt, cinnamon, cloves and nutmeg; mix well and set aside.

2. Pour pumpkin purée, water, oil and vinegar into the bread machine baking pan. Add eggs and egg whites.

3. Select the **Dough Cycle**. As the bread machine is mixing, gradually add the dry ingredients, scraping bottom and sides of pan with a rubber spatula. Try to incorporate all the dry ingredients within 1 to 2 minutes. When the mixing and kneading are complete, remove the kneading blade, leaving the bread pan in the bread machine. Quickly smooth the top of the loaf. Allow the cycle to finish. Turn off the bread machine.

4. Select the **Bake Cycle**. Set time to 60 minutes and temperature to 350°F (180°C). Allow the cycle to finish. Do not turn machine off before taking the internal temperature of the loaf with an instant-read thermometer. It should be 200°F (100°C). If it's between 180°F (85°C) and 200°F (100°C), leave machine on the **Keep Warm Cycle** until baked. If it's below 180°F (85°C), turn on the **Bake Cycle** and check the internal temperature every 10 minutes. (Some bread machines are automatically set for 60 minutes; others need to be set by 10-minute intervals.)

5. Once the loaf has reached 200°F (100°C), remove it from the pan immediately and let cool completely on a rack.

Pumpkin Spread

MAKES 2¼ CUPS
(550 ML)
2 tbsp (25 mL)
per serving

One taste of this addictive spread and you'll love it as much as we do. It's fabulous in place of butter, layered over any of the autumn-themed breads in this book.

Tips

Recipe can be doubled to use a whole 28-oz (796 mL) can of pumpkin purée.

If you prefer a smoother spread, purée in a food processor or blender.

Variation

For a slightly tangier version, use apple cider instead of the applesauce.

1¾ cups	canned pumpkin purée (not pie filling)	425 mL
¾ cup	unsweetened applesauce	175 mL
⅓ cup	packed brown sugar	75 mL
1 tsp	ground cinnamon	5 mL
¼ tsp	ground allspice	1 mL
¼ tsp	ground cloves	1 mL
1 tsp	freshly squeezed lemon juice	5 mL

1. In a saucepan, combine pumpkin, applesauce, brown sugar, cinnamon, allspice and cloves. Bring to a boil over medium heat, stirring constantly. Reduce heat to low and simmer gently, stirring frequently, for 5 minutes. Remove from heat and stir in lemon juice. Store in the refrigerator for up to 2 weeks or freeze for up to 3 months.

NUTRITIONAL VALUES per serving	
Calories	28
Fat, total	0 g
Fat, saturated	0 g
Cholesterol	0 mg
Sodium	3 mg
Carbohydrate	7 g
Fiber	1 g
Protein	0 g
Calcium	12 mg
Iron	1 mg

Quick 'n' Easy Mixes

Our bread mixes were one of the most popular features in *125 Best Gluten-Free Bread Machine Recipes*, and we've had many requests for versions of these mixes made without nuts or rice. We're happy to oblige, and have given you a nut-free variation of our White Bread Mix and five recipes to make with it, as well as a rice-free variation of our Brown Bread Mix and five recipes to make with it. As a bonus, we've added a cornbread mix and seven recipes to make with it.

Single-Loaf Nut-Free Creamy Bread Mix

*We've received many
emails asking how to
substitute for the nut
flour in our original
White Bread Mix.
Here's the answer to your
requests! Try this single-
loaf mix before making
the larger batches on
pages 185 and 186. You
can use this mix to make
Nut-Free Sandwich
Bread (page 188), Nut-
Free Orange Chocolate
Chip Loaf (page 190),
Nut-Free Dinner Rolls
(page 187), Nut-Free
Cheese Rolls (page 192)
or Nut-Free Rosemary
Breadsticks (page 193).
It's sure to become your
favorite nutritious
bread mix.*

1½ cups	brown rice flour	375 mL
⅔ cup	amaranth flour	150 mL
½ cup	quinoa flour	125 mL
⅓ cup	potato starch	75 mL
¼ cup	tapioca starch	60 mL
1 tbsp	xanthan gum	15 mL
1¼ tsp	bread machine or instant yeast	6 mL
1¼ tsp	salt	6 mL

1. In a large bowl, combine brown rice flour, amaranth flour, quinoa flour, potato starch, tapioca starch, xanthan gum, yeast and salt; mix well.

2. Use right away or seal tightly in a plastic bag, removing as much air as possible. Store at room temperature for up to 3 days or in the freezer for up to 6 months.

Working with Bread Mix

- Label and date the package if not using bread mix immediately. We add the page number of the recipe to the label as a quick reference.
- Let bread mix warm to room temperature, and mix well before using.

NUTRITIONAL VALUES
per serving

Calories	119
Fat, total	1 g
Fat, saturated	0 g
Cholesterol	0 mg
Sodium	238 mg
Carbohydrate	26 g
Fiber	2 g
Protein	3 g
Calcium	9 mg
Iron	1 mg

Four-Loaf Nut-Free Creamy Bread Mix

**MAKES ABOUT
14 CUPS (3.5 L),
ENOUGH FOR
4 LOAVES**
(1/4 cup/60 mL per
serving)

*Here's the four-loaf
version of our Nut-Free
Creamy Bread mix. Use
it to make the recipes on
pages 187–193.*

Tips

For accuracy, use a 1-cup
(250 mL) dry measure
several times to measure
each type of flour and
starch. If you use a 4-cup
(1 L) liquid measure, it's
difficult to get an accurate
volume and you'll end up
with extra flour in the mix.

We used a large roasting
pan to combine all the
ingredients.

	NUTRITIONAL VALUES per serving	
Calories	114
Fat, total	1 g
Fat, saturated	0 g
Cholesterol	0 mg
Sodium	238 mg
Carbohydrate	25 g
Fiber	2 g
Protein	3 g
Calcium	9 mg
Iron	1 mg

6 cups	brown rice flour	1500 mL
2 2/3 cups	amaranth flour	650 mL
2 cups	quinoa flour	500 mL
1 1/3 cups	potato starch	325 mL
1 cup	tapioca starch	250 mL
1/4 cup	xanthan gum	60 mL
2 tbsp	bread machine or instant yeast	30 mL
2 tbsp	salt	30 mL

1. In a very large container, combine brown rice flour, amaranth flour, quinoa flour, potato starch, tapioca starch, xanthan gum, yeast and salt; mix well.

2. Divide into 4 equal portions of about 3 1/2 cups (875 mL) each. Seal tightly in plastic bags, removing as much air as possible. Store at room temperature for up to 3 days or in the freezer for up to 6 weeks.

Working with Bread Mix

- In step 2, stir the mix before spooning it very lightly into the dry measures. Do not pack.

- Be sure to divide the mix into equal portions. Depending on how much air you incorporate into the mix, and the texture of the individual gluten-free flours, the total volume of the mix can vary slightly. The important thing is to make the number of portions specified in the recipe.

- Label and date the packages before storing. We add the page number of the recipe to the labels as a quick reference.

- Let bread mix warm to room temperature, and mix well before using.

Six-Loaf Nut-Free Creamy Bread Mix

*When you want to
make a really big batch
of bread mix, this is the
recipe for you. Use it
to make the recipes on
pages 187–193.*

Tips

For accuracy, use a 1-cup
(250 mL) dry measure
several times to measure
each type of flour and
starch. If you use a 4-cup
(1 L) liquid measure, it's
difficult to get an accurate
volume and you'll end up
with extra flour in the mix.

We used a large roasting
pan to combine all the
ingredients.

NUTRITIONAL VALUES per serving	
Calories	119
Fat, total	1 g
Fat, saturated	0 g
Cholesterol	0 mg
Sodium	238 mg
Carbohydrate	26 g
Fiber	2 g
Protein	3 g
Calcium	9 mg
Iron	1 mg

9¼ cups	brown rice flour	2300 mL
4¼ cups	amaranth flour	1060 mL
3 cups	quinoa flour	750 mL
2¼ cups	potato starch	550 mL
1½ cups	tapioca starch	375 mL
⅓ cup	xanthan gum	75 mL
3 tbsp	bread machine or instant yeast	45 mL
3 tbsp	salt	45 mL

1. In a very large container, combine brown rice flour, amaranth flour, quinoa flour, potato starch, tapioca starch, xanthan gum, yeast and salt; mix well. (When working with this large a volume of ingredients, it is especially important to mix them very well before portioning.)

2. Divide into 6 equal portions of about 3½ cups (875 mL) each. Seal tightly in plastic bags, removing as much air as possible. Store at room temperature for up to 3 days or freeze for up to 6 weeks.

Working with Bread Mix

- In step 2, stir the mix before spooning it very lightly into the dry measures. Do not pack.
- Be sure to divide the mix into equal portions. Depending on how much air you incorporate into the mix, and the texture of the individual gluten-free flours, the total volume of the mix can vary slightly. The important thing is to make the number of portions specified in the recipe.
- Label and date the packages before storing. We add the page number of the recipe to the labels as a quick reference.
- Let bread mix warm to room temperature, and mix well before using.

Nut-Free Dinner Rolls

These nut-free all-purpose dinner rolls are a cinch to prepare and a delight to eat.

Tips

To ensure success, see page 14 for information on using your bread machine and page 18 for general tips on bread machine baking.

For a softer crust, brush the rolls with melted butter as soon as you remove them from the oven.

You can use ½ cup (125 mL) liquid whole eggs and 2 tbsp (30 mL) liquid egg white, if you prefer.

◆ 12-cup muffin tin, lightly greased

1¼ cups	water	300 mL
2 tbsp	vegetable oil	30 mL
¼ cup	liquid honey	60 mL
1 tsp	cider vinegar	5 mL
2	eggs, lightly beaten	2
1	egg white, lightly beaten	1
3½ cups	Nut-Free Creamy Bread Mix (pages 184–186)	875 mL

1. Pour water, oil, honey and vinegar into the bread machine baking pan. Add eggs and egg white.

2. Select the **Dough Cycle**. As the bread machine is mixing, gradually add the bread mix, scraping bottom and sides of pan with a rubber spatula. Try to incorporate all the bread mix within 1 to 2 minutes. Stop bread machine as soon as the kneading portion of the cycle is complete. Do not let bread machine finish the cycle.

3. Using a ¼-cup (60 mL) scoop, divide dough into 12 equal amounts and place in cups of prepared muffin tin. Let rise, uncovered, in a warm, draft-free place for 60 to 75 minutes or until dough has risen to the top of the cups. Meanwhile, preheat oven to 350°F (180°C).

4. Bake for 18 to 20 minutes or until internal temperature of rolls registers 200°F (100°C) on an instant-read thermometer. Remove from the tin immediately and let cool completely on a rack.

NUTRITIONAL VALUES per serving	
Calories	197
Fat, total	4 g
Fat, saturated	1 g
Cholesterol	27 mg
Sodium	264 mg
Carbohydrate	37 g
Fiber	3 g
Protein	4 g
Calcium	15 mg
Iron	1 mg

Nut-Free Sandwich Bread

This nut-free version of our nutritious white sandwich bread is destined to become your favorite.

Tip

To ensure success, see page 14 for information on using your bread machine and page 18 for general tips on bread machine baking.

1¼ cups	water	300 mL
¼ cup	vegetable oil	60 mL
2 tbsp	liquid honey	30 mL
1 tsp	cider vinegar	5 mL
2	eggs, lightly beaten	2
2	egg whites, lightly beaten	2
3½ cups	Nut-Free Creamy Bread Mix (pages 184–186)	875 mL

1. Pour water, oil, honey and vinegar into the bread machine baking pan. Add eggs and egg whites.

2. Select the **Gluten-Free Cycle**. As the bread machine is mixing, gradually add the bread mix, scraping bottom and sides of pan with a rubber spatula. Try to incorporate all the bread mix within 1 to 2 minutes. When the mixing and kneading are complete, remove the kneading blade, leaving the bread pan in the bread machine. Quickly smooth the top of the loaf. Allow the cycle to finish.

3. At the end of the cycle, take the temperature of the loaf using an instant-read thermometer. It is baked at 200°F (100°C). If it's between 180°F (85°C) and 200°F (100°C), leave machine on the **Keep Warm Cycle** until baked. If it's below 180°F (85°C), turn on the **Bake Cycle** and check the internal temperature every 10 minutes. (Some bread machines are automatically set for 60 minutes; others need to be set by 10-minute intervals.)

4. Once the loaf has reached 200°F (100°C), remove it from the pan immediately and let cool completely on a rack.

NUTRITIONAL VALUES
per serving

Calories	166
Fat, total	5 g
Fat, saturated	1 g
Cholesterol	22 mg
Sodium	215 mg
Carbohydrate	27 g
Fiber	2 g
Protein	4 g
Calcium	12 mg
Iron	1 mg

Tip

Always store bread at room temperature or wrapped airtight in the freezer. The refrigerator accelerates the staling process.

Variation

To turn this into a raisin loaf, add ½ cup (125 mL) raisins and 1 tsp (5 mL) ground cinnamon with the bread mix.

Dough Cycle and Bake Cycle

If your bread machine does not have a Gluten-Free Cycle, use the Dough Cycle followed by the Bake Cycle.

1. Pour water, oil, honey and vinegar into the bread machine baking pan. Add eggs and egg whites.

2. Select the **Dough Cycle**. As the bread machine is mixing, gradually add the bread mix, scraping bottom and sides of pan with a rubber spatula. Try to incorporate all the bread mix within 1 to 2 minutes. When the mixing and kneading are complete, remove the kneading blade, leaving the bread pan in the bread machine. Quickly smooth the top of the loaf. Allow the cycle to finish. Turn off the bread machine.

3. Select the **Bake Cycle**. Set time to 60 minutes and temperature to 350°F (180°C). Allow the cycle to finish. Do not turn machine off before taking the internal temperature of the loaf with an instant-read thermometer. It should be 200°F (100°C). If it's between 180°F (85°C) and 200°F (100°C), leave machine on the **Keep Warm Cycle** until baked. If it's below 180°F (85°C), turn on the **Bake Cycle** and check the internal temperature every 10 minutes. (Some bread machines are automatically set for 60 minutes; others need to be set by 10-minute intervals.)

4. Once the loaf has reached 200°F (100°C), remove it from the pan immediately and let cool completely on a rack.

Nut-Free Orange Chocolate Chip Loaf

Our original Orange Chocolate Chip Loaf was a big hit. We've adapted the recipe to be nut-free so that those of you who are allergic to nuts can learn to love it too! Serve it warm for a quick snack.

Tips

To ensure success, see page 14 for information on using your bread machine and page 18 for general tips on bread machine baking.

Chocolate chips partially melt in most bread machines, giving a marbled effect to the bread.

¾ cup	water	175 mL
1 tbsp	grated orange zest	15 mL
¾ cup	freshly squeezed orange juice	175 mL
¼ cup	liquid honey	60 mL
2 tbsp	vegetable oil	30 mL
1 tsp	cider vinegar	5 mL
2	eggs, lightly beaten	2
1	egg white, lightly beaten	1
3½ cups	Nut-Free Creamy Bread Mix (pages 184–186)	875 mL
1 cup	jumbo or mini semisweet chocolate chips	250 mL

1. Pour water, orange zest, orange juice, honey, oil and vinegar into the bread machine baking pan. Add eggs and egg white.

2. Select the **Gluten-Free Cycle**. As the bread machine is mixing, gradually add the bread mix and chocolate chips, scraping bottom and sides of pan with a rubber spatula. Try to incorporate all the dry ingredients within 1 to 2 minutes. When the mixing and kneading are complete, remove the kneading blade, leaving the bread pan in the bread machine. Quickly smooth the top of the loaf. Allow the cycle to finish.

3. At the end of the cycle, take the temperature of the loaf using an instant-read thermometer. It is baked at 200°F (100°C). If it's between 180°F (85°C) and 200°F (100°C), leave machine on the **Keep Warm Cycle** until baked. If it's below 180°F (85°C), turn on the **Bake Cycle** and check the internal temperature every 10 minutes. (Some bread machines are automatically set for 60 minutes; others need to be set by 10-minute intervals.)

4. Once the loaf has reached 200°F (100°C), remove it from the pan immediately and let cool completely on a rack.

NUTRITIONAL VALUES
per serving

Calories	238
Fat, total	8 g
Fat, saturated	3 g
Cholesterol	22 mg
Sodium	211 mg
Carbohydrate	41 g
Fiber	3 g
Protein	4 g
Calcium	14 mg
Iron	1 mg

Tips

Use a zester to make long, thin strips of orange zest. Be sure to remove only the colored outer layer, avoiding the bitter white pith beneath.

Freshly squeezed orange juice enhances the flavor. Roll the orange on the counter or between your hands to loosen the juice.

Keep an orange in the freezer. Zest while frozen, then juice after warming in the microwave.

Dough Cycle and Bake Cycle

If your bread machine does not have a Gluten-Free Cycle, use the Dough Cycle followed by the Bake Cycle.

1. Pour water, orange zest, orange juice, honey, oil and vinegar into the bread machine baking pan. Add eggs and egg white.

2. Select the **Dough Cycle**. As the bread machine is mixing, gradually add the bread mix and chocolate chips, scraping bottom and sides of pan with a rubber spatula. Try to incorporate all the dry ingredients within 1 to 2 minutes. When the mixing and kneading are complete, remove the kneading blade, leaving the bread pan in the bread machine. Quickly smooth the top of the loaf. Allow the cycle to finish. Turn off the bread machine.

3. Select the **Bake Cycle**. Set time to 60 minutes and temperature to 350°F (180°C). Allow the cycle to finish. Do not turn machine off before taking the internal temperature of the loaf with an instant-read thermometer. It should be 200°F (100°C). If it's between 180°F (85°C) and 200°F (100°C), leave machine on the **Keep Warm Cycle** until baked. If it's below 180°F (85°C), turn on the **Bake Cycle** and check the internal temperature every 10 minutes. (Some bread machines are automatically set for 60 minutes; others need to be set by 10-minute intervals.)

4. Once the loaf has reached 200°F (100°C), remove it from the pan immediately and let cool completely on a rack.

Nut-Free Cheese Rolls

When it comes to cheese rolls, this nut-free version of our original recipe is hard to beat. They're so delicious, and so easy to make from our mix!

Tips

To ensure success, see page 14 for information on using your bread machine and page 18 for general tips on bread machine baking.

For a sharper flavor, double the amount of cayenne pepper.

Variation

Make 10 larger rolls to serve as buns for hamburgers. Spoon batter onto a baking sheet lined with parchment paper and flatten the tops slightly. Let rise, uncovered, in a warm, draft-free place for 1 hour. Bake for 20 to 23 minutes.

NUTRITIONAL VALUES
per serving

Calories	215
Fat, total	5 g
Fat, saturated	2 g
Cholesterol	36 mg
Sodium	351 mg
Carbohydrate	37 g
Fiber	3 g
Protein	7 g
Calcium	96 mg
Iron	1 mg

◆ **12-cup muffin tin, lightly greased**

3$\frac{1}{2}$ cups	Nut-Free Creamy Bread Mix (pages 184–186)	875 mL
$\frac{3}{4}$ cup	shredded sharp (old) Cheddar cheese	175 mL
$\frac{1}{4}$ cup	freshly grated Parmesan cheese	60 mL
$\frac{1}{2}$ tsp	bread machine or instant yeast	2 mL
$\frac{1}{8}$ tsp	dry mustard	0.5 mL
$\frac{1}{8}$ tsp	cayenne pepper	0.5 mL
1$\frac{1}{4}$ cups	water	300 mL
$\frac{1}{4}$ cup	liquid honey	60 mL
1 tsp	cider vinegar	5 mL
2	eggs, lightly beaten	2
1	egg white, lightly beaten	1

1. In a large bowl or plastic bag, combine bread mix, Cheddar, Parmesan, yeast, mustard and cayenne; mix well and set aside.

2. Pour water, honey and vinegar into the bread machine baking pan. Add eggs and egg white.

3. Select the **Dough Cycle**. As the bread machine is mixing, gradually add the bread mix, scraping bottom and sides of pan with a rubber spatula. Try to incorporate all the bread mix within 1 to 2 minutes. Stop bread machine as soon as the kneading portion of the cycle is complete. Do not let bread machine finish the cycle.

4. Using a $\frac{1}{4}$-cup (60 mL) scoop, divide dough into 12 equal amounts and place in cups of prepared muffin tin. Let rise, uncovered, in a warm, draft-free place for 60 to 75 minutes or until dough has risen to the top of the cups. Meanwhile, preheat oven to 350°F (180°C).

5. Bake for 18 to 20 minutes or until internal temperature of rolls registers 200°F (100°C) on an instant-read thermometer. Remove from the tin immediately and let cool completely on a rack.

Figgy Apricot Bread (page 150)

Quinoa and Seed Bread (page 154)
and Orange Poppy Seed Loaf (page 156)

Chocolate Banana Bread (page 164)
and Coconut Banana Bread (page 166)

Cornbread with
Cheese and Broccoli (page 207)

EF Ancient Grains Bread (page 240)
and EF Honey Walnut Bread (page 242)

EF Hazelnut Ciabatta (page 252)

Mediterranean Pizza (page 288)

Soy-Free Golden Sesame Wafers (page 293)

Nut-Free Rosemary Breadsticks

These crunchy breadsticks are baked twice for a warm, golden brown, crisp crust.

Tips

To ensure success, see page 14 for information on using your bread machine and page 18 for general tips on bread machine baking.

For uniform breadsticks, cut bread in half, then lengthwise into quarters. Finally, cut each quarter lengthwise into 3 strips.

If breadsticks become soft during storage, crisp them in a toaster oven or conventional oven at 350°F (180°C) for a few minutes.

Variation

Substitute snipped fresh thyme or tarragon, or a combination of herbs, for the rosemary.

NUTRITIONAL VALUES
per serving

Calories	94
Fat, total	3 g
Fat, saturated	1 g
Cholesterol	3 mg
Sodium	167 mg
Carbohydrate	16 g
Fiber	1 g
Protein	3 g
Calcium	38 mg
Iron	1 mg

◆ **Two 9-inch (23 cm) square baking pans, lightly greased**
◆ **Baking sheets, ungreased**

2 cups	water	500 mL
2 tbsp	extra virgin olive oil	30 mL
1 tsp	cider vinegar	5 mL
3½ cups	Nut-Free Creamy Bread Mix (pages 184–186)	875 mL
½ cup	snipped fresh rosemary	125 mL
1 tsp	granulated sugar	5 mL
½ tsp	freshly ground black pepper	2 mL
½ cup	freshly grated Parmesan cheese, divided	125 mL

1. Pour water, oil and vinegar into the bread machine baking pan.

2. Select the **Dough Cycle**. As the bread machine is mixing, gradually add the bread mix, rosemary, sugar and pepper, scraping bottom and sides of pan with a rubber spatula. Try to incorporate all the dry ingredients within 1 to 2 minutes. Stop bread machine as soon as the kneading portion of the cycle is complete. Do not let bread machine finish the cycle.

3. Sprinkle 2 tbsp (30 mL) of the Parmesan in the bottom of each prepared pan. Drop dough by spoonfuls over the Parmesan. Using a moistened rubber spatula, spread dough evenly to the edges of the pan. Sprinkle each with 2 tbsp (30 mL) Parmesan. Let rise, uncovered, in a warm, draft-free place for 30 minutes. Meanwhile, preheat oven to 400°F (200°C).

4. Bake for 12 to 15 minutes or until light brown. Remove from pan and transfer immediately to a cutting board. Reduce oven temperature to 350°F (180°C). Using a pizza wheel or a sharp knife, cut bread into 12 equal strips.

5. Arrange breadsticks, cut side up, at least ½ inch (1 cm) apart on baking sheets. Bake for 20 to 25 minutes or until dry, crisp and golden brown. Turn off oven and let breadsticks cool completely in oven.

6. Store in an airtight container at room temperature for up to 1 week.

Single-Loaf Rice-Free Brown Bread Mix

We are still amazed at how often we meet people who cannot tolerate rice. Just for you, we've adapted our original Brown Bread Mix to create this rice-free version you can use to make Rice-Free Maritime (Boston) Brown Bread (page 196), Rice-Free Mock Bran Bread (page 198), Rice-Free Mock Pumpernickel Bread (page 200), Rice-Free Brown Pizza Crusts (page 202) or Rice-Free Brown Pan Rolls (page 203).

1$\frac{2}{3}$ cups	sorghum flour	400 mL
1$\frac{1}{4}$ cups	whole bean flour	300 mL
$\frac{1}{3}$ cup	tapioca starch	75 mL
2 tbsp	packed brown sugar	30 mL
1 tbsp	xanthan gum	15 mL
1$\frac{1}{2}$ tsp	bread machine or instant yeast	7 mL
1$\frac{1}{2}$ tsp	salt	7 mL

1. In a large bowl, combine sorghum flour, whole bean flour, tapioca starch, brown sugar, xanthan gum, yeast and salt; mix well.

2. Use right away or seal tightly in a plastic bag, removing as much air as possible. Store at room temperature for up to 3 days or in the freezer for up to 6 weeks.

Working with Bread Mix

- Be sure the brown sugar is well distributed and any lumps are broken up; it clumps easily when mixed with other dry ingredients.
- Label and date the package if not using bread mix immediately. We add the page number of the recipe to the label as a quick reference.
- Let bread mix warm to room temperature, and mix well before using.

NUTRITIONAL VALUES per serving	
Calories	121
Fat, total	1 g
Fat, saturated	0 g
Cholesterol	0 mg
Sodium	234 mg
Carbohydrate	24 g
Fiber	3 g
Protein	5 g
Calcium	11 mg
Iron	1 mg

Four-Loaf Rice-Free Brown Bread Mix

*After you've tried
the single-loaf mix
(page 194), you'll want
to have extras ready in
the freezer. Use them
to make the recipes on
pages 196–203.*

Tips

For accuracy, use a 1-cup
(250 mL) dry measure
several times to measure
each type of flour and
starch. If you use a 4-cup
(1 L) liquid measure, it's
difficult to get an accurate
volume and you'll end up
with extra flour in the mix.

We used a large roasting
pan to combine all the
ingredients.

NUTRITIONAL VALUES per serving	
Calories	121
Fat, total	1 g
Fat, saturated	0 g
Cholesterol	0 mg
Sodium	234 mg
Carbohydrate	24 g
Fiber	3 g
Protein	5 g
Calcium	11 mg
Iron	1 mg

6²⁄₃ cups	sorghum flour	1650 mL
5 cups	whole bean flour	1250 mL
1¹⁄₃ cups	tapioca starch	325 mL
½ cup	packed brown sugar	125 mL
¼ cup	xanthan gum	60 mL
2 tbsp	bread machine or instant yeast	30 mL
2 tbsp	salt	30 mL

1. In a very large container, combine sorghum flour, whole bean flour, tapioca starch, brown sugar, xanthan gum, yeast and salt; mix well.

2. Divide into 4 equal portions of about 3½ cups (875 mL) each. Seal tightly in plastic bags, removing as much air as possible. Store at room temperature for up to 3 days or in the freezer for up to 6 weeks.

Working with Bread Mix

- Be sure the brown sugar is well distributed and any lumps are broken up; it clumps easily when mixed with other dry ingredients.
- In step 2, stir the mix before spooning it very lightly into the dry measures. Do not pack.
- Be sure to divide the mix into equal portions. Depending on how much air you incorporate into the mix, and the texture of the individual gluten-free flours, the total volume of the mix can vary. The important thing is to make the number of portions specified in the recipe.
- Label and date the packages before storing. We add the page number of the recipe to the labels as a quick reference.
- Let bread mix warm to room temperature, and mix well before using.

Rice-Free Maritime (Boston) Brown Bread

If you cannot tolerate rice and are looking for a good basic brown bread for sandwiches, this is the loaf for you.

Tips

To ensure success, see page 14 for information on using your bread machine and page 18 for general tips on bread machine baking.

Measuring the oil before the molasses ensures that the molasses slides out of the measure. If the molasses is really thick or is straight out of the refrigerator, warm it slightly in the microwave before measuring.

1¼ cups	water	300 mL
3 tbsp	vegetable oil	45 mL
2 tbsp	light (fancy) molasses	30 mL
1 tsp	cider vinegar	5 mL
2	eggs, lightly beaten	2
2	egg whites, lightly beaten	2
3½ cups	Rice-Free Brown Bread Mix (pages 194–195)	875 mL

1. Pour water, oil, molasses and vinegar into the bread machine baking pan. Add eggs and egg whites.

2. Select the **Gluten-Free Cycle**. As the bread machine is mixing, gradually add the bread mix, scraping bottom and sides of pan with a rubber spatula. Try to incorporate all the bread mix within 1 to 2 minutes. When the mixing and kneading are complete, remove the kneading blade, leaving the bread pan in the bread machine. Quickly smooth the top of the loaf. Allow the cycle to finish.

3. At the end of the cycle, take the temperature of the loaf using an instant-read thermometer. It is baked at 200°F (100°C). If it's between 180°F (85°C) and 200°F (100°C), leave machine on the **Keep Warm Cycle** until baked. If it's below 180°F (85°C), turn on the **Bake Cycle** and check the internal temperature every 10 minutes. (Some bread machines are automatically set for 60 minutes; others need to be set by 10-minute intervals.)

4. Once the loaf has reached 200°F (100°C), remove it from the pan immediately and let cool completely on a rack.

NUTRITIONAL VALUES	
per serving	
Calories	164
Fat, total	5 g
Fat, saturated	0 g
Cholesterol	22 mg
Sodium	251 mg
Carbohydrate	26 g
Fiber	3 g
Protein	6 g
Calcium	22 mg
Iron	2 mg

Tips

Slice this or any bread with an electric knife for thin, even sandwich slices.

Always store bread at room temperature or wrapped airtight in the freezer. The refrigerator accelerates the staling process.

Variation

Add ½ cup (125 mL) raisins or chopped walnuts with the bread mix.

Dough Cycle and Bake Cycle

If your bread machine does not have a Gluten-Free Cycle, use the Dough Cycle followed by the Bake Cycle.

1. Pour water, oil, molasses and vinegar into the bread machine baking pan. Add eggs and egg whites.

2. Select the **Dough Cycle**. As the bread machine is mixing, gradually add the bread mix, scraping bottom and sides of pan with a rubber spatula. Try to incorporate all the bread mix within 1 to 2 minutes. When the mixing and kneading are complete, remove the kneading blade, leaving the bread pan in the bread machine. Quickly smooth the top of the loaf. Allow the cycle to finish. Turn off the bread machine.

3. Select the **Bake Cycle**. Set time to 60 minutes and temperature to 350°F (180°C). Allow the cycle to finish. Do not turn machine off before taking the internal temperature of the loaf with an instant-read thermometer. It should be 200°F (100°C). If it's between 180°F (85°C) and 200°F (100°C), leave machine on the **Keep Warm Cycle** until baked. If it's below 180°F (85°C), turn on the **Bake Cycle** and check the internal temperature every 10 minutes. (Some bread machines are automatically set for 60 minutes; others need to be set by 10-minute intervals.)

4. Once the loaf has reached 200°F (100°C), remove it from the pan immediately and let cool completely on a rack.

Rice-Free Mock Bran Bread

Here's another delicious sandwich bread for those who cannot tolerate rice. This one is a sweeter, higher-fiber version of our basic Brown Bread (page 40).

Tips

To ensure success, see page 14 for information on using your bread machine and page 18 for general tips on bread machine baking.

Warm up GF oat bran that has been stored in the refrigerator or freezer to room temperature.

2 tbsp	GF oat bran	30 mL
3½ cups	Rice-Free Brown Bread Mix (pages 194–195)	875 mL
1½ cups	water	375 mL
3 tbsp	vegetable oil	45 mL
1 tbsp	liquid honey	15 mL
1 tbsp	light (fancy) molasses	15 mL
1 tsp	cider vinegar	5 mL
2	eggs, lightly beaten	2
2	egg whites, lightly beaten	2

1. Add oat bran to the bread mix; mix well and set aside.

2. Pour water, oil, honey, molasses and vinegar into the bread machine baking pan. Add eggs and egg whites.

3. Select the **Gluten-Free Cycle**. As the bread machine is mixing, gradually add the bread mix, scraping bottom and sides of pan with a rubber spatula. Try to incorporate all the bread mix within 1 to 2 minutes. When the mixing and kneading are complete, remove the kneading blade, leaving the bread pan in the bread machine. Quickly smooth the top of the loaf. Allow the cycle to finish.

4. At the end of the cycle, take the temperature of the loaf using an instant-read thermometer. It is baked at 200°F (100°C). If it's between 180°F (85°C) and 200°F (100°C), leave machine on the **Keep Warm Cycle** until baked. If it's below 180°F (85°C), turn on the **Bake Cycle** and check the internal temperature every 10 minutes. (Some bread machines are automatically set for 60 minutes; others need to be set by 10-minute intervals.)

5. Once the loaf has reached 200°F (100°C), remove it from the pan immediately and let cool completely on a rack.

NUTRITIONAL VALUES
per serving

Calories	166
Fat, total	5 g
Fat, saturated	0 g
Cholesterol	22 mg
Sodium	250 mg
Carbohydrate	26 g
Fiber	3 g
Protein	6 g
Calcium	19 mg
Iron	2 mg

Dough Cycle and Bake Cycle

If your bread machine does not have a Gluten-Free Cycle, use the Dough Cycle followed by the Bake Cycle.

1. Add oat bran to the bread mix; mix well and set aside.

2. Pour water, oil, honey, molasses and vinegar into the bread machine baking pan. Add eggs and egg whites.

3. Select the **Dough Cycle**. As the bread machine is mixing, gradually add the bread mix, scraping bottom and sides of pan with a rubber spatula. Try to incorporate all the bread mix within 1 to 2 minutes. When the mixing and kneading are complete, remove the kneading blade, leaving the bread pan in the bread machine. Quickly smooth the top of the loaf. Allow the cycle to finish. Turn off the bread machine.

4. Select the **Bake Cycle**. Set time to 60 minutes and temperature to 350°F (180°C). Allow the cycle to finish. Do not turn machine off before taking the internal temperature of the loaf with an instant-read thermometer. It should be 200°F (100°C). If it's between 180°F (85°C) and 200°F (100°C), leave machine on the **Keep Warm Cycle** until baked. If it's below 180°F (85°C), turn on the **Bake Cycle** and check the internal temperature every 10 minutes. (Some bread machines are automatically set for 60 minutes; others need to be set by 10-minute intervals.)

5. Once the loaf has reached 200°F (100°C), remove it from the pan immediately and let cool completely on a rack.

Rice-Free Mock Pumpernickel Bread

MAKES 15 SLICES
(1 per serving)

Coffee and cocoa bring out the strong molasses flavor in this loaf.

Tips

To ensure success, see page 14 for information on using your bread machine and page 18 for general tips on bread machine baking.

Sift cocoa just before using, as it lumps easily.

1 tbsp	instant coffee granules	15 mL
1 tbsp	unsweetened cocoa powder, sifted	15 mL
½ tsp	ground ginger	2 mL
3½ cups	Rice-Free Brown Bread Mix (pages 194–195)	875 mL
1½ cups	water	375 mL
3 tbsp	vegetable oil	45 mL
2 tbsp	light (fancy) molasses	30 mL
1 tsp	cider vinegar	5 mL
2	eggs, lightly beaten	2
2	egg whites, lightly beaten	2

1. Add coffee granules, cocoa and ginger to the bread mix; mix well and set aside.

2. Pour water, oil, molasses and vinegar into the bread machine baking pan. Add eggs and egg whites.

3. Select the **Gluten-Free Cycle**. As the bread machine is mixing, gradually add the bread mix, scraping bottom and sides of pan with a rubber spatula. Try to incorporate all the bread mix within 1 to 2 minutes. When the mixing and kneading are complete, remove the kneading blade, leaving the bread pan in the bread machine. Quickly smooth the top of the loaf. Allow the cycle to finish.

4. At the end of the cycle, take the temperature of the loaf using an instant-read thermometer. It is baked at 200°F (100°C). If it's between 180°F (85°C) and 200°F (100°C), leave machine on the **Keep Warm Cycle** until baked. If it's below 180°F (85°C), turn on the **Bake Cycle** and check the internal temperature every 10 minutes. (Some bread machines are automatically set for 60 minutes; others need to be set by 10-minute intervals.)

5. Once the loaf has reached 200°F (100°C), remove it from the pan immediately and let cool completely on a rack.

NUTRITIONAL VALUES
per serving

Calories	166
Fat, total	5 g
Fat, saturated	0 g
Cholesterol	22 mg
Sodium	251 mg
Carbohydrate	26 g
Fiber	3 g
Protein	6 g
Calcium	22 mg
Iron	2 mg

Variations

Add 2 tbsp (30 mL) caraway, fennel or anise seeds with the bread mix.

Substitute an equal quantity of strong brewed room-temperature coffee for the water

Dough Cycle and Bake Cycle

If your bread machine does not have a Gluten-Free Cycle, use the Dough Cycle followed by the Bake Cycle.

1. Add coffee granules, cocoa and ginger to the bread mix; mix well and set aside.

2. Pour water, oil, molasses and vinegar into the bread machine baking pan. Add eggs and egg whites.

3. Select the **Dough Cycle**. As the bread machine is mixing, gradually add the bread mix, scraping bottom and sides of pan with a rubber spatula. Try to incorporate all the bread mix within 1 to 2 minutes. When the mixing and kneading are complete, remove the kneading blade, leaving the bread pan in the bread machine. Quickly smooth the top of the loaf. Allow the cycle to finish. Turn off the bread machine.

4. Select the **Bake Cycle**. Set time to 60 minutes and temperature to 350°F (180°C). Allow the cycle to finish. Do not turn machine off before taking the internal temperature of the loaf with an instant-read thermometer. It should be 200°F (100°C). If it's between 180°F (85°C) and 200°F (100°C), leave machine on the **Keep Warm Cycle** until baked. If it's below 180°F (85°C), turn on the **Bake Cycle** and check the internal temperature every 10 minutes. (Some bread machines are automatically set for 60 minutes; others need to be set by 10-minute intervals.)

5. Once the loaf has reached 200°F (100°C), remove it from the pan immediately and let cool completely on a rack.

Rice-Free Brown Pizza Crusts

*This recipe makes
enough dough for two
pizzas. Make one now
and freeze the other.*

Tips

To ensure success, see
page 14 for information on
using your bread machine
and page 18 for general tips
on bread machine baking.

Pizza toppings stick better
during baking when you don't
smooth the top of the crust.

Partially baked pizza crust
can be wrapped airtight and
frozen for up to 1 month.
Thaw in the refrigerator
overnight before using.

Variation

If you like a thick crust, leave
the dough in one piece, spread
it in the pan and let rise for
30 minutes before baking.

NUTRITIONAL VALUES per serving	
Calories	147
Fat, total	5 g
Fat, saturated	1 g
Cholesterol	0 mg
Sodium	220 mg
Carbohydrate	22 g
Fiber	3 g
Protein	5 g
Calcium	10 mg
Iron	1 mg

◆ **Two 15- by 10-inch (40 by 25 cm) rimmed baking sheets,
generously greased and dusted with cornmeal**

2 tsp	bread machine or instant yeast	10 mL
3½ cups	Rice-Free Brown Bread Mix (pages 194–195)	875 mL
2¼ cups	water	550 mL
¼ cup	extra virgin olive oil	60 mL
1 tbsp	cider vinegar	15 mL

1. Add yeast to the bread mix; mix well and set aside.

2. Pour water, oil and vinegar into the bread machine baking
pan.

3. Select the **Dough Cycle**. As the bread machine is mixing,
gradually add the bread mix, scraping bottom and sides of
pan with a rubber spatula. Try to incorporate all the bread
mix within 1 to 2 minutes. Stop bread machine as soon as
the kneading portion of the cycle is complete. Do not let
bread machine finish the cycle.

4. Meanwhile preheat oven to 400°F (200°C).

5. Divide dough in half. Place half the dough in each prepared
pan and, using a moistened rubber spatula, spread evenly to
the edges. Do not smooth tops.

6. Bake for 12 minutes or until bottom is golden and crust is
partially baked.

7. Use right away to make pizza with your favorite toppings
(see pages 287–290 for some topping suggestions and
baking instructions), or wrap airtight and store in the
freezer for up to 1 month.

Rice-Free Brown Pan Rolls

We've made these traditional pan rolls rice-free just for you.

Tip

To ensure success, see page 14 for information on using your bread machine and page 18 for general tips on bread machine baking.

◆ 9-inch (23 cm) square baking pan, lightly greased

2 tbsp	packed brown sugar	30 mL
1 tsp	bread machine or instant yeast	5 mL
3½ cups	Rice-Free Brown Bread Mix (pages 194–195)	875 mL
1¼ cups	water	300 mL
3 tbsp	vegetable oil	45 mL
1 tsp	cider vinegar	5 mL
2	eggs, lightly beaten	2
2	egg whites, lightly beaten	2

1. Add brown sugar and yeast to the bread mix; mix well and set aside.

2. Pour water, oil and vinegar into the bread machine baking pan. Add eggs and egg whites.

3. Select the **Dough Cycle**. As the bread machine is mixing, gradually add the bread mix, scraping bottom and sides of pan with a rubber spatula. Try to incorporate all the bread mix within 1 to 2 minutes. Stop bread machine as soon as the kneading portion of the cycle is complete. Do not let bread machine finish the cycle.

4. Using a ¼-cup (60 mL) scoop, divide dough into 16 equal amounts and arrange in four rows of four in prepared pan. Let rise, uncovered, in a warm, draft-free place for 60 to 75 minutes or until dough has risen to the top of the pan. Meanwhile, preheat oven to 350°F (180°C)

5. Bake for 22 to 24 minutes or until internal temperature of rolls registers 200°F (100°C) on an instant-read thermometer. Remove from the pan immediately and let cool completely on a rack.

NUTRITIONAL VALUES
per serving

Calories	153
Fat, total	4 g
Fat, saturated	0 g
Cholesterol	21 mg
Sodium	235 mg
Carbohydrate	24 g
Fiber	3 g
Protein	6 g
Calcium	15 mg
Iron	1 mg

Single-Loaf Cornbread Mix

**MAKES ABOUT
3¹/₂ CUPS (875 ML),
ENOUGH FOR
1 LOAF**
(¹/₄ cup/60 mL per
serving)

*Every time Donna
visits Texas, she gets a
request for a gluten-free
cornbread mix. Here it is!
Use it to make the recipes
on pages 207–218.*

1 cup	cornmeal	250 mL
1 cup	brown rice flour	250 mL
³/₄ cup	amaranth flour	175 mL
¹/₃ cup	tapioca starch	75 mL
3 tbsp	granulated sugar	45 mL
1 tbsp	xanthan gum	15 mL
2 tsp	bread machine or instant yeast	10 mL
1¹/₂ tsp	salt	7 mL

1. In a large bowl, combine cornmeal, brown rice flour, amaranth flour, tapioca starch, sugar, xanthan gum, yeast and salt; mix well.

2. Use right away or seal tightly in a plastic bag, removing as much air as possible. Store at room temperature for up to 3 days or in the freezer for up to 6 months.

Working with Bread Mix

- Label and date the package if not using bread mix immediately. We add the page number of the recipe to the label as a quick reference.
- Let bread mix warm to room temperature, and mix well before using.

NUTRITIONAL VALUES
per serving

Calories	119
Fat, total	1 g
Fat, saturated	0 g
Cholesterol	0 mg
Sodium	237 mg
Carbohydrate	26 g
Fiber	2 g
Protein	3 g
Calcium	9 mg
Iron	1 mg

Four-Loaf Cornbread Mix

**MAKES ABOUT
14 CUPS (3.5 L),
ENOUGH FOR
4 LOAVES**
(¼ cup/60 mL per
serving)

*It's so handy to have this
cornbread mix on hand
in the freezer — just
thaw one portion and it
can be ready for dinner.
Use it to make the recipes
on pages 207–218.*

Tips

For accuracy, use a 1-cup
(250 mL) dry measure
several times to measure
each type of flour and
starch. If you use a 4-cup
(1 L) liquid measure, it's
difficult to get an accurate
volume and you'll end up
with extra flour in the mix.

We used a large roasting
pan to combine all the
ingredients.

NUTRITIONAL VALUES
per serving

Calories	119
Fat, total	1 g
Fat, saturated	0 g
Cholesterol	0 mg
Sodium	237 mg
Carbohydrate	26 g
Fiber	2 g
Protein	3 g
Calcium	9 mg
Iron	1 mg

4 cups	cornmeal	1000 mL
4 cups	brown rice flour	1000 mL
3 cups	amaranth flour	750 mL
1⅓ cups	tapioca starch	325 mL
¾ cup	granulated sugar	175 mL
¼ cup	xanthan gum	60 mL
3 tbsp	bread machine or instant yeast	45 mL
2 tbsp	salt	30 mL

1. In a very large container, combine cornmeal, brown rice flour, amaranth flour, tapioca starch, sugar, xanthan gum, yeast and salt; mix well.

2. Divide into 4 equal portions of about 3½ cups (875 mL) each. Seal tightly in plastic bags, removing as much air as possible. Store at room temperature for up to 3 days or in the freezer for up to 6 months.

Working with Bread Mix

- In step 2, stir the mix before spooning it very lightly into the dry measures. Do not pack.
- Be sure to divide the mix into equal portions. Depending on how much air you incorporate into the mix, and the texture of the individual gluten-free flours, the total volume of the mix can vary slightly. The important thing is to make the number of portions specified in the recipe.
- Label and date the packages if not using bread mix immediately. We add the page number of the recipe to the label as a quick reference.
- Let bread mix warm to room temperature, and mix well before using.

Eight-Loaf Cornbread Mix

**MAKES ABOUT
28 CUPS (7 L),
ENOUGH FOR
8 LOAVES**
(1/4 cup/60 mL per
serving)

*In response to an email
request, here's a recipe
for a large batch of
cornbread mix. Use it
to make the recipes on
pages 207–218.*

Tips

For accuracy, use a 1-cup
(250 mL) dry measure
several times to measure
each type of flour and
starch. If you use a 4-cup
(1 L) liquid measure, it's
difficult to get an accurate
volume and you'll end up
with extra flour in the mix.

We used a large roasting
pan to combine all the
ingredients. Your pan must
be large enough to hold
36 cups (9 L).

NUTRITIONAL VALUES per serving	
Calories	119
Fat, total	1 g
Fat, saturated	0 g
Cholesterol	0 mg
Sodium	237 mg
Carbohydrate	26 g
Fiber	2 g
Protein	3 g
Calcium	9 mg
Iron	1 mg

8 cups	cornmeal	2000 mL
8 cups	brown rice flour	2000 mL
6 cups	amaranth flour	1500 mL
2²/₃ cups	tapioca starch	650 mL
1¹/₂ cups	granulated sugar	375 mL
¹/₂ cup	xanthan gum	125 mL
¹/₂ cup	bread machine or instant yeast	125 mL
¹/₄ cup	salt	60 mL

1. In a very large container, combine cornmeal, brown rice flour, amaranth flour, tapioca starch, sugar, xanthan gum, yeast and salt; mix well.

2. Divide into 8 equal portions of about 3¹/₂ cups (875 mL) each. Seal tightly in plastic bags, removing as much air as possible. Store at room temperature for up to 3 days or in the freezer for up to 6 months.

Working with Bread Mix

- In step 2, stir the mix before spooning it very lightly into the dry measures. Do not pack.
- Be sure to divide the mix into equal portions. Depending on how much air you incorporate into the mix, and the texture of the individual gluten-free flours, the total volume of the mix can vary slightly. The important thing is to make the number of portions specified in the recipe.
- Label and date the packages if not using bread mix immediately. We add the page number of the recipe to the label as a quick reference.
- Let bread mix warm to room temperature, and mix well before using.

Cornbread with Cheese and Broccoli

Broccoli and three different cheeses combine to make an outstanding cornbread!

Tips

To ensure success, see page 14 for information on using your bread machine and page 18 for general tips on bread machine baking.

For the amount of cheese to purchase, see the weight/volume equivalents in the Ingredient Glossary, pages 302 and 300.

We like to cut this loaf into 1½-inch (3.5 cm) squares and serve them as hors d'oeuvres.

NUTRITIONAL VALUES
per serving

Calories	281
Fat, total	12 g
Fat, saturated	4 g
Cholesterol	54 mg
Sodium	440 mg
Carbohydrate	36 g
Fiber	3 g
Protein	9 g
Calcium	136 mg
Iron	2 mg

◆ **9-inch (23 cm) square baking pan, lightly greased**

½ cup	shredded Havarti cheese	125 mL
¼ cup	shredded Asiago cheese	60 mL
¼ cup	freshly grated Parmesan cheese	60 mL
½ tsp	dry mustard	2 mL
3½ cups	Cornbread Mix (pages 204–206)	875 mL
¾ cup	GF cream-style corn	175 mL
½ cup	water	125 mL
¼ cup	vegetable oil	60 mL
1 tsp	cider vinegar	5 mL
3	eggs, lightly beaten	3
2	egg whites, lightly beaten	2
1½ cups	small broccoli florets	375 mL

1. Add Havarti, Asiago, Parmesan and mustard to the cornbread mix; mix well and set aside.

2. Pour corn, water, oil and vinegar into the bread machine baking pan. Add eggs and egg whites.

3. Select the **Dough Cycle**. As the bread machine is mixing, gradually add the cornbread mix, scraping bottom and sides of pan with a rubber spatula. Try to incorporate all the cornbread mix within 1 to 2 minutes. Stop bread machine as soon as the kneading portion of the cycle is complete. Do not let bread machine finish the cycle. Using a rubber spatula, stir in broccoli just to combine.

4. Place dough in prepared pan and, using a moistened rubber spatula, spread evenly to the edges. Let rise, uncovered, in a warm, draft-free place for 40 to 50 minutes or until dough has risen to the top of the pan. Meanwhile, preheat oven to 350°F (180°C).

5. Bake for 32 to 36 minutes or until top is golden and internal temperature of loaf registers 200°F (100°C) on an instant-read thermometer. Remove from the pan immediately and let cool completely on a rack.

Cornbread Loaf (Johnny Cake)

Moist, soft, and with a good corn flavor, this is a loaf you're bound to enjoy frequently.

Tips

To ensure success, see page 14 for information on using your bread machine and page 18 for general tips on bread machine baking.

For the best flavor, plan for the loaf to be ready when dinner is, and serve warm.

1¼ cups	water	300 mL
¼ cup	vegetable oil	60 mL
1 tsp	cider vinegar	5 mL
3	eggs, lightly beaten	3
1	egg white, lightly beaten	1
3½ cups	Cornbread Mix (pages 204–206)	875 mL

1. Pour water, oil and vinegar into the bread machine baking pan. Add eggs and egg white.

2. Select the **Gluten-Free Cycle**. As the bread machine is mixing, gradually add the cornbread mix, scraping bottom and sides of pan with a rubber spatula. Try to incorporate all the cornbread mix within 1 to 2 minutes. When the mixing and kneading are complete, remove the kneading blade, leaving the bread pan in the bread machine. Quickly smooth the top of the loaf. Allow the cycle to finish.

3. At the end of the cycle, take the temperature of the loaf using an instant-read thermometer. It is baked at 200°F (100°C). If it's between 180°F (85°C) and 200°F (100°C), leave machine on the **Keep Warm Cycle** until baked. If it's below 180°F (85°C), turn on the **Bake Cycle** and check the internal temperature every 10 minutes. (Some bread machines are automatically set for 60 minutes; others need to be set by 10-minute intervals.)

4. Once the loaf has reached 200°F (100°C), remove it from the pan immediately and let cool on a rack. Serve warm.

NUTRITIONAL VALUES
per serving

Calories	165
Fat, total	6 g
Fat, saturated	1 g
Cholesterol	33 mg
Sodium	253 mg
Carbohydrate	26 g
Fiber	2 g
Protein	4 g
Calcium	14 mg
Iron	1 mg

Tips

Slice this or any bread with an electric knife for thin, even sandwich slices.

Always store bread at room temperature or wrapped airtight in the freezer. The refrigerator accelerates the staling process.

Dough Cycle and Bake Cycle

If your bread machine does not have a Gluten-Free Cycle, use the Dough Cycle followed by the Bake Cycle.

1. Pour water, oil and vinegar into the bread machine baking pan. Add eggs and egg white.

2. Select the **Dough Cycle**. As the bread machine is mixing, gradually add the cornbread mix, scraping bottom and sides of pan with a rubber spatula. Try to incorporate all the cornbread mix within 1 to 2 minutes. When the mixing and kneading are complete, remove the kneading blade, leaving the bread pan in the bread machine. Quickly smooth the top of the loaf. Allow the cycle to finish. Turn off the bread machine.

3. Select the **Bake Cycle**. Set time to 60 minutes and temperature to 350°F (180°C). Allow the cycle to finish. Do not turn machine off before taking the internal temperature of the loaf with an instant-read thermometer. It should be 200°F (100°C). If it's between 180°F (85°C) and 200°F (100°C), leave machine on the **Keep Warm Cycle** until baked. If it's below 180°F (85°C), turn on the **Bake Cycle** and check the internal temperature every 10 minutes. (Some bread machines are automatically set for 60 minutes; others need to be set by 10-minute intervals.)

4. Once the loaf has reached 200°F (100°C), remove it from the pan immediately and let cool completely on a rack.

Sun-Dried Tomato Basil Cornbread

Sun-dried tomatoes give this cornbread delicious tang — don't skimp on them.

Tip

To ensure success, see page 14 for information on using your bread machine and page 18 for general tips on bread machine baking.

1 cup	snipped dry-packed sun-dried tomatoes	250 mL
¼ cup	snipped fresh basil	60 mL
3½ cups	Cornbread Mix (pages 204–206)	875 mL
1¼ cups	water	300 mL
¼ cup	vegetable oil	60 mL
1 tsp	cider vinegar	5 mL
3	eggs, lightly beaten	3
1	egg white, lightly beaten	1

1. Add sun-dried tomatoes and basil to the cornbread mix; mix well and set aside.

2. Pour water, oil and vinegar into the bread machine baking pan. Add eggs and egg white.

3. Select the **Gluten-Free Cycle**. As the bread machine is mixing, gradually add the cornbread mix, scraping bottom and sides of pan with a rubber spatula. Try to incorporate all the cornbread mix within 1 to 2 minutes. When the mixing and kneading are complete, remove the kneading blade, leaving the bread pan in the bread machine. Quickly smooth the top of the loaf. Allow the cycle to finish.

4. At the end of the cycle, take the temperature of the loaf using an instant-read thermometer. It is baked at 200°F (100°C). If it's between 180°F (85°C) and 200°F (100°C), leave machine on the **Keep Warm Cycle** until baked. If it's below 180°F (85°C), turn on the **Bake Cycle** and check the internal temperature every 10 minutes. (Some bread machines are automatically set for 60 minutes; others need to be set by 10-minute intervals.)

5. Once the loaf has reached 200°F (100°C), remove it from the pan immediately and let cool completely on a rack.

NUTRITIONAL VALUES
per serving

Calories	174
Fat, total	6 g
Fat, saturated	1 g
Cholesterol	33 mg
Sodium	329 mg
Carbohydrate	28 g
Fiber	2 g
Protein	4 g
Calcium	19 mg
Iron	2 mg

Dough Cycle and Bake Cycle

If your bread machine does not have a Gluten-Free Cycle, use the Dough Cycle followed by the Bake Cycle.

1. Add sun-dried tomatoes and basil to the cornbread mix; mix well and set aside.

2. Pour water, oil and vinegar into the bread machine baking pan. Add eggs and egg white.

3. Select the **Dough Cycle**. As the bread machine is mixing, gradually add the cornbread mix, scraping bottom and sides of pan with a rubber spatula. Try to incorporate all the cornbread mix within 1 to 2 minutes. When the mixing and kneading are complete, remove the kneading blade, leaving the bread pan in the bread machine. Quickly smooth the top of the loaf. Allow the cycle to finish. Turn off the bread machine.

4. Select the **Bake Cycle**. Set time to 60 minutes and temperature to 350°F (180°C). Allow the cycle to finish. Do not turn machine off before taking the internal temperature of the loaf with an instant-read thermometer. It should be 200°F (100°C). If it's between 180°F (85°C) and 200°F (100°C), leave machine on the **Keep Warm Cycle** until baked. If it's below 180°F (85°C), turn on the **Bake Cycle** and check the internal temperature every 10 minutes. (Some bread machines are automatically set for 60 minutes; others need to be set by 10-minute intervals.)

5. Once the loaf has reached 200°F (100°C), remove it from the pan immediately and let cool completely on a rack.

Provolone and Sage Cornbread

You'll love this moist and savory treat!

Tips

To ensure success, see page 14 for information on using your bread machine and page 18 for general tips on bread machine baking.

For the amount of cheese to purchase, see the weight/volume equivalents in the Ingredient Glossary, page 304.

1 cup	shredded provolone cheese	250 mL
1/3 cup	buttermilk powder	75 mL
2 tbsp	dried sage	30 mL
1/2 tsp	ground white pepper	2 mL
1/8 tsp	cayenne pepper	0.5 mL
3 1/2 cups	Cornbread Mix (pages 204–206)	875 mL
1 1/4 cups	water	300 mL
1/4 cup	vegetable oil	60 mL
1 tsp	cider vinegar	5 mL
3	eggs, lightly beaten	3
1	egg white, lightly beaten	1

1. Add cheese, buttermilk powder, sage, white pepper and cayenne to the cornbread mix; mix well and set aside.

2. Pour water, oil and vinegar into the bread machine baking pan. Add eggs and egg white.

3. Select the **Gluten-Free Cycle**. As the bread machine is mixing, gradually add the cornbread mix, scraping bottom and sides of pan with a rubber spatula. Try to incorporate all the cornbread mix within 1 to 2 minutes. When the mixing and kneading are complete, remove the kneading blade, leaving the bread pan in the bread machine. Quickly smooth the top of the loaf. Allow the cycle to finish.

4. At the end of the cycle, take the temperature of the loaf using an instant-read thermometer. It is baked at 200°F (100°C). If it's between 180°F (85°C) and 200°F (100°C), leave machine on the **Keep Warm Cycle** until baked. If it's below 180°F (85°C), turn on the **Bake Cycle** and check the internal temperature every 10 minutes. (Some bread machines are automatically set for 60 minutes; others need to be set by 10-minute intervals.)

5. Once the loaf has reached 200°F (100°C), remove it from the pan immediately and let cool completely on a rack.

NUTRITIONAL VALUES
per serving

Calories	189
Fat, total	7 g
Fat, saturated	2 g
Cholesterol	37 mg
Sodium	322 mg
Carbohydrate	27 g
Fiber	2 g
Protein	6 g
Calcium	82 mg
Iron	1 mg

You can purchase buttermilk powder in bulk stores and health food stores.

Always store bread at room temperature or wrapped airtight in the freezer. The refrigerator accelerates the staling process.

Dough Cycle and Bake Cycle

If your bread machine does not have a Gluten-Free Cycle, use the Dough Cycle followed by the Bake Cycle.

1. Add cheese, buttermilk powder, sage, white pepper and cayenne to the cornbread mix; mix well and set aside.

2. Pour water, oil and vinegar into the bread machine baking pan. Add eggs and egg white.

3. Select the **Dough Cycle**. As the bread machine is mixing, gradually add the cornbread mix, scraping bottom and sides of pan with a rubber spatula. Try to incorporate all the cornbread mix within 1 to 2 minutes. When the mixing and kneading are complete, remove the kneading blade, leaving the bread pan in the bread machine. Quickly smooth the top of the loaf. Allow the cycle to finish. Turn off the bread machine.

4. Select the **Bake Cycle**. Set time to 60 minutes and temperature to 350°F (180°C). Allow the cycle to finish. Do not turn machine off before taking the internal temperature of the loaf with an instant-read thermometer. It should be 200°F (100°C). If it's between 180°F (85°C) and 200°F (100°C), leave machine on the **Keep Warm Cycle** until baked. If it's below 180°F (85°C), turn on the **Bake Cycle** and check the internal temperature every 10 minutes. (Some bread machines are automatically set for 60 minutes; others need to be set by 10-minute intervals.)

5. Once the loaf has reached 200°F (100°C), remove it from the pan immediately and let cool completely on a rack.

Bacon Cheddar Cornbread

**MAKES
12 SERVINGS**

This is a seriously kid-friendly combination, sure to get a stamp of approval from any little ones in your life. Adults will have trouble resisting too!

Tips

To ensure success, see page 14 for information on using your bread machine and page 18 for general tips on bread machine baking.

For the amount of cheese to purchase, see the weight/volume equivalents in the Ingredient Glossary, page 301.

◆ **9-inch (23 cm) square baking pan, lightly greased**

8	slices GF bacon, cooked crisp and crumbled	8
1 cup	shredded sharp (old) Cheddar cheese	250 mL
½ tsp	dry mustard	2 mL
3½ cups	Cornbread Mix (pages 204–206)	875 mL
¾ cup	GF cream-style corn	175 mL
½ cup	water	125 mL
¼ cup	vegetable oil	60 mL
1 tsp	cider vinegar	5 mL
3	eggs, lightly beaten	3
1	egg white, lightly beaten	1

1. Add bacon, cheese and mustard to the cornbread mix; mix well and set aside.

2. Pour corn, water, oil and vinegar into the bread machine baking pan. Add eggs and egg white.

3. Select the **Gluten-Free Cycle**. As the bread machine is mixing, gradually add the cornbread mix, scraping bottom and sides of pan with a rubber spatula. Try to incorporate all the cornbread mix within 1 to 2 minutes. When the mixing and kneading are complete, remove the kneading blade, leaving the bread pan in the bread machine. Quickly smooth the top of the loaf. Allow the cycle to finish.

4. At the end of the cycle, take the temperature of the loaf using an instant-read thermometer. It is baked at 200°F (100°C). If it's between 180°F (85°C) and 200°F (100°C), leave machine on the **Keep Warm Cycle** until baked. If it's below 180°F (85°C), turn on the **Bake Cycle** and check the internal temperature every 10 minutes. (Some bread machines are automatically set for 60 minutes; others need to be set by 10-minute intervals.)

5. Once the loaf has reached 200°F (100°C), remove it from the pan immediately and let cool completely on a rack.

NUTRITIONAL VALUES
per serving

Calories	283
Fat, total	12 g
Fat, saturated	4 g
Cholesterol	55 mg
Sodium	506 mg
Carbohydrate	36 g
Fiber	3 g
Protein	9 g
Calcium	69 mg
Iron	2 mg

Tips
Use an orange-colored Cheddar for a richer golden color.

We like to cut this loaf into 1½-inch (3.5 cm) squares and serve them as hors d'oeuvres.

Dough Cycle and Bake Cycle

If your bread machine does not have a Gluten-Free Cycle, use the Dough Cycle followed by the Bake Cycle.

1. Add bacon, cheese and mustard to the cornbread mix; mix well and set aside.

2. Pour corn, water, oil and vinegar into the bread machine baking pan. Add eggs and egg white.

3. Select the **Dough Cycle**. As the bread machine is mixing, gradually add the cornbread mix, scraping bottom and sides of pan with a rubber spatula. Try to incorporate all the cornbread mix within 1 to 2 minutes. When the mixing and kneading are complete, remove the kneading blade, leaving the bread pan in the bread machine. Quickly smooth the top of the loaf. Allow the cycle to finish. Turn off the bread machine.

4. Select the **Bake Cycle**. Set time to 60 minutes and temperature to 350°F (180°C). Allow the cycle to finish. Do not turn machine off before taking the internal temperature of the loaf with an instant-read thermometer. It should be 200°F (100°C). If it's between 180°F (85°C) and 200°F (100°C), leave machine on the **Keep Warm Cycle** until baked. If it's below 180°F (85°C), turn on the **Bake Cycle** and check the internal temperature every 10 minutes. (Some bread machines are automatically set for 60 minutes; others need to be set by 10-minute intervals.)

5. Once the loaf has reached 200°F (100°C), remove it from the pan immediately and let cool completely on a rack.

Blueberry Cornbread

Here's a moist, colorful cornbread that's quick to make thanks to our mix.

Tips

To ensure success, see page 14 for information on using your bread machine and page 18 for general tips on bread machine baking.

You can use cooked fresh, thawed frozen or well-drained canned corn.

¾ cup	dried blueberries	175 mL
2 tsp	lemon zest	10 mL
3½ cups	Cornbread Mix (pages 204–206)	875 mL
1¼ cups	water	300 mL
¾ cup	corn kernels, well drained	175 mL
¼ cup	vegetable oil	60 mL
2 tsp	freshly squeezed lemon juice	10 mL
3	eggs, lightly beaten	3
1	egg white, lightly beaten	1

1. Add blueberries and lemon zest to the cornbread mix; mix well and set aside.

2. Pour water, corn, oil and lemon juice into the bread machine baking pan. Add eggs and egg white.

3. Select the **Gluten-Free Cycle**. As the bread machine is mixing, gradually add the cornbread mix, scraping bottom and sides of pan with a rubber spatula. Try to incorporate all the cornbread mix within 1 to 2 minutes. When the mixing and kneading are complete, remove the kneading blade, leaving the bread pan in the bread machine. Quickly smooth the top of the loaf. Allow the cycle to finish.

4. At the end of the cycle, take the temperature of the loaf using an instant-read thermometer. It is baked at 200°F (100°C). If it's between 180°F (85°C) and 200°F (100°C), leave machine on the **Keep Warm Cycle** until baked. If it's below 180°F (85°C), turn on the **Bake Cycle** and check the internal temperature every 10 minutes. (Some bread machines are automatically set for 60 minutes; others need to be set by 10-minute intervals.)

5. Once the loaf has reached 200°F (100°C), remove it from the pan immediately and let cool completely on a rack.

NUTRITIONAL VALUES
per serving

Calories	199
Fat, total	6 g
Fat, saturated	1 g
Cholesterol	34 mg
Sodium	280 mg
Carbohydrate	33 g
Fiber	3 g
Protein	4 g
Calcium	15 mg
Iron	1 mg

Variation
Replace the blueberries with an equal amount of dried cranberries for an attractive red and yellow loaf.

Dough Cycle and Bake Cycle

If your bread machine does not have a Gluten-Free Cycle, use the Dough Cycle followed by the Bake Cycle.

1. Add blueberries and lemon zest to the cornbread mix; mix well and set aside.

2. Pour water, corn, oil and lemon juice into the bread machine baking pan. Add eggs and egg white.

3. Select the **Dough Cycle**. As the bread machine is mixing, gradually add the cornbread mix, scraping bottom and sides of pan with a rubber spatula. Try to incorporate all the cornbread mix within 1 to 2 minutes. When the mixing and kneading are complete, remove the kneading blade, leaving the bread pan in the bread machine. Quickly smooth the top of the loaf. Allow the cycle to finish. Turn off the bread machine.

4. Select the **Bake Cycle**. Set time to 60 minutes and temperature to 350°F (180°C). Allow the cycle to finish. Do not turn machine off before taking the internal temperature of the loaf with an instant-read thermometer. It should be 200°F (100°C). If it's between 180°F (85°C) and 200°F (100°C), leave machine on the **Keep Warm Cycle** until baked. If it's below 180°F (85°C), turn on the **Bake Cycle** and check the internal temperature every 10 minutes. (Some bread machines are automatically set for 60 minutes; others need to be set by 10-minute intervals.)

5. Once the loaf has reached 200°F (100°C), remove it from the pan immediately and let cool completely on a rack.

Cornbread English Muffins

The cornmeal provides extra crunch in these English muffins. Just split with a fork and toast.

Tips

To ensure success, see page 14 for information on using your bread machine and page 18 for general tips on bread machine baking.

To serve, use a fork to split each English muffin horizontally in half. Toast until golden and serve warm.

Variation

Cinnamon Raisin Cornbread English Muffins: Add ¼ cup (60 mL) raisins and ¼ tsp (1 mL) ground cinnamon with the yeast in step 1.

◆ **Baking sheets, lined with parchment and generously sprinkled with cornmeal**

2 tsp	bread machine or instant yeast	10 mL
3½ cups	Cornbread Mix (pages 204–206)	875 mL
1½ cups	milk, at room temperature	375 mL
⅓ cup	vegetable oil	75 mL
2 tsp	cider vinegar	10 mL
2	eggs, lightly beaten	2
1	egg white, lightly beaten	1
½ cup	cornmeal	125 mL

1. Add yeast to the cornbread mix; mix well and set aside.

2. Pour milk, oil and vinegar into the bread machine baking pan. Add eggs and egg white.

3. Select the **Dough Cycle**. As the bread machine is mixing, gradually add the cornbread mix, scraping bottom and sides of pan with a rubber spatula. Try to incorporate all the cornbread mix within 1 to 2 minutes. Stop bread machine as soon as the kneading portion of the cycle is complete. Do not let bread machine finish the cycle.

4. Using a ¼-cup (60 mL) scoop, drop 18 scoops of dough at least 2 inches (5 cm) apart onto prepared baking sheets. Sprinkle each generously with cornmeal. Using an egg lifter, gently pat each scoop into a ¾-inch (2 cm) thick circle. Let rise, uncovered, in a warm, draft-free place for 30 minutes. Meanwhile, preheat oven to 400°F (200°C).

5. Bake for 13 to 15 minutes or until internal temperature of English muffins registers 200°F (100°C) on an instant-read thermometer. Remove from the pan immediately and let cool completely on a rack.

NUTRITIONAL VALUES per serving	
Calories	169
Fat, total	6 g
Fat, saturated	1 g
Cholesterol	19 mg
Sodium	219 mg
Carbohydrate	27 g
Fiber	2 g
Protein	4 g
Calcium	36 mg
Iron	1 mg

Egg-Free Breads

We've been surprised by the number of people at conferences who have purchased our *Complete Gluten-Free Cookbook* specifically because it includes egg-free variations. We didn't know there were so many of you who cannot tolerate eggs. But now that we know, here's a whole bunch of egg-free bread recipes to satisfy your needs.

Egg-Free Baking

Eggs have several different roles in baking — they are used for leavening or lightness, and as a binder to help hold baked goods together. Eggs provide extra structure in gluten-free bread; therefore, when you eliminate them, the resulting loaves may be shorter. The tops of egg-free loaves are often flat or slightly concave, even when you use a ground flaxseed gel or commercial egg replacer in place of eggs.

Ground Flaxseed Gel

Ground flaxseed can replace eggs in many baking recipes. The ground flaxseed you use can be flax flour, milled flaxseed, sprouted flax flour or grind-your-own flaxseed. When you combine it with warm water and let it stand for at least 5 minutes, it forms a thick gel, about the consistency of a raw egg white.

In many baking recipes, each egg can be replaced with 2 tbsp (30 mL) ground flaxseed and $\frac{1}{4}$ cup (60 mL) warm tap water. However, this may need to be adjusted to create a product similar to the original. Wait to add the flaxseed gel until the bread machine begins to mix. Add the gel before the dry ingredients, allowing it to combine with the liquids.

Baked goods made with ground flaxseed tend to brown more quickly than those made with eggs and sometimes need to be tented with foil to prevent burning. However, many require an extra couple of minutes of baking time to reach the internal temperature of 200°F (100°C).

Commercial Egg Replacer

Egg replacer is a white powder containing a combination of baking powder and starches. It is added with the dry ingredients so that it is well mixed in before it touches the liquids. The oil or other fat in the recipe may have to be increased slightly.

Note: The egg substitutes sold in most supermarkets contain egg products and should not be confused with commercial egg replacer.

Tips for Successful Starters

Using the Starter

- It is normal for a starter to separate. The grayish liquid rises to the top, while the very thick part settles to the bottom of the storage container. Stir well before each use.

- The starter should have the consistency of pancake batter. If it's too thick, add a small amount of water before measuring.

- After refrigerating, bring the starter to room temperature by placing it in a bowl of warm water for 15 minutes before measuring.

- Until the starter becomes established and is working well, remove only 1 cup (250 mL) at a time.

- Make sure all utensils and pans that come into contact with the starter go through the dishwasher or are sanitized with a mild solution of water and bleach.

Feeding the Starter

- To replace each cup (250 mL) of starter used in preparing a recipe, add to the remaining starter:

¾ cup	water	175 mL
¾ cup	teff flour	175 mL
1 tsp	granulated sugar	5 mL

  Stir well, cover with a double layer of cheesecloth or a loose-fitting lid and let stand at room temperature for at least 24 hours or until bubbly and sour-smelling. Refrigerate, loosely covered.

- If not used regularly, stir in 1 tsp (5 mL) granulated sugar every 10 days.

Teff Sourdough Starter

Begin by making this starter, and you'll be on your way to enjoying egg-free, gluten-free sourdough teff breads.

Tips

If the starter liquid turns green, pink or orange — or develops mold — throw it out and start again.

During hot weather, use a triple layer of cheesecloth to cover the sourdough starter when it is at room temperature. A loose-fitting lid on a large casserole dish works well too.

3 cups	warm water	750 mL
2 tbsp	granulated sugar	30 mL
2 tbsp	bread machine or instant yeast	30 mL
3 cups	teff flour	750 mL

1. In a very large glass bowl, combine water and sugar. Sprinkle with yeast, gently stir to moisten and let stand for 10 minutes.
2. Add teff flour and whisk until smooth.
3. Cover with a double layer of cheesecloth or a loose-fitting lid. Secure so that it is not touching the starter. Let stand at room temperature for 2 to 4 days, stirring two to three times a day. When ready to use, starter has a sour smell, with small bubbles rising to the surface.
4. Store, loosely covered, in the refrigerator until needed. If not used regularly, stir in 1 tsp (5 mL) granulated sugar every 10 days.

NUTRITIONAL VALUES per serving	
Calories	435
Fat, total	4 g
Fat, saturated	0 g
Cholesterol	0 mg
Sodium	24 mg
Carbohydrate	85 g
Fiber	15 g
Protein	16 g
Calcium	176 mg
Iron	8 mg

EF Sourdough Teff Walnut Raisin Hearth Bread

MAKES 8 WEDGES
(1 per serving)

Here's an egg-free version of a traditional French Canadian sourdough hearth bread. Serve it for dessert, with fresh fruit.

Tip

To ensure success, see page 14 for information on using your bread machine, page 18 for general tips on bread machine baking and page 221 for tips on using and feeding the starter.

Variation

To make this nut-free, use double the raisins or substitute dried cranberries for the walnuts.

NUTRITIONAL VALUES
per serving

Calories	458
Fat, total	21 g
Fat, saturated	1 g
Cholesterol	0 mg
Sodium	89 mg
Carbohydrate	60 g
Fiber	11 g
Protein	13 g
Calcium	99 mg
Iron	5 mg

◆ **9-inch (23 cm) round baking pan, lightly greased**

²⁄₃ cup	flax flour or ground flaxseed	150 mL
³⁄₄ cup	warm water	175 mL
1¼ cups	amaranth flour	300 mL
²⁄₃ cup	teff flour	150 mL
²⁄₃ cup	tapioca starch	150 mL
¼ cup	packed brown sugar	60 mL
1 tbsp	xanthan gum	15 mL
1 tbsp	bread machine or instant yeast	15 mL
1¼ tsp	salt	6 mL
½ cup	raisins	125 mL
1 cup	coarsely chopped toasted walnuts	250 mL
1 cup	Teff Sourdough Starter (page 222), at room temperature	250 mL
²⁄₃ cup	water	150 mL
¼ cup	vegetable oil	60 mL

1. In a small bowl or measuring cup, combine flax flour and warm water; mix well. Let stand for 5 minutes.

2. In a large bowl or plastic bag, combine amaranth flour, teff flour, tapioca starch, brown sugar, xanthan gum, yeast, salt, raisins and walnuts; mix well and set aside.

3. Pour sourdough starter, water and oil into the bread machine baking pan.

4. Select the **Dough Cycle**. As the bread machine is mixing, add the flax flour mixture. Gradually add the dry ingredients, scraping bottom and sides of pan with a rubber spatula. Try to incorporate all the dry ingredients within 1 to 2 minutes. Stop bread machine as soon as the kneading portion of the cycle is complete. Do not let bread machine finish the cycle.

5. Gently transfer dough to prepared pan and spread evenly to the edges, leaving the top rough and uneven. Let rise, uncovered, in a warm, draft-free place for 40 to 50 minutes or until almost doubled in volume. Meanwhile, preheat oven to 375°F (190°C).

6. Bake for 30 to 33 minutes or until internal temperature of loaf registers 200°F (100°C) on an instant-read thermometer. Remove from the pan immediately and let cool on a rack. Cut into 8 wedges and serve warm.

EF Sourdough Teff Loaf

Teff and flax flours provide a tangy aroma in this exceptionally tasty loaf.

Tips

To ensure success, see page 14 for information on using your bread machine, page 18 for general tips on bread machine baking and page 221 for tips on using and feeding the starter.

For a light-colored loaf, choose white teff flour.

¾ cup	flax flour or ground flaxseed	175 mL
¾ cup	warm water	175 mL
1 cup	amaranth flour	250 mL
¾ cup	teff flour	175 mL
½ cup	potato starch	125 mL
3 tbsp	granulated sugar	45 mL
1 tbsp	xanthan gum	15 mL
1 tbsp	bread machine or instant yeast	15 mL
1½ tsp	salt	7 mL
1 cup	Teff Sourdough Starter (page 222), at room temperature	250 mL
½ cup	water	125 mL
¼ cup	vegetable oil	60 mL

1. In a small bowl or measuring cup, combine flax flour and warm water; mix well. Let stand for 5 minutes.

2. In a large bowl or plastic bag, combine amaranth flour, teff flour, potato starch, sugar, xanthan gum, yeast and salt; mix well and set aside.

3. Pour sourdough starter, water and oil into the bread machine baking pan.

4. Select the **Gluten-Free Cycle**. As the bread machine is mixing, add the flax flour mixture. Gradually add the dry ingredients, scraping bottom and sides of pan with a rubber spatula. Try to incorporate all the dry ingredients within 1 to 2 minutes. When the mixing and kneading are complete, remove the kneading blade, leaving the bread pan in the bread machine. Quickly smooth the top of the loaf. Allow the cycle to finish.

5. At the end of the cycle, take the temperature of the loaf using an instant-read thermometer. It is baked at 200°F (100°C). If it's between 180°F (85°C) and 200°F (100°C), leave machine on the **Keep Warm Cycle** until baked. If it's below 180°F (85°C), turn on the **Bake Cycle** and check the internal temperature every 10 minutes. (Some bread machines are automatically set for 60 minutes; others need to be set by 10-minute intervals.)

6. Once the loaf has reached 200°F (100°C), remove it from the pan immediately and let cool completely on a rack.

NUTRITIONAL VALUES per serving	
Calories	172
Fat, total	7 g
Fat, saturated	0 g
Cholesterol	0 mg
Sodium	238 mg
Carbohydrate	26 g
Fiber	5 g
Protein	5 g
Calcium	42 mg
Iron	2 mg

Dough Cycle and Bake Cycle

If your bread machine does not have a Gluten-Free Cycle, use the Dough Cycle followed by the Bake Cycle.

1. In a small bowl or measuring cup, combine flax flour and warm water; mix well. Let stand for 5 minutes.

2. In a large bowl or plastic bag, combine amaranth flour, teff flour, potato starch, sugar, xanthan gum, yeast and salt; mix well and set aside.

3. Pour sourdough starter, water and oil into the bread machine baking pan.

4. Select the **Dough Cycle**. As the bread machine is mixing, add the flax flour mixture. Gradually add the dry ingredients, scraping bottom and sides of pan with a rubber spatula. Try to incorporate all the dry ingredients within 1 to 2 minutes. When the mixing and kneading are complete, remove the kneading blade, leaving the bread pan in the bread machine. Quickly smooth the top of the loaf. Allow the cycle to finish. Turn off the bread machine.

5. Select the **Bake Cycle**. Set time to 60 minutes and temperature to 350°F (180°C). Allow the cycle to finish. Do not turn machine off before taking the internal temperature of the loaf with an instant-read thermometer. It should be 200°F (100°C). If it's between 180°F (85°C) and 200°F (100°C), leave machine on the **Keep Warm Cycle** until baked. If it's below 180°F (85°C), turn on the **Bake Cycle** and check the internal temperature every 10 minutes. (Some bread machines are automatically set for 60 minutes; others need to be set by 10-minute intervals.)

6. Once the loaf has reached 200°F (100°C), remove it from the pan immediately and let cool completely on a rack.

EF Sourdough Teff Brown Bread

This bread is highly nutritious and has a delicious, tangy flavor.

Tips

To ensure success, see page 14 for information on using your bread machine, page 18 for general tips on bread machine baking and page 221 for tips on using and feeding the starter.

Don't forget about the sourdough starter sitting in your refrigerator. If you haven't used it to make a loaf in the last 10 days, see page 221 for information on feeding it.

⅔ cup	flax flour or ground flaxseed	150 mL
¾ cup	warm water	175 mL
1 cup	sorghum flour	250 mL
¾ cup	teff flour	175 mL
2 tbsp	rice bran	30 mL
½ cup	tapioca starch	125 mL
1 tbsp	xanthan gum	15 mL
1 tbsp	bread machine or instant yeast	15 mL
1¼ tsp	salt	6 mL
1 cup	Teff Sourdough Starter (page 222), at room temperature	250 mL
½ cup	water	125 mL
2 tbsp	vegetable oil	30 mL
3 tbsp	liquid honey	45 mL
2 tbsp	light (fancy) molasses	30 mL

1. In a small bowl or measuring cup, combine flax flour and warm water; mix well. Let stand for 5 minutes.

2. In a large bowl or plastic bag, combine sorghum flour, teff flour, rice bran, tapioca starch, xanthan gum, yeast and salt; mix well and set aside.

3. Pour sourdough starter, water, oil, honey and molasses into the bread machine baking pan.

4. Select the **Gluten-Free Cycle**. As the bread machine is mixing, add the flax flour mixture. Gradually add the dry ingredients, scraping bottom and sides of pan with a rubber spatula. Try to incorporate all the dry ingredients within 1 to 2 minutes. When the mixing and kneading are complete, remove the kneading blade, leaving the bread pan in the bread machine. Quickly smooth the top of the loaf. Allow the cycle to finish.

5. At the end of the cycle, take the temperature of the loaf using an instant-read thermometer. It is baked at 200°F (100°C). If it's between 180°F (85°C) and 200°F (100°C), leave machine on the **Keep Warm Cycle** until baked. If it's below 180°F (85°C), turn on the **Bake Cycle** and check the internal temperature every 10 minutes. (Some bread machines are automatically set for 60 minutes; others need to be set by 10-minute intervals.)

NUTRITIONAL VALUES per serving	
Calories	164
Fat, total	4 g
Fat, saturated	0 g
Cholesterol	0 mg
Sodium	199 mg
Carbohydrate	29 g
Fiber	5 g
Protein	5 g
Calcium	38 mg
Iron	2 mg

Tip

It is easier to measure honey and molasses if they are warmed in the microwave for a few seconds, or set in a pan of hot water for a few minutes. Measure the oil first, then measure the honey and molasses; they will slide off the measuring spoon more easily that way.

Variation

Substitute ¼ cup (60 mL) packed brown sugar for the honey and the molasses.

6. Once the loaf has reached 200°F (100°C), remove it from the pan immediately and let cool completely on a rack.

Dough Cycle and Bake Cycle

If your bread machine does not have a Gluten-Free Cycle, use the Dough Cycle followed by the Bake Cycle.

1. In a small bowl or measuring cup, combine flax flour and warm water; mix well. Let stand for 5 minutes.

2. In a large bowl or plastic bag, combine sorghum flour, teff flour, rice bran, tapioca starch, xanthan gum, yeast and salt; mix well and set aside.

3. Pour sourdough starter, water, oil, honey and molasses into the bread machine baking pan.

4. Select the **Dough Cycle**. As the bread machine is mixing, add the flax flour mixture. Gradually add the dry ingredients, scraping bottom and sides of pan with a rubber spatula. Try to incorporate all the dry ingredients within 1 to 2 minutes. When the mixing and kneading are complete, remove the kneading blade, leaving the bread pan in the bread machine. Quickly smooth the top of the loaf. Allow the cycle to finish. Turn off the bread machine.

5. Select the **Bake Cycle**. Set time to 60 minutes and temperature to 350°F (180°C). Allow the cycle to finish. Do not turn machine off before taking the internal temperature of the loaf with an instant-read thermometer. It should be 200°F (100°C). If it's between 180°F (85°C) and 200°F (100°C), leave machine on the **Keep Warm Cycle** until baked. If it's below 180°F (85°C), turn on the **Bake Cycle** and check the internal temperature every 10 minutes. (Some bread machines are automatically set for 60 minutes; others need to be set by 10-minute intervals.)

6. Once the loaf has reached 200°F (100°C), remove it from the pan immediately and let cool completely on a rack.

EF Sourdough Teff Savory Ciabatta

MAKES 8 WEDGES
(1 per serving)

This egg-free ciabatta has the "tuggy" texture of sourdough.

Tips

To ensure success, see page 14 for information on using your bread machine, page 18 for general tips on bread machine baking and page 221 for tips on using and feeding the starter.

We like this ciabatta best served hot out of the oven.

◆ **8-inch (20 cm) round baking pan, lightly greased and floured with teff flour**

⅓ cup	flax flour or ground flaxseed	75 mL
½ cup	warm water	125 mL
½ cup	amaranth flour	125 mL
⅓ cup	teff flour	75 mL
¼ cup	tapioca starch	60 mL
1 tbsp	granulated sugar	15 mL
2 tsp	xanthan gum	10 mL
2 tbsp	bread machine or instant yeast	30 mL
½ tsp	salt	2 mL
⅓ cup	packed fresh savory, snipped	75 mL
1 cup	Teff Sourdough Starter (page 222), at room temperature	250 mL
¼ cup	water	60 mL
2 tbsp	extra virgin olive oil	30 mL
1 to 2 tbsp	teff flour	15 to 30 mL

1. In a small bowl or measuring cup, combine flax flour and warm water; mix well. Let stand for 5 minutes.

2. In a large bowl or plastic bag, combine amaranth flour, teff flour, tapioca starch, sugar, xanthan gum, yeast, salt and savory; mix well and set aside.

3. Pour sourdough starter, water and oil into the bread machine baking pan.

4. Select the **Dough Cycle**. As the bread machine is mixing, add the flax flour mixture. Gradually add the dry ingredients, scraping bottom and sides of pan with a rubber spatula. Try to incorporate all the dry ingredients within 1 to 2 minutes. Stop bread machine as soon as the kneading portion of the cycle is complete. Do not let bread machine finish the cycle.

NUTRITIONAL VALUES per serving	
Calories	189
Fat, total	6 g
Fat, saturated	1 g
Cholesterol	0 mg
Sodium	155 mg
Carbohydrate	29 g
Fiber	7 g
Protein	6 g
Calcium	4 mg
Iron	3 mg

5. Gently transfer dough to prepared pan and spread evenly to the edges, leaving the top rough and uneven. Lightly dust top with teff flour. With well-floured fingers, make deep indents all over the dough, pressing all the way down to the pan. Let rise, uncovered, in a warm, draft-free place for 40 to 50 minutes or until almost doubled in volume. Meanwhile, preheat oven to 425°F (220°C).

6. Bake for 13 to 15 minutes or until top is golden. Remove from the pan immediately and let cool on a rack. Cut into 8 wedges and serve warm.

EF Sunflower Flax Mini Loaves

MAKES 3 LOAVES, 6 SLICES EACH
(1 slice per serving)

Enjoy a thick slice for a snack, along with a chunk of old (sharp) Cheddar cheese.

Tips

To ensure success, see page 14 for information on using your bread machine and page 18 for general tips on bread machine baking.

For information on grinding and cracking flaxseed, see the Technique Glossary, page 307.

◆ **Three 5³⁄₄- by 3¹⁄₄-inch (14 by 8 cm) loaf pans, lightly greased**

¹⁄₂ cup	flax flour or ground flaxseed	125 mL
²⁄₃ cup	warm water	150 mL
1 cup	sorghum flour	250 mL
¹⁄₃ cup	amaranth flour	75 mL
¹⁄₄ cup	flax flour or ground flaxseed	60 mL
¹⁄₃ cup	tapioca starch	75 mL
¹⁄₄ cup	cornstarch	60 mL
2 tbsp	granulated sugar	30 mL
2¹⁄₂ tsp	xanthan gum	12 mL
1 tbsp	bread machine or instant yeast	15 mL
1¹⁄₄ tsp	salt	6 mL
¹⁄₂ cup	cracked flaxseed	125 mL
¹⁄₂ cup	unsalted raw sunflower seeds	125 mL
1 cup	water	250 mL
3 tbsp	vegetable oil	45 mL
2 tsp	cider vinegar	10 mL

1. In a small bowl or measuring cup, combine ¹⁄₂ cup (125 mL) flax flour and warm water; mix well. Let stand for 5 minutes.

2. In a large bowl or plastic bag, combine sorghum flour, amaranth flour, ¹⁄₄ cup (60 mL) flax flour, tapioca starch, cornstarch, sugar, xanthan gum, yeast, salt, flaxseed and sunflower seeds; mix well and set aside.

3. Pour water, oil and vinegar into the bread machine baking pan.

NUTRITIONAL VALUES	
per serving	
Calories	140
Fat, total	8 g
Fat, saturated	1 g
Cholesterol	0 mg
Sodium	164 mg
Carbohydrate	16 g
Fiber	5 g
Protein	4 g
Calcium	22 mg
Iron	1 mg

4. Select the **Dough Cycle**. As the bread machine is mixing, add the flax flour–water mixture. Gradually add the dry ingredients, scraping bottom and sides of pan with a rubber spatula. Try to incorporate all the dry ingredients within 1 to 2 minutes. Stop bread machine as soon as the kneading portion of the cycle is complete. Do not let bread machine finish the cycle.

5. Spoon dough into prepared pans, dividing evenly. Let rise, uncovered, in a warm, draft-free place for 50 minutes. Meanwhile, preheat oven to 350°F (180°C).

6. Bake for 33 to 36 minutes or until internal temperature of loaves registers 200°F (100°C) on an instant-read thermometer. Remove from the pan immediately and let cool completely on a rack.

EF Brown Bread

MAKES 15 SLICES
(1 per serving)

Here's a good basic brown bread for sandwiches and everyday use. This egg-free version has a hint of flax flavor. It's especially good with homemade baked beans.

Tips

To ensure success, see page 14 for information on using your bread machine and page 18 for general tips on bread machine baking.

⅓ cup	flax flour or ground flaxseed	75 mL
⅔ cup	warm water	150 mL
1¼ cups	sorghum flour	300 mL
⅔ cup	whole bean flour	150 mL
½ cup	brown rice flour	125 mL
2 tbsp	quinoa flour	30 mL
¼ cup	potato starch	60 mL
3 tbsp	tapioca starch	45 mL
2 tbsp	packed brown sugar	30 mL
1 tbsp	xanthan gum	15 mL
1½ tsp	bread machine or instant yeast	7 mL
1½ tsp	salt	7 mL
1¼ cups	water	300 mL
3 tbsp	vegetable oil	45 mL
2 tbsp	light (fancy) molasses	30 mL
1 tsp	cider vinegar	5 mL

1. In a small bowl or measuring cup, combine flax flour and warm water; mix well. Let stand for 5 minutes.

2. In a large bowl or plastic bag, combine sorghum flour, whole bean flour, brown rice flour, quinoa flour, potato starch, tapioca starch, brown sugar, xanthan gum, yeast and salt; mix well and set aside.

3. Pour water, oil, molasses and vinegar into the bread machine baking pan.

4. Select the **Gluten-Free Cycle**. As the bread machine is mixing, add the flax flour mixture. Gradually add the dry ingredients, scraping bottom and sides of pan with a rubber spatula. Try to incorporate all the dry ingredients within 1 to 2 minutes. When the mixing and kneading are complete, remove the kneading blade, leaving the bread pan in the bread machine. Quickly smooth the top of the loaf. Allow the cycle to finish.

5. At the end of the cycle, take the temperature of the loaf using an instant-read thermometer. It is baked at 200°F (100°C). If it's between 180°F (85°C) and 200°F (100°C), leave machine on the **Keep Warm Cycle** until baked. If it's below 180°F (85°C), turn on the **Bake Cycle** and check the internal temperature every 10 minutes. (Some bread machines are automatically set for 60 minutes; others need to be set by 10-minute intervals.)

NUTRITIONAL VALUES
per serving

Calories	157
Fat, total	5 g
Fat, saturated	0 g
Cholesterol	0 mg
Sodium	236 mg
Carbohydrate	26 g
Fiber	3 g
Protein	4 g
Calcium	18 mg
Iron	1 mg

Measuring the oil before the molasses ensures that the molasses slides out of the measure. We enjoy using the Oxo sloped ¼-cup (60 mL) measure for this. If the molasses is really thick or is straight out of the refrigerator, warm it slightly in the microwave before measuring.

Variation

Add ½ cup (125 mL) raisins or chopped walnuts with the dry ingredients.

6. Once the loaf has reached 200°F (100°C), remove it from the pan immediately and let cool completely on a rack.

Dough Cycle and Bake Cycle

If your bread machine does not have a Gluten-Free Cycle, use the Dough Cycle followed by the Bake Cycle.

1. In a small bowl or measuring cup, combine flax flour and warm water; mix well. Let stand for 5 minutes.

2. In a large bowl or plastic bag, combine sorghum flour, whole bean flour, brown rice flour, quinoa flour, potato starch, tapioca starch, brown sugar, xanthan gum, yeast and salt; mix well and set aside.

3. Pour water, oil, molasses and vinegar into the bread machine baking pan.

4. Select the **Dough Cycle**. As the bread machine is mixing, add the flax flour mixture. Gradually add the dry ingredients, scraping bottom and sides of pan with a rubber spatula. Try to incorporate all the dry ingredients within 1 to 2 minutes. When the mixing and kneading are complete, remove the kneading blade, leaving the bread pan in the bread machine. Quickly smooth the top of the loaf. Allow the cycle to finish. Turn off the bread machine.

5. Select the **Bake Cycle**. Set time to 60 minutes and temperature to 350°F (180°C). Allow the cycle to finish. Do not turn machine off before taking the internal temperature of the loaf with an instant-read thermometer. It should be 200°F (100°C). If it's between 180°F (85°C) and 200°F (100°C), leave machine on the **Keep Warm Cycle** until baked. If it's below 180°F (85°C), turn on the **Bake Cycle** and check the internal temperature every 10 minutes. (Some bread machines are automatically set for 60 minutes; others need to be set by 10-minute intervals.)

6. Once the loaf has reached 200°F (100°C), remove it from the pan immediately and let cool completely on a rack.

EF Mock Pumpernickel Loaf

MAKES 15 SLICES
(1 per serving)

*Coffee and cocoa powder
intensify the flavors
of this loaf, resulting
in a taste similar to
pumpernickel.*

Tips

To ensure success, see
page 14 for information on
using your bread machine
and page 18 for general tips
on bread machine baking.

Pea flour, like soy flour, has
a distinctive odor when wet
that disappears with baking.

½ cup	flax flour or ground flaxseed	125 mL
½ cup	warm water	125 mL
1¼ cups	sorghum flour	300 mL
1 cup	pea flour	250 mL
½ cup	cornstarch	125 mL
⅓ cup	tapioca starch	75 mL
3 tbsp	packed brown sugar	45 mL
1 tbsp	xanthan gum	15 mL
1 tsp	bread machine or instant yeast	5 mL
1½ tsp	salt	7 mL
2 tsp	instant coffee granules	10 mL
2 tsp	unsweetened cocoa powder, sifted	10 mL
1⅔ cups	water	400 mL
2 tbsp	vegetable oil	30 mL
3 tbsp	light (fancy) molasses	45 mL
1 tsp	cider vinegar	5 mL

1. In a small bowl or measuring cup, combine flax flour and warm water; mix well. Let stand for 5 minutes.

2. In a large bowl or plastic bag, combine sorghum flour, pea flour, cornstarch, tapioca starch, brown sugar, xanthan gum, yeast, salt, coffee granules and cocoa; mix well and set aside.

3. Pour water, oil, molasses and vinegar into the bread machine baking pan.

4. Select the **Gluten-Free Cycle**. As the bread machine is mixing, add the flax flour mixture. Gradually add the dry ingredients, scraping bottom and sides of pan with a rubber spatula. Try to incorporate all the dry ingredients within 1 to 2 minutes. When the mixing and kneading are complete, remove the kneading blade, leaving the bread pan in the bread machine. Quickly smooth the top of the loaf. Allow the cycle to finish.

5. At the end of the cycle, take the temperature of the loaf using an instant-read thermometer. It is baked at 200°F (100°C). If it's between 180°F (85°C) and 200°F (100°C), leave machine on the **Keep Warm Cycle** until baked. If it's below 180°F (85°C), turn on the **Bake Cycle** and check the internal temperature every 10 minutes. (Some

NUTRITIONAL VALUES
per serving

Calories	158
Fat, total	3 g
Fat, saturated	0 g
Cholesterol	0 mg
Sodium	238 mg
Carbohydrate	29 g
Fiber	6 g
Protein	5 g
Calcium	20 mg
Iron	2 mg

Sift cocoa just before using, as it lumps easily.

Measuring the oil before the molasses ensures that the molasses slides out of the measure. If the molasses is really thick or is straight out of the refrigerator, warm it slightly in the microwave before measuring.

Variation

Any type of bean flour can be substituted for the pea flour.

bread machines are automatically set for 60 minutes; others need to be set by 10-minute intervals.)

6. Once the loaf has reached 200°F (100°C), remove it from the pan immediately and let cool completely on a rack.

Dough Cycle and Bake Cycle

If your bread machine does not have a Gluten-Free Cycle, use the Dough Cycle followed by the Bake Cycle.

1. In a small bowl or measuring cup, combine flax flour and warm water; mix well. Let stand for 5 minutes.

2. In a large bowl or plastic bag, combine sorghum flour, pea flour, cornstarch, tapioca starch, brown sugar, xanthan gum, yeast, salt, coffee granules and cocoa; mix well and set aside.

3. Pour water, oil, molasses and vinegar into the bread machine baking pan.

4. Select the **Dough Cycle**. As the bread machine is mixing, add the flax flour mixture. Gradually add the dry ingredients, scraping bottom and sides of pan with a rubber spatula. Try to incorporate all the dry ingredients within 1 to 2 minutes. When the mixing and kneading are complete, remove the kneading blade, leaving the bread pan in the bread machine. Quickly smooth the top of the loaf. Allow the cycle to finish. Turn off the bread machine.

5. Select the **Bake Cycle**. Set time to 60 minutes and temperature to 350°F (180°C). Allow the cycle to finish. Do not turn machine off before taking the internal temperature of the loaf with an instant-read thermometer. It should be 200°F (100°C). If it's between 180°F (85°C) and 200°F (100°C), leave machine on the **Keep Warm Cycle** until baked. If it's below 180°F (85°C), turn on the **Bake Cycle** and check the internal temperature every 10 minutes. (Some bread machines are automatically set for 60 minutes; others need to be set by 10-minute intervals.)

6. Once the loaf has reached 200°F (100°C), remove it from the pan immediately and let cool completely on a rack.

EF Flax Bread

Flax bread is the new white bread!

Tips

To ensure success, see page 14 for information on using your bread machine and page 18 for general tips on bread machine baking.

For a warmer-colored loaf, choose golden flax flour and golden flaxseed rather than brown.

$2/3$ cup	flax flour or ground flaxseed	150 mL
$2/3$ cup	warm water	150 mL
2 cups	brown rice flour	500 mL
$2/3$ cup	potato starch	150 mL
$1/3$ cup	tapioca starch	75 mL
$1/3$ cup	cracked flaxseed	75 mL
$1/4$ cup	granulated sugar	60 mL
$2^1/2$ tsp	xanthan gum	12 mL
$2^1/4$ tsp	bread machine or instant yeast	11 mL
$1^1/2$ tsp	salt	7 mL
$1^1/2$ cups	milk, warmed to room temperature	375 mL
$1/4$ cup	vegetable oil	60 mL
1 tsp	cider vinegar	5 mL

1. In a small bowl or measuring cup, combine flax flour and warm water; mix well. Let stand for 5 minutes.

2. In a large bowl or plastic bag, combine brown rice flour, potato starch, tapioca starch, flaxseed, sugar, xanthan gum, yeast and salt; mix well and set aside.

3. Pour milk, oil and vinegar into the bread machine baking pan.

4. Select the **Gluten-Free Cycle**. As the bread machine is mixing, add the flax flour mixture. Gradually add the dry ingredients, scraping bottom and sides of pan with a rubber spatula. Try to incorporate all the dry ingredients within 1 to 2 minutes. When the mixing and kneading are complete, remove the kneading blade, leaving the bread pan in the bread machine. Quickly smooth the top of the loaf. Allow the cycle to finish.

5. At the end of the cycle, take the temperature of the loaf using an instant-read thermometer. It is baked at 200°F (100°C). If it's between 180°F (85°C) and 200°F (100°C), leave machine on the **Keep Warm Cycle** until baked. If it's below 180°F (85°C), turn on the **Bake Cycle** and check the internal temperature every 10 minutes. (Some bread machines are automatically set for 60 minutes; others need to be set by 10-minute intervals.)

6. Once the loaf has reached 200°F (100°C), remove it from the pan immediately and let cool completely on a rack.

For information on grinding and cracking flaxseed, see the Technique Glossary, page 307.

For instructions on warming milk, see the Technique Glossary, page 308.

Dough Cycle and Bake Cycle

If your bread machine does not have a Gluten-Free Cycle, use the Dough Cycle followed by the Bake Cycle.

1. In a small bowl or measuring cup, combine flax flour and warm water; mix well. Let stand for 5 minutes.

2. In a large bowl or plastic bag, combine brown rice flour, potato starch, tapioca starch, flaxseed, sugar, xanthan gum, yeast and salt; mix well and set aside.

3. Pour milk, oil and vinegar into the bread machine baking pan.

4. Select the **Dough Cycle**. As the bread machine is mixing, add the flax flour mixture. Gradually add the dry ingredients, scraping bottom and sides of pan with a rubber spatula. Try to incorporate all the dry ingredients within 1 to 2 minutes. When the mixing and kneading are complete, remove the kneading blade, leaving the bread pan in the bread machine. Quickly smooth the top of the loaf. Allow the cycle to finish. Turn off the bread machine.

5. Select the **Bake Cycle**. Set time to 60 minutes and temperature to 350°F (180°C). Allow the cycle to finish. Do not turn machine off before taking the internal temperature of the loaf with an instant-read thermometer. It should be 200°F (100°C). If it's between 180°F (85°C) and 200°F (100°C), leave machine on the **Keep Warm Cycle** until baked. If it's below 180°F (85°C), turn on the **Bake Cycle** and check the internal temperature every 10 minutes. (Some bread machines are automatically set for 60 minutes; others need to be set by 10-minute intervals.)

6. Once the loaf has reached 200°F (100°C), remove it from the pan immediately and let cool completely on a rack.

EF Teff Bread

This yummy bread is a great introduction to the most nutritious and smallest grain available.

Tips

To ensure success, see page 14 for information on using your bread machine and page 18 for general tips on bread machine baking.

See the Technique Glossary, page 307, for information on grinding flaxseed.

⅓ cup	flax flour or ground flaxseed	75 mL
⅔ cup	warm water	150 mL
¾ cup	brown rice flour	175 mL
¾ cup	teff flour	175 mL
⅓ cup	GF oat flour	75 mL
½ cup	potato starch	125 mL
¼ cup	teff grain	60 mL
2 tbsp	ground flaxseed	30 mL
1 tbsp	xanthan gum	15 mL
2¼ tsp	bread machine or instant yeast	11 mL
1½ tsp	salt	7 mL
2 tbsp	grated orange zest	30 mL
1 cup	water	250 mL
¼ cup	vegetable oil	60 mL
¼ cup	liquid honey	60 mL
2 tsp	cider vinegar	10 mL

1. In a small bowl or measuring cup, combine flax flour and warm water; mix well. Let stand for 5 minutes.

2. In a large bowl or plastic bag, combine brown rice flour, teff flour, oat flour, potato starch, teff grain, flaxseed, xanthan gum, yeast, salt and orange zest; mix well and set aside.

3. Pour water, oil, honey and vinegar into the bread machine baking pan.

4. Select the **Gluten-Free Cycle**. As the bread machine is mixing, add the flax flour mixture. Gradually add the dry ingredients, scraping bottom and sides of pan with a rubber spatula. Try to incorporate all the dry ingredients within 1 to 2 minutes. When the mixing and kneading are complete, remove the kneading blade, leaving the bread pan in the bread machine. Quickly smooth the top of the loaf. Allow the cycle to finish.

5. At the end of the cycle, take the temperature of the loaf using an instant-read thermometer. It is baked at 200°F (100°C). If it's between 180°F (85°C) and 200°F (100°C), leave machine on the **Keep Warm Cycle** until baked. If it's below 180°F (85°C), turn on the **Bake Cycle** and check the internal temperature every 10 minutes. (Some bread machines are automatically set for 60 minutes; others need to be set by 10-minute intervals.)

NUTRITIONAL VALUES per serving	
Calories	157
Fat, total	6 g
Fat, saturated	0 g
Cholesterol	0 mg
Sodium	237 mg
Carbohydrate	26 g
Fiber	3 g
Protein	3 g
Calcium	23 mg
Iron	1 mg

Teff flour can be stored at room temperature in an airtight container for up to 1 month. Refrigerate for up to 6 months or freeze for longer storage.

Choose brown teff flour for a sweet, nutty flavor and a darker color; choose white teff flour for a milder flavor.

Variation

If you can't find teff grain, substitute ¼ cup (60 mL) poppy seeds or amaranth grain.

6. Once the loaf has reached 200°F (100°C), remove it from the pan immediately and let cool completely on a rack.

Dough Cycle and Bake Cycle

If your bread machine does not have a Gluten-Free Cycle, use the Dough Cycle followed by the Bake Cycle.

1. In a small bowl or measuring cup, combine flax flour and warm water; mix well. Let stand for 5 minutes.

2. In a large bowl or plastic bag, combine brown rice flour, teff flour, oat flour, potato starch, teff grain, flaxseed, xanthan gum, yeast, salt and orange zest; mix well and set aside.

3. Pour water, oil, honey and vinegar into the bread machine baking pan.

4. Select the **Dough Cycle**. As the bread machine is mixing, add the flax flour mixture. Gradually add the dry ingredients, scraping bottom and sides of pan with a rubber spatula. Try to incorporate all the dry ingredients within 1 to 2 minutes. When the mixing and kneading are complete, remove the kneading blade, leaving the bread pan in the bread machine. Quickly smooth the top of the loaf. Allow the cycle to finish. Turn off the bread machine.

5. Select the **Bake Cycle**. Set time to 60 minutes and temperature to 350°F (180°C). Allow the cycle to finish. Do not turn machine off before taking the internal temperature of the loaf with an instant-read thermometer. It should be 200°F (100°C). If it's between 180°F (85°C) and 200°F (100°C), leave machine on the **Keep Warm Cycle** until baked. If it's below 180°F (85°C), turn on the **Bake Cycle** and check the internal temperature every 10 minutes. (Some bread machines are automatically set for 60 minutes; others need to be set by 10-minute intervals.)

6. Once the loaf has reached 200°F (100°C), remove it from the pan immediately and let cool completely on a rack.

EF Ancient Grains Bread

*One of our favorites —
made egg-free for you!*

Tips

This flavorful egg-free loaf
is shorter than some.

To ensure success, see
page 14 for information on
using your bread machine
and page 18 for general tips
on bread machine baking.

1/2 cup	flax flour or ground flaxseed	125 mL
3/4 cup	warm water	175 mL
1 cup	sorghum flour	250 mL
3/4 cup	amaranth flour	175 mL
3/4 cup	cornmeal	175 mL
1/4 cup	quinoa flour	60 mL
1/2 cup	tapioca starch	125 mL
1/3 cup	packed brown sugar	75 mL
1 tbsp	xanthan gum	15 mL
2 tsp	bread machine or instant yeast	10 mL
1 1/2 tsp	salt	7 mL
1 1/4 cups	water	300 mL
2 tbsp	vegetable oil	30 mL
2 tsp	cider vinegar	10 mL

1. In a small bowl or measuring cup, combine flax flour and warm water; mix well. Let stand for 5 minutes.

2. In a large bowl or plastic bag, combine sorghum flour, amaranth flour, cornmeal, quinoa flour, tapioca starch, brown sugar, xanthan gum, yeast and salt; mix well and set aside.

3. Pour water, oil and vinegar into the bread machine baking pan.

4. Select the **Gluten-Free Cycle**. As the bread machine is mixing, add the flax flour mixture. Gradually add the dry ingredients, scraping bottom and sides of pan with a rubber spatula. Try to incorporate all the dry ingredients within 1 to 2 minutes. When the mixing and kneading are complete, remove the kneading blade, leaving the bread pan in the bread machine. Quickly smooth the top of the loaf. Allow the cycle to finish.

5. At the end of the cycle, take the temperature of the loaf using an instant-read thermometer. It is baked at 200°F (100°C). If it's between 180°F (85°C) and 200°F (100°C), leave machine on the **Keep Warm Cycle** until baked. If it's below 180°F (85°C), turn on the **Bake Cycle** and check the internal temperature every 10 minutes. (Some bread machines are automatically set for 60 minutes; others need to be set by 10-minute intervals.)

NUTRITIONAL VALUES
per serving

Calories	157
Fat, total	4 g
Fat, saturated	0 g
Cholesterol	0 mg
Sodium	237 mg
Carbohydrate	28 g
Fiber	4 g
Protein	4 g
Calcium	19 mg
Iron	2 mg

Thoroughly mix the dry ingredients before adding them to the liquids — they are powder-fine and could clump together.

Slice this or any bread with an electric knife for thin, even sandwich slices.

6. Once the loaf has reached 200°F (100°C), remove it from the pan immediately and let cool completely on a rack.

Dough Cycle and Bake Cycle

If your bread machine does not have a Gluten-Free Cycle, use the Dough Cycle followed by the Bake Cycle.

1. In a small bowl or measuring cup, combine flax flour and warm water; mix well. Let stand for 5 minutes.

2. In a large bowl or plastic bag, combine sorghum flour, amaranth flour, cornmeal, quinoa flour, tapioca starch, brown sugar, xanthan gum, yeast and salt; mix well and set aside.

3. Pour water, oil and vinegar into the bread machine baking pan.

4. Select the **Dough Cycle**. As the bread machine is mixing, add the flax flour mixture. Gradually add the dry ingredients, scraping bottom and sides of pan with a rubber spatula. Try to incorporate all the dry ingredients within 1 to 2 minutes. When the mixing and kneading are complete, remove the kneading blade, leaving the bread pan in the bread machine. Quickly smooth the top of the loaf. Allow the cycle to finish. Turn off the bread machine.

5. Select the **Bake Cycle**. Set time to 60 minutes and temperature to 350°F (180°C). Allow the cycle to finish. Do not turn machine off before taking the internal temperature of the loaf with an instant-read thermometer. It should be 200°F (100°C). If it's between 180°F (85°C) and 200°F (100°C), leave machine on the **Keep Warm Cycle** until baked. If it's below 180°F (85°C), turn on the **Bake Cycle** and check the internal temperature every 10 minutes. (Some bread machines are automatically set for 60 minutes; others need to be set by 10-minute intervals.)

6. Once the loaf has reached 200°F (100°C), remove it from the pan immediately and let cool completely on a rack.

EF Honey Walnut Bread

Ground flax intensifies the nutty flavor of this loaf.

Tips

To ensure success, see page 14 for information on using your bread machine and page 18 for general tips on bread machine baking.

It's worth the time to toast the walnuts (for instructions, see the Technique Glossary, page 308). No need to let them cool; just add to the dry ingredients. Toast more walnuts than you need for this recipe. Cool and store the extra in a sealable plastic bag in the refrigerator.

⅓ cup	flax flour or ground flaxseed	75 mL
½ cup	warm water	125 mL
1½ cups	sorghum flour	375 mL
¾ cup	brown rice flour	175 mL
½ cup	cornstarch	125 mL
½ cup	rice bran	125 mL
1 tbsp	xanthan gum	15 mL
1½ tsp	bread machine or instant yeast	7 mL
1½ tsp	salt	7 mL
1 cup	coarsely chopped walnuts, toasted (see tip, at left)	250 mL
1¼ cups	water	300 mL
2 tbsp	walnut oil or vegetable oil	30 mL
⅓ cup	liquid honey	75 mL
1 tsp	cider vinegar	5 mL

1. In a small bowl or measuring cup, combine flax flour and warm water; mix well. Let stand for 5 minutes.

2. In a large bowl or plastic bag, combine sorghum flour, brown rice flour, cornstarch, rice bran, xanthan gum, yeast, salt and walnuts; mix well and set aside.

3. Pour water, oil, honey and vinegar into the bread machine baking pan.

4. Select the **Gluten-Free Cycle**. As the bread machine is mixing, add the flax flour mixture. Gradually add the dry ingredients, scraping bottom and sides of pan with a rubber spatula. Try to incorporate all the dry ingredients within 1 to 2 minutes. When the mixing and kneading are complete, remove the kneading blade, leaving the bread pan in the bread machine. Quickly smooth the top of the loaf. Allow the cycle to finish.

5. At the end of the cycle, take the temperature of the loaf using an instant-read thermometer. It is baked at 200°F (100°C). If it's between 180°F (85°C) and 200°F (100°C), leave machine on the **Keep Warm Cycle** until baked. If it's below 180°F (85°C), turn on the **Bake Cycle** and check the internal temperature every 10 minutes. (Some bread machines are automatically set for 60 minutes; others need to be set by 10-minute intervals.)

NUTRITIONAL VALUES
per serving

Calories	213
Fat, total	9 g
Fat, saturated	1 g
Cholesterol	0 mg
Sodium	235 mg
Carbohydrate	31 g
Fiber	4 g
Protein	5 g
Calcium	9 mg
Iron	2 mg

Tips

Store brown rice flour and rice bran in the refrigerator.

Warm up rice bran that has been stored in the refrigerator or freezer to room temperature.

Always store bread at room temperature or wrapped airtight in the freezer. The refrigerator accelerates the staling process.

6. Once the loaf has reached 200°F (100°C), remove it from the pan immediately and let cool completely on a rack.

Dough Cycle and Bake Cycle

If your bread machine does not have a Gluten-Free Cycle, use the Dough Cycle followed by the Bake Cycle.

1. In a small bowl or measuring cup, combine flax flour and warm water; mix well. Let stand for 5 minutes.

2. In a large bowl or plastic bag, combine sorghum flour, brown rice flour, cornstarch, rice bran, xanthan gum, yeast, salt and walnuts; mix well and set aside.

3. Pour water, oil, honey and vinegar into the bread machine baking pan.

4. Select the **Dough Cycle**. As the bread machine is mixing, add the flax flour mixture. Gradually add the dry ingredients, scraping bottom and sides of pan with a rubber spatula. Try to incorporate all the dry ingredients within 1 to 2 minutes. When the mixing and kneading are complete, remove the kneading blade, leaving the bread pan in the bread machine. Quickly smooth the top of the loaf. Allow the cycle to finish. Turn off the bread machine.

5. Select the **Bake Cycle**. Set time to 60 minutes and temperature to 350°F (180°C). Allow the cycle to finish. Do not turn machine off before taking the internal temperature of the loaf with an instant-read thermometer. It should be 200°F (100°C). If it's between 180°F (85°C) and 200°F (100°C), leave machine on the **Keep Warm Cycle** until baked. If it's below 180°F (85°C), turn on the **Bake Cycle** and check the internal temperature every 10 minutes. (Some bread machines are automatically set for 60 minutes; others need to be set by 10-minute intervals.)

6. Once the loaf has reached 200°F (100°C), remove it from the pan immediately and let cool completely on a rack.

EF Double Apple Oatmeal Bread

Make this loaf in the fall, when fresh apple cider is available.

Tips

To ensure success, see page 14 for information on using your bread machine and page 18 for general tips on bread machine baking.

Warm the apple cider and applesauce gently in the microwave if they have been stored in the refrigerator.

1/3 cup	flax flour or ground flaxseed	75 mL
1/2 cup	warm unsweetened apple cider	125 mL
1 1/3 cups	sorghum flour	325 mL
1/2 cup	GF oats	125 mL
1/2 cup	GF oat flour	125 mL
1/3 cup	tapioca starch	75 mL
3 tbsp	packed brown sugar	45 mL
1 tbsp	xanthan gum	15 mL
1 tbsp	bread machine or instant yeast	15 mL
1 1/2 tsp	salt	7 mL
1 1/2 tsp	GF apple pie spice	7 mL
3/4 cup	unsweetened apple cider, at room temperature	175 mL
1/2 cup	unsweetened applesauce, at room temperature	125 mL
2 tbsp	vegetable oil	30 mL

1. In a small bowl or measuring cup, combine flax flour and warm apple cider; mix well. Let stand for 5 minutes.

2. In a large bowl or plastic bag, combine sorghum flour, oats, oat flour, tapioca starch, brown sugar, xanthan gum, yeast, salt and apple pie spice; mix well and set aside.

3. Pour apple cider, applesauce and oil into the bread machine baking pan.

4. Select the **Gluten-Free Cycle**. As the bread machine is mixing, add the flax flour mixture. Gradually add the dry ingredients, scraping bottom and sides of pan with a rubber spatula. Try to incorporate all the dry ingredients within 1 to 2 minutes. When the mixing and kneading are complete, remove the kneading blade, leaving the bread pan in the bread machine. Quickly smooth the top of the loaf. Allow the cycle to finish.

5. At the end of the cycle, take the temperature of the loaf using an instant-read thermometer. It is baked at 200°F (100°C). If it's between 180°F (85°C) and 200°F (100°C), leave machine on the **Keep Warm Cycle** until baked. If it's below 180°F (85°C), turn on the **Bake Cycle** and check the internal temperature every 10 minutes. (Some bread machines are automatically set for 60 minutes; others need to be set by 10-minute intervals.)

NUTRITIONAL VALUES per serving	
Calories	129
Fat, total	4 g
Fat, saturated	0 g
Cholesterol	0 mg
Sodium	237 mg
Carbohydrate	23 g
Fiber	3 g
Protein	3 g
Calcium	10 mg
Iron	1 mg

Variations

For a tasty sandwich bread, omit the apple pie spice.

If you don't have apple pie spice, use ¾ tsp (3 mL) ground cinnamon, ½ tsp (2 mL) ground nutmeg and a pinch each of ground allspice and either ground cloves or ground ginger.

6. Once the loaf has reached 200°F (100°C), remove it from the pan immediately and let cool completely on a rack.

Dough Cycle and Bake Cycle

If your bread machine does not have a Gluten-Free Cycle, use the Dough Cycle followed by the Bake Cycle.

1. In a small bowl or measuring cup, combine flax flour and warm apple cider; mix well. Let stand for 5 minutes.

2. In a large bowl or plastic bag, combine sorghum flour, oats, oat flour, tapioca starch, brown sugar, xanthan gum, yeast, salt and apple pie spice; mix well and set aside.

3. Pour apple cider, applesauce and oil into the bread machine baking pan.

4. Select the **Dough Cycle**. As the bread machine is mixing, add the flax flour mixture. Gradually add the dry ingredients, scraping bottom and sides of pan with a rubber spatula. Try to incorporate all the dry ingredients within 1 to 2 minutes. When the mixing and kneading are complete, remove the kneading blade, leaving the bread pan in the bread machine. Quickly smooth the top of the loaf. Allow the cycle to finish. Turn off the bread machine.

5. Select the **Bake Cycle**. Set time to 60 minutes and temperature to 350°F (180°C). Allow the cycle to finish. Do not turn machine off before taking the internal temperature of the loaf with an instant-read thermometer. It should be 200°F (100°C). If it's between 180°F (85°C) and 200°F (100°C), leave machine on the **Keep Warm Cycle** until baked. If it's below 180°F (85°C), turn on the **Bake Cycle** and check the internal temperature every 10 minutes. (Some bread machines are automatically set for 60 minutes; others need to be set by 10-minute intervals.)

6. Once the loaf has reached 200°F (100°C), remove it from the pan immediately and let cool completely on a rack.

EF Cranberry Pumpkin Seed Bread

This loaf was made to be served with Thanksgiving dinner, and the leftovers make perfect turkey salad sandwiches.

Tips

To ensure success, see page 14 for information on using your bread machine and page 18 for general tips on bread machine baking.

See the Technique Glossary for information on grinding flaxseed to make flax flour (page 307).

²⁄₃ cup	flax flour or ground flaxseed	150 mL
¾ cup	warm water	175 mL
1½ cups	sorghum flour	375 mL
⅓ cup	flax flour	75 mL
¼ cup	quinoa flour	60 mL
½ cup	tapioca starch	125 mL
⅓ cup	cornstarch	75 mL
¼ cup	granulated sugar	60 mL
2½ tsp	xanthan gum	12 mL
1 tbsp	bread machine or instant yeast	15 mL
1½ tsp	salt	7 mL
1 tsp	ground cinnamon	5 mL
½ tsp	ground nutmeg	2 mL
¼ tsp	ground cloves	1 mL
¾ cup	dried cranberries	175 mL
½ cup	unsalted green pumpkin seeds	125 mL
1⅓ cups	pumpkin purée (not pie filling)	325 mL
⅓ cup	water	75 mL
¼ cup	vegetable oil	60 mL
2 tsp	cider vinegar	10 mL

1. In a small bowl or measuring cup, combine flax flour and warm water; mix well. Let stand for 5 minutes.

2. In a large bowl or plastic bag, combine sorghum flour, flax flour, quinoa flour, tapioca starch, cornstarch, sugar, xanthan gum, yeast, salt, cinnamon, nutmeg, cloves, cranberries and pumpkin seeds; mix well and set aside.

3. Pour pumpkin purée, water, oil and vinegar into the bread machine baking pan.

4. Select the **Gluten-Free Cycle**. As the bread machine is mixing, add the flax flour mixture. Gradually add the dry ingredients, scraping bottom and sides of pan with a rubber spatula. Try to incorporate all the dry ingredients within 1 to 2 minutes. When the mixing and kneading are complete, remove the kneading blade, leaving the bread pan in the bread machine. Quickly smooth the top of the loaf. Allow the cycle to finish.

5. At the end of the cycle, take the temperature of the loaf using an instant-read thermometer. It is baked at 200°F (100°C). If it's between 180°F (85°C) and 200°F (100°C), leave machine on the **Keep Warm Cycle** until baked. If it's below 180°F (85°C), turn on the **Bake Cycle** and

NUTRITIONAL VALUES per serving	
Calories	206
Fat, total	9 g
Fat, saturated	1 g
Cholesterol	0 mg
Sodium	236 mg
Carbohydrate	30 g
Fiber	5 g
Protein	5 g
Calcium	20 mg
Iron	2 mg

check the internal temperature every 10 minutes. (Some bread machines are automatically set for 60 minutes; others need to be set by 10-minute intervals.)

6. Once the loaf has reached 200°F (100°C), remove it from the pan immediately and let cool completely on a rack.

Dough Cycle and Bake Cycle
If your bread machine does not have a Gluten-Free Cycle, use the Dough Cycle followed by the Bake Cycle.

1. In a small bowl or measuring cup, combine flax flour and warm water; mix well. Let stand for 5 minutes.

2. In a large bowl or plastic bag, combine sorghum flour, flax flour, quinoa flour, tapioca starch, cornstarch, sugar, xanthan gum, yeast, salt, cinnamon, nutmeg, cloves, cranberries and pumpkin seeds; mix well and set aside.

3. Pour pumpkin purée, water, oil and vinegar into the bread machine baking pan.

4. Select the **Dough Cycle**. As the bread machine is mixing, add the flax flour mixture. Gradually add the dry ingredients, scraping bottom and sides of pan with a rubber spatula. Try to incorporate all the dry ingredients within 1 to 2 minutes. When the mixing and kneading are complete, remove the kneading blade, leaving the bread pan in the bread machine. Quickly smooth the top of the loaf. Allow the cycle to finish. Turn off the bread machine.

5. Select the **Bake Cycle**. Set time to 60 minutes and temperature to 350°F (180°C). Allow the cycle to finish. Do not turn machine off before taking the internal temperature of the loaf with an instant-read thermometer. It should be 200°F (100°C). If it's between 180°F (85°C) and 200°F (100°C), leave machine on the **Keep Warm Cycle** until baked. If it's below 180°F (85°C), turn on the **Bake Cycle** and check the internal temperature every 10 minutes. (Some bread machines are automatically set for 60 minutes; others need to be set by 10-minute intervals.)

6. Once the loaf has reached 200°F (100°C), remove it from the pan immediately and let cool completely on a rack.

EF Banana Raisin Bread

The idea for this bread came from a gluten-free summer camp menu — kids love it!

Tips

To ensure success, see page 14 for information on using your bread machine and page 18 for general tips on bread machine baking.

If you use thawed frozen bananas, don't use any thin, watery parts, just the thicker banana.

²⁄₃ cup	flax flour or ground flaxseed	150 mL
¾ cup	warm water	175 mL
1 cup	sorghum flour	250 mL
1 cup	whole bean flour	250 mL
½ cup	potato starch	125 mL
¼ cup	tapioca starch	60 mL
2½ tsp	xanthan gum	12 mL
1 tbsp	bread machine or instant yeast	15 mL
1¼ tsp	salt	6 mL
1½ tsp	ground cinnamon	7 mL
¾ cup	raisins	175 mL
1 cup	water	250 mL
¾ cup	mashed bananas	175 mL
¼ cup	vegetable oil	60 mL
3 tbsp	liquid honey	45 mL
2 tsp	cider vinegar	10 mL

1. In a small bowl or measuring cup, combine flax flour and warm water; mix well. Let stand for 5 minutes.

2. In a large bowl or plastic bag, combine sorghum flour, whole bean flour, potato starch, tapioca starch, xanthan gum, yeast, salt, cinnamon and raisins; mix well and set aside.

3. Pour water, bananas, oil, honey and vinegar into the bread machine baking pan.

4. Select the **Gluten-Free Cycle**. As the bread machine is mixing, add the flax flour mixture. Gradually add the dry ingredients, scraping bottom and sides of pan with a rubber spatula. Try to incorporate all the dry ingredients within 1 to 2 minutes. When the mixing and kneading are complete, remove the kneading blade, leaving the bread pan in the bread machine. Quickly smooth the top of the loaf. Allow the cycle to finish.

5. At the end of the cycle, take the temperature of the loaf using an instant-read thermometer. It is baked at 200°F (100°C). If it's between 180°F (85°C) and 200°F (100°C), leave machine on the **Keep Warm Cycle** until baked. If it's below 180°F (85°C), turn on the **Bake Cycle** and check the internal temperature every 10 minutes. (Some bread machines are automatically set for 60 minutes; others need to be set by 10-minute intervals.)

NUTRITIONAL VALUES
per serving

Calories	207
Fat, total	6 g
Fat, saturated	0 g
Cholesterol	0 mg
Sodium	197 mg
Carbohydrate	34 g
Fiber	5 g
Protein	5 g
Calcium	22 mg
Iron	2 mg

Tips
Thoroughly mix the dry ingredients before adding them to the liquids — they are powder-fine and could clump together.

Slice this or any bread with an electric knife for thin, even sandwich slices.

6. Once the loaf has reached 200°F (100°C), remove it from the pan immediately and let cool completely on a rack.

Dough Cycle and Bake Cycle

If your bread machine does not have a Gluten-Free Cycle, use the Dough Cycle followed by the Bake Cycle.

1. In a small bowl or measuring cup, combine flax flour and warm water; mix well. Let stand for 5 minutes.

2. In a large bowl or plastic bag, combine sorghum flour, whole bean flour, potato starch, tapioca starch, xanthan gum, yeast, salt, cinnamon and raisins; mix well and set aside.

3. Pour water, bananas, oil, honey and vinegar into the bread machine baking pan.

4. Select the **Dough Cycle**. As the bread machine is mixing, add the flax flour mixture. Gradually add the dry ingredients, scraping bottom and sides of pan with a rubber spatula. Try to incorporate all the dry ingredients within 1 to 2 minutes. When the mixing and kneading are complete, remove the kneading blade, leaving the bread pan in the bread machine. Quickly smooth the top of the loaf. Allow the cycle to finish. Turn off the bread machine.

5. Select the **Bake Cycle**. Set time to 60 minutes and temperature to 350°F (180°C). Allow the cycle to finish. Do not turn machine off before taking the internal temperature of the loaf with an instant-read thermometer. It should be 200°F (100°C). If it's between 180°F (85°C) and 200°F (100°C), leave machine on the **Keep Warm Cycle** until baked. If it's below 180°F (85°C), turn on the **Bake Cycle** and check the internal temperature every 10 minutes. (Some bread machines are automatically set for 60 minutes; others need to be set by 10-minute intervals.)

6. Once the loaf has reached 200°F (100°C), remove it from the pan immediately and let cool completely on a rack.

EF Cinnamon Raisin Bread

Cinnamon raisin bread is a true classic, and we've made it egg-free just for you.

Tips

To ensure success, see page 14 for information on using your bread machine and page 18 for general tips on bread machine baking.

Thoroughly mix the dry ingredients before adding them to the liquids — they are powder-fine and can clump together.

⅓ cup	flax flour or ground flaxseed	75 mL
⅔ cup	warm water	150 mL
1¾ cups	brown rice flour	425 mL
⅓ cup	potato starch	75 mL
¼ cup	tapioca starch	60 mL
⅓ cup	granulated sugar	75 mL
¼ cup	nonfat dry milk or skim milk powder	60 mL
1 tbsp	xanthan gum	15 mL
1 tbsp	bread machine or instant yeast	15 mL
1¼ tsp	salt	6 mL
1 tbsp	ground cinnamon	15 mL
1 cup	raisins	250 mL
1 cup	water	250 mL
2 tbsp	vegetable oil	30 mL
2 tsp	cider vinegar	10 mL

1. In a small bowl or measuring cup, combine flax flour and warm water; mix well. Let stand for 5 minutes.

2. In a large bowl or plastic bag, combine brown rice flour, potato starch, tapioca starch, sugar, dry milk, xanthan gum, yeast, salt, cinnamon and raisins; mix well and set aside.

3. Pour water, oil and vinegar into the bread machine baking pan.

4. Select the **Gluten-Free Cycle**. As the bread machine is mixing, add the flax flour mixture. Gradually add the dry ingredients, scraping bottom and sides of pan with a rubber spatula. Try to incorporate all the dry ingredients within 1 to 2 minutes. When the mixing and kneading are complete, remove the kneading blade, leaving the bread pan in the bread machine. Quickly smooth the top of the loaf. Allow the cycle to finish.

5. At the end of the cycle, take the temperature of the loaf using an instant-read thermometer. It is baked at 200°F (100°C). If it's between 180°F (85°C) and 200°F (100°C), leave machine on the **Keep Warm Cycle** until baked. If it's below 180°F (85°C), turn on the **Bake Cycle** and check the internal temperature every 10 minutes. (Some bread machines are automatically set for 60 minutes; others need to be set by 10-minute intervals.)

NUTRITIONAL VALUES per serving	
Calories	173
Fat, total	3 g
Fat, saturated	0 g
Cholesterol	0 mg
Sodium	207 mg
Carbohydrate	35 g
Fiber	3 g
Protein	3 g
Calcium	29 mg
Iron	1 mg

Tip
See the Technique Glossary for information on grinding flaxseed to make flax flour (page 307).

Variation
Substitute other dried fruits for the raisins — try cranberries, currants, snipped apricots or a mixture.

6. Once the loaf has reached 200°F (100°C), remove it from the pan immediately and let cool completely on a rack.

Dough Cycle and Bake Cycle

If your bread machine does not have a Gluten-Free Cycle, use the Dough Cycle followed by the Bake Cycle.

1. In a small bowl or measuring cup, combine flax flour and warm water; mix well. Let stand for 5 minutes.

2. In a large bowl or plastic bag, combine brown rice flour, potato starch, tapioca starch, sugar, dry milk, xanthan gum, yeast, salt, cinnamon and raisins; mix well and set aside.

3. Pour water, oil and vinegar into the bread machine baking.

4. Select the **Dough Cycle**. As the bread machine is mixing, add the flax flour mixture. Gradually add the dry ingredients, scraping bottom and sides of pan with a rubber spatula. Try to incorporate all the dry ingredients within 1 to 2 minutes. When the mixing and kneading are complete, remove the kneading blade, leaving the bread pan in the bread machine. Quickly smooth the top of the loaf. Allow the cycle to finish. Turn off the bread machine.

5. Select the **Bake Cycle**. Set time to 60 minutes and temperature to 350°F (180°C). Allow the cycle to finish. Do not turn machine off before taking the internal temperature of the loaf with an instant-read thermometer. It should be 200°F (100°C). If it's between 180°F (85°C) and 200°F (100°C), leave machine on the **Keep Warm Cycle** until baked. If it's below 180°F (85°C), turn on the **Bake Cycle** and check the internal temperature every 10 minutes. (Some bread machines are automatically set for 60 minutes; others need to be set by 10-minute intervals.)

6. Once the loaf has reached 200°F (100°C), remove it from the pan immediately and let cool completely on a rack.

EF Hazelnut Ciabatta

Hazelnuts and rosemary lend a unique flavor to an otherwise ordinary — but egg-free — ciabatta.

Tips

To ensure success, see page 14 for information on using your bread machine and page 18 for general tips on bread machine baking.

For more information on making your own hazelnut flour, see the Technique Glossary, page 308.

◆ 8-inch (20 cm) round baking pan, lightly greased

½ cup	flax flour or ground flaxseed	125 mL
¼ cup	warm water	60 mL
½ cup	hazelnut flour	125 mL
½ cup	whole bean flour	125 mL
¼ cup	quinoa flour	60 mL
¼ cup	tapioca starch	60 mL
2 tbsp	granulated sugar	30 mL
2 tsp	xanthan gum	10 mL
1 tbsp	bread machine or instant yeast	15 mL
1 tsp	salt	5 mL
2 tbsp	dried rosemary	30 mL
¾ cup	water	175 mL
2 tbsp	extra virgin olive oil	30 mL
1 tsp	cider vinegar	5 mL
1 cup	chopped hazelnuts	250 mL
1 to 2 tbsp	sweet rice flour, brown rice flour or whole bean flour	15 to 30 mL

1. In a small bowl or measuring cup, combine flax flour and warm water; mix well. Let stand for 5 minutes.

2. In a large bowl or plastic bag, combine hazelnut flour, whole bean flour, quinoa flour, tapioca starch, sugar, xanthan gum, yeast, salt and rosemary; mix well and set aside.

3. Pour water, oil and vinegar into the bread machine baking pan.

NUTRITIONAL VALUES
per serving

Calories	286
Fat, total	20 g
Fat, saturated	2 g
Cholesterol	0 mg
Sodium	294 mg
Carbohydrate	23 g
Fiber	7 g
Protein	8 g
Calcium	57 mg
Iron	3 mg

Tip
When dusting with sweet rice flour, use a flour sifter for a light, even sprinkle.

Variation
Substitute pecan flour for the hazelnut flour and pecans for the hazelnuts.

4. Select the **Dough Cycle**. As the bread machine is mixing, add the flax flour mixture. Gradually add the dry ingredients, scraping bottom and sides of pan with a rubber spatula. Try to incorporate all the dry ingredients within 1 to 2 minutes. Stop bread machine as soon as the kneading portion of the cycle is complete. Do not let bread machine finish the cycle. Remove baking pan from the bread machine. Fold in hazelnuts.

5. Gently transfer dough to prepared pan and spread evenly to the edges, leaving the top rough and uneven. Generously dust top with sweet rice flour. With well-floured fingers, make deep indents all over the dough, pressing all the way down to the pan. Let rise, uncovered, in a warm, draft-free place for 60 to 75 minutes, or until almost doubled in volume. Meanwhile, preheat oven to 400°F (200°C).

6. Bake for 20 to 25 minutes or until top is golden. Remove from the pan immediately and let cool on a rack. Cut into 8 wedges and serve warm.

EF Hamburger Buns

Toast these buns on the barbecue just before filling. Be sure to keep them separate from wheat flour buns to avoid cross-contamination.

Tips

To ensure success, see page 14 for information on using your bread machine and page 18 for general tips on bread machine baking.

If you don't have a hamburger bun pan, try a cast-iron corncob-shaped bread pan or English muffin rings, or make free-form buns on a lightly greased baking sheet. Decrease the water by 2 tbsp (30 mL) for free-form buns.

◆ Hamburger bun baking pan, lightly greased

⅓ cup	flax flour or ground flaxseed	75 mL
⅔ cup	warm water	150 mL
1¾ cups	brown rice flour	425 mL
⅔ cup	potato starch	150 mL
⅓ cup	tapioca starch	75 mL
¼ cup	nonfat dry milk or skim milk powder	60 mL
¼ cup	granulated sugar	60 mL
2½ tsp	xanthan gum	12 mL
1 tbsp	bread machine or instant yeast	15 mL
1½ tsp	salt	7 mL
1¼ cups	water	300 mL
¼ cup	vegetable oil	60 mL
1 tsp	cider vinegar	5 mL

1. In a small bowl or measuring cup, combine flax flour and warm water; mix well. Let stand for 5 minutes.

2. In a large bowl or plastic bag, combine brown rice flour, potato starch, tapioca starch, dry milk, sugar, xanthan gum, yeast and salt; mix well and set aside.

3. Pour water, oil and vinegar into the bread machine baking pan.

4. Select the **Dough Cycle**. As the bread machine is mixing, add the flax flour mixture. Gradually add the dry ingredients, scraping bottom and sides of pan with a rubber spatula. Try to incorporate all the dry ingredients within 1 to 2 minutes. Stop bread machine as soon as the kneading portion of the cycle is complete. Do not let bread machine finish the cycle.

NUTRITIONAL VALUES
per serving

Calories	413
Fat, total	13 g
Fat, saturated	1 g
Cholesterol	1 mg
Sodium	606 mg
Carbohydrate	73 g
Fiber	5 g
Protein	7 g
Calcium	46 mg
Iron	1 mg

Tip
Always store bread at room temperature or wrapped airtight in the freezer. The refrigerator accelerates the staling process.

Variation
Sprinkle the tops with sesame seeds before the dough rises. The seeds will toast as the buns bake.

5. Spoon ⅔ cup (150 mL) dough into each cup of prepared pan (see tip, page 254), mounding toward the center of each bun. Smooth the tops with a moistened rubber spatula. Let rise in a warm, draft-free place for 30 to 45 minutes or until dough has almost doubled in volume. Do not allow dough to over-rise. Meanwhile, preheat oven to 350°F (180°C).

6. Bake for 20 to 23 minutes or until internal temperature of buns registers 200°F (100°C) on an instant-read thermometer. Remove from the pan immediately and let cool completely on a rack.

EF Flaxseed Sandwich Buns

Golden flaxseed provides the warm speckled color in these large buns. Fill with pulled pork for a weekend lunch.

Tips

To ensure success, see page 14 for information on using your bread machine and page 18 for general tips on bread machine baking.

If you don't have a hamburger bun pan, try a cast-iron corncob-shaped bread pan or English muffin rings, or make free-form buns on a lightly greased baking sheet. Decrease the water by 2 tbsp (30 mL) for free-form buns.

◆ **Hamburger bun baking pan, lightly greased**

1/3 cup	flax flour or ground flaxseed	75 mL
2/3 cup	warm water	150 mL
1¾ cups	brown rice flour	425 mL
2/3 cup	potato starch	150 mL
1/3 cup	flax flour or ground flaxseed	75 mL
1/2 cup	buttermilk powder	125 mL
1/4 cup	packed brown sugar	60 mL
2½ tsp	xanthan gum	12 mL
1 tbsp	bread machine or instant yeast	15 mL
1½ tsp	salt	7 mL
1/4 cup	cracked golden flaxseed	60 mL
1¼ cups	water	300 mL
1/4 cup	vegetable oil	60 mL
1 tsp	cider vinegar	5 mL

1. In a small bowl or measuring cup, combine flax flour and warm water; mix well. Let stand for 5 minutes.

2. In a large bowl or plastic bag, combine brown rice flour, potato starch, flax flour, buttermilk powder, brown sugar, xanthan gum, yeast, salt and flaxseed; mix well and set aside.

3. Pour water, oil and vinegar into the bread machine baking pan.

4. Select the **Dough Cycle**. As the bread machine is mixing, add the flax flour mixture. Gradually add the dry ingredients, scraping bottom and sides of pan with a rubber spatula. Try to incorporate all the dry ingredients within 1 to 2 minutes. Stop bread machine as soon as the kneading portion of the cycle is complete. Do not let bread machine finish the cycle.

NUTRITIONAL VALUES per serving	
Calories	449
Fat, total	15 g
Fat, saturated	1 g
Cholesterol	1 mg
Sodium	609 mg
Carbohydrate	75 g
Fiber	7 g
Protein	8 g
Calcium	59 mg
Iron	2 mg

Tips

For information on grinding and cracking flaxseed, see the Technique Glossary, page 307.

You can purchase buttermilk powder in bulk stores and health food stores.

Variation

Sprinkle the tops with sesame seeds before the dough rises. The seeds will toast as the buns bake.

5. Spoon ⅔ cup (150 mL) dough into each cup of prepared pan (see tip, page 256), mounding toward the center of each bun. Smooth the tops with a moistened rubber spatula. Let rise in a warm, draft-free place for 30 to 45 minutes or until dough has almost doubled in volume. Do not allow dough to over-rise. Meanwhile, preheat oven to 350°F (180°C).

6. Bake for 20 to 23 minutes or until internal temperature of buns registers 200°F (100°C) on an instant-read thermometer. Remove from the pan immediately and let cool completely on a rack.

Everything-Free White Dinner Rolls

If you have multiple sensitivities, these rolls are sure to become a staple in your diet!

Tips

To ensure success, see page 14 for information on using your bread machine and page 18 for general tips on bread machine baking.

Xanthan gum is important to the success of this recipe, so don't omit it. If you are allergic to soy, check the label to be sure it is soy-free. If you have a corn allergy, don't worry: although xanthan gum is made from corn sugar, the allergens are removed during processing. For more information, see page 33.

NUTRITIONAL VALUES
per serving

Calories	140
Fat, total	4 g
Fat, saturated	0 g
Cholesterol	0 mg
Sodium	245 mg
Carbohydrate	25 g
Fiber	3 g
Protein	3 g
Calcium	9 mg
Iron	1 mg

◆ **12-cup muffin tin, lightly greased**

¼ cup	flax flour or ground flaxseed	60 mL
⅓ cup	warm water	75 mL
1½ cups	sorghum flour	375 mL
⅓ cup	amaranth flour	75 mL
⅓ cup	potato starch	75 mL
¼ cup	tapioca starch	60 mL
2 tbsp	granulated sugar	30 mL
2½ tsp	xanthan gum	12 mL
1 tbsp	bread machine or instant yeast	15 mL
1¼ tsp	salt	6 mL
1⅓ cups	water	325 mL
2 tbsp	vegetable oil	30 mL
2 tsp	cider vinegar	10 mL

1. In a small bowl or measuring cup, combine flax flour and warm water; mix well. Let stand for 5 minutes.

2. In a large bowl or plastic bag, combine sorghum flour, amaranth flour, potato starch, tapioca starch, sugar, xanthan gum, yeast and salt; mix well and set aside.

3. Pour water, oil and vinegar into the bread machine baking pan.

4. Select the **Dough Cycle**. As the bread machine is mixing, add the flax flour mixture. Gradually add the dry ingredients, scraping bottom and sides of pan with a rubber spatula. Try to incorporate all the dry ingredients within 1 to 2 minutes. Stop bread machine as soon as the kneading portion of the cycle is complete. Do not let bread machine finish the cycle.

Variations

Add ½ cup (125 mL) unsalted raw sunflower seeds or green pumpkin seeds with the dry ingredients.

For larger buns or rolls, drop 10 scoops of dough at least 2 inches (5 cm) apart onto a lightly greased baking sheet. Let rise as directed in step 5, and bake for 25 minutes or until internal temperature of rolls registers 200°F (100°C) on an instant-read thermometer.

5. Using a ¼-cup (60 mL) scoop, divide dough into 12 equal amounts and place in cups of prepared muffin tin. Let rise, uncovered, in a warm, draft-free place for 60 minutes. Meanwhile, preheat oven to 350°F (180°C).

6. Bake for 20 to 22 minutes or until internal temperature of rolls registers 200°F (100°C) on an instant-read thermometer. Remove from the pan immediately and let cool completely on a rack.

EF Brown Seed Dinner Rolls

When it's time for a tasty change, make these crunchy brown dinner rolls in place of white ones.

Tips

To ensure success, see page 14 for information on using your bread machine and page 18 for general tips on bread machine baking.

If you don't have a scoop, use a large serving spoon and drop dough into muffin cups by large rounded spoonfuls.

If you don't have a muffin tin, drop 12 spoonfuls of dough at least 2 inches (5 cm) apart onto a lightly greased baking sheet.

NUTRITIONAL VALUES per serving	
Calories	226
Fat, total	12 g
Fat, saturated	1 g
Cholesterol	0 mg
Sodium	252 mg
Carbohydrate	26 g
Fiber	5 g
Protein	7 g
Calcium	36 mg
Iron	2 mg

◆ **12-cup muffin tin, lightly greased**

⅓ cup	flax flour or ground flaxseed	75 mL
¼ cup	warm water	60 mL
¾ cup	sorghum flour	175 mL
¾ cup	whole bean flour	175 mL
¼ cup	potato starch	60 mL
¼ cup	rice bran	60 mL
2½ tsp	xanthan gum	12 mL
1 tbsp	bread machine or instant yeast	15 mL
1¼ tsp	salt	6 mL
⅓ cup	unsalted green pumpkin seeds	75 mL
⅓ cup	unsalted raw sunflower seeds	75 mL
¼ cup	sesame seeds	60 mL
1¼ cups	water	300 mL
¼ cup	vegetable oil	60 mL
2 tbsp	liquid honey	30 mL
2 tbsp	light (fancy) molasses	30 mL
1 tsp	cider vinegar	5 mL

1. In a small bowl or measuring cup, combine flax flour and warm water; mix well. Let stand for 5 minutes.

2. In a large bowl or plastic bag, combine sorghum flour, whole bean flour, potato starch, rice bran, xanthan gum, yeast, salt, pumpkin seeds, sunflower seeds and sesame seeds; mix well and set aside.

3. Pour water, oil, honey, molasses and vinegar into the bread machine baking pan.

4. Select the **Dough Cycle**. As the bread machine is mixing, add the flax flour mixture. Gradually add the dry ingredients, scraping bottom and sides of pan with a rubber spatula. Try to incorporate all the dry ingredients within 1 to 2 minutes. Stop bread machine as soon as the kneading portion of the cycle is complete. Do not let bread machine finish the cycle.

5. Using a ¼-cup (60 mL) scoop, divide dough into 12 equal amounts and place in cups of prepared muffin tin. Let rise, uncovered, in a warm, draft-free place for 60 minutes. Meanwhile, preheat oven to 350°F (180°C).

6. Bake for 18 to 20 minutes or until internal temperature of rolls registers 200°F (100°C) on an instant-read thermometer. Remove from the pan immediately and let cool completely on a rack.

EF Rich Dinner Rolls

Almond flour and yogurt give these white rolls a softer texture and deeper flavor than most.

Tips

To ensure success, see page 14 for information on using your bread machine and page 18 for general tips on bread machine baking.

If only a 12-cup muffin tin is available, fill the empty cups one-quarter full with water before baking.

To make a dozen dinner rolls, double the ingredients, except for the xanthan gum and the yeast.

◆ **6-cup muffin tin, lightly greased**

½ cup	almond flour	125 mL
½ cup	brown rice flour	125 mL
¼ cup	amaranth flour	60 mL
¼ cup	potato starch	60 mL
1 tbsp	powdered egg replacer	15 mL
2 tsp	xanthan gum	10 mL
1¾ tsp	bread machine or instant yeast	8 mL
¾ tsp	salt	3 mL
¾ cup	plain yogurt	175 mL
¼ cup	water	60 mL
2 tbsp	vegetable oil	30 mL
2 tbsp	liquid honey	30 mL

1. In a large bowl or plastic bag, combine almond flour, brown rice flour, amaranth flour, potato starch, egg replacer, xanthan gum, yeast and salt; mix well and set aside.

2. Pour yogurt, water, oil and honey into the bread machine baking pan.

3. Select the **Dough Cycle**. As the bread machine is mixing, gradually add the dry ingredients, scraping bottom and sides of pan with a rubber spatula. Try to incorporate all the dry ingredients within 1 to 2 minutes. Stop bread machine as soon as the kneading portion of the cycle is complete. Do not let bread machine finish the cycle.

4. Using a ¼-cup (60 mL) scoop, divide dough into 6 equal amounts and place in cups of prepared muffin tin. Let rise, uncovered, in a warm, draft-free place for 60 minutes. Meanwhile, preheat oven to 400°F (200°C).

5. Bake for 18 to 20 minutes or until internal temperature of rolls registers 200°F (100°C) on an instant-read thermometer. Remove from the pan immediately and let cool completely on a rack.

NUTRITIONAL VALUES per serving	
Calories	236
Fat, total	11 g
Fat, saturated	1 g
Cholesterol	2 mg
Sodium	320 mg
Carbohydrate	33 g
Fiber	3 g
Protein	6 g
Calcium	124 mg
Iron	1 mg

EF Oatmeal Dinner Rolls

These healthy dinner rolls offer a lovely sweet flavor.

Tips

To ensure success, see page 14 for information on using your bread machine and page 18 for general tips on bread machine baking.

The batter will appear thinner than most as you are incorporating the dry ingredients, but it will thicken; don't adjust any of the ingredient amounts.

For a softer crust, brush the rolls with melted butter as soon as you remove them from the oven.

See the Technique Glossary, page 309, for information on toasting seeds.

NUTRITIONAL VALUES per serving	
Calories	169
Fat, total	5 g
Fat, saturated	0 g
Cholesterol	2 mg
Sodium	262 mg
Carbohydrate	28 g
Fiber	4 g
Protein	5 g
Calcium	50 mg
Iron	1 mg

◆ **12-cup muffin tin, lightly greased**

1/3 cup	flax flour or ground flaxseed	75 mL
1/2 cup	warm water	125 mL
1 1/2 cups	sorghum flour	375 mL
1/2 cup	GF oats	125 mL
1/2 cup	GF oat flour	125 mL
1/3 cup	tapioca starch	75 mL
1/4 cup	packed brown sugar	60 mL
1 tbsp	xanthan gum	15 mL
1 tbsp	bread machine or instant yeast	15 mL
1 1/4 tsp	salt	6 mL
1 1/2 tsp	ground ginger	7 mL
1 1/2 cups	milk, warmed to room temperature	375 mL
2 tbsp	vegetable oil	30 mL
1 tsp	cider vinegar	5 mL

1. In a small bowl or measuring cup, combine flax flour and warm water; mix well. Let stand for 5 minutes.

2. In a large bowl or plastic bag, combine sorghum flour, oats, oat flour, tapioca starch, brown sugar, xanthan gum, yeast, salt and ginger; mix well and set aside.

3. Pour milk, oil and vinegar into the bread machine baking pan.

4. Select the **Dough Cycle**. As the bread machine is mixing, add the flax flour mixture. Gradually add the dry ingredients, scraping bottom and sides of pan with a rubber spatula. Try to incorporate all the dry ingredients within 1 to 2 minutes. Stop bread machine as soon as the kneading portion of the cycle is complete. Do not let bread machine finish the cycle.

5. Using a 1/4-cup (60 mL) scoop, divide dough into 12 equal amounts and place in cups of prepared muffin tin. Let rise, uncovered, in a warm, draft-free place for 60 to 75 minutes or until dough has risen to the top of the cups. Meanwhile, preheat oven to 350°F (180°C).

6. Bake for 18 to 20 minutes or until internal temperature of rolls registers 200°F (100°C) on an instant-read thermometer. Remove from the pan immediately and let cool completely on a rack.

EF Mock Rye Rolls

This recipe adds yet another flavor to a basketful of dinner rolls. Take these to your next celiac support group potluck.

Tip

To ensure success, see page 14 for information on using your bread machine and page 18 for general tips on bread machine baking.

◆ **12-cup muffin tin, lightly greased**

1/2 cup	flax flour or ground flaxseed	125 mL
3/4 cup	warm water	175 mL
1 1/4 cups	sorghum flour	300 mL
1 cup	whole bean flour	250 mL
1/2 cup	tapioca starch	125 mL
1/4 cup	packed brown sugar	60 mL
1 tbsp	xanthan gum	15 mL
1 1/4 tsp	bread machine or instant yeast	6 mL
1 1/4 tsp	salt	6 mL
1 1/4 cups	water	300 mL
2 tbsp	vegetable oil	30 mL
1 tsp	cider vinegar	5 mL

1. In a small bowl or measuring cup, combine flax flour and warm water; mix well. Let stand for 5 minutes.

2. In a large bowl or plastic bag, combine sorghum flour, whole bean flour, tapioca starch, brown sugar, xanthan gum, yeast and salt; mix well and set aside.

3. Pour water, oil and vinegar into the bread machine baking pan.

4. Select the **Dough Cycle**. As the bread machine is mixing, add the flax flour mixture. Gradually add the dry ingredients, scraping bottom and sides of pan with a rubber spatula. Try to incorporate all the dry ingredients within 1 to 2 minutes. Stop bread machine as soon as the kneading portion of the cycle is complete. Do not let bread machine finish the cycle.

5. Using a 1/4-cup (60 mL) scoop, divide dough into 12 equal amounts and place in cups of prepared muffin tin. Let rise, uncovered, in a warm, draft-free place for 60 minutes. Meanwhile, preheat oven to 350°F (180°C).

6. Bake for 20 to 22 minutes or until internal temperature of buns registers 200°F (100°C) on an instant-read thermometer. Remove from the pan immediately and let cool completely on a rack.

NUTRITIONAL VALUES per serving	
Calories	176
Fat, total	5 g
Fat, saturated	0 g
Cholesterol	0 mg
Sodium	245 mg
Carbohydrate	29 g
Fiber	4 g
Protein	6 g
Calcium	20 mg
Iron	2 mg

Flatbreads, Filled Breads, Pizzas and Snacks

Today's busy lifestyle means we eat on the run much of the time. Your bread machine makes it easier to prepare the dough for breads to go.

Teff Ciabatta

This ciabatta is soft-textured, with a crunchy crust. Slice wedges in half horizontally and fill, for a carried lunch.

Tips

To ensure success, see page 14 for information on using your bread machine and page 18 for general tips on bread machine baking.

When dusting with sweet rice flour, use a flour sifter for a light, even sprinkle.

This bread freezes well. Cut into wedges and freeze individually for sandwiches.

◆ **8-inch (20 cm) round baking pan, lightly floured with brown rice flour**

⅔ cup	teff flour	150 mL
½ cup	brown rice flour	125 mL
½ cup	tapioca starch	125 mL
2 tbsp	granulated sugar	30 mL
2 tsp	xanthan gum	10 mL
1 tbsp	bread machine or instant yeast	15 mL
½ tsp	salt	2 mL
¾ cup	water	175 mL
2 tbsp	extra virgin olive oil	30 mL
1 tsp	cider vinegar	5 mL
1	egg, lightly beaten	1
2	egg whites, lightly beaten	2
2 to 3 tbsp	sweet rice flour	30 to 45 mL

1. In a large bowl or plastic bag, combine teff flour, brown rice flour, tapioca starch, sugar, xanthan gum, yeast and salt; mix well and set aside.

2. Pour water, oil and vinegar into the bread machine baking pan. Add egg and egg whites.

3. Select the **Dough Cycle**. As the bread machine is mixing, gradually add the dry ingredients, scraping bottom and sides of pan with a rubber spatula. Try to incorporate all the dry ingredients within 1 to 2 minutes. Stop bread machine as soon as the kneading portion of the cycle is complete. Do not let bread machine finish the cycle.

4. Gently transfer dough to prepared pan and spread evenly to the edges, leaving the top rough and uneven. Generously dust top with sweet rice flour. With well-floured fingers, make deep indents all over the dough, pressing all the way down to the pan. Let rise, uncovered, in a warm, draft-free place for 40 to 50 minutes or until almost doubled in volume. Meanwhile, preheat oven to 425°F (220°C).

5. Bake for 13 to 15 minutes or until top is golden. Remove from the pan immediately and let cool on a rack. Cut into 8 wedges and serve warm.

NUTRITIONAL VALUES per serving	
Calories	166
Fat, total	5 g
Fat, saturated	1 g
Cholesterol	21 mg
Sodium	172 mg
Carbohydrate	28 g
Fiber	3 g
Protein	4 g
Calcium	21 mg
Iron	1 mg

Black Olive Goat Cheese Ciabatta

One of the softest-textured breads in this book!

Tips

To ensure success, see page 14 for information on using your bread machine and page 18 for general tips on bread machine baking.

When dusting with sweet rice flour, use a flour sifter for a light, even sprinkle.

If using canned olives, rinse under cold water and drain well.

Variations

Dust with either brown rice flour or whole bean flour instead of the sweet rice flour.

Substitute GF Stilton for the goat cheese.

NUTRITIONAL VALUES per serving	
Calories	253
Fat, total	14 g
Fat, saturated	3 g
Cholesterol	47 mg
Sodium	429 mg
Carbohydrate	25 g
Fiber	3 g
Protein	9 g
Calcium	53 mg
Iron	2 mg

◆ **8-inch (20 cm) round baking pan, lightly greased and floured with sweet rice flour**

¾ cup	whole bean flour	175 mL
½ cup	amaranth flour	125 mL
¼ cup	tapioca starch	60 mL
2 tbsp	granulated sugar	30 mL
2 tsp	xanthan gum	10 mL
1 tbsp	bread machine or instant yeast	15 mL
½ tsp	freshly ground black pepper	2 mL
¼ tsp	salt	1 mL
¾ cup	water	175 mL
2 tbsp	vegetable oil	30 mL
1 tsp	cider vinegar	5 mL
½ cup	crumbled goat cheese	125 mL
2	eggs, lightly beaten	2
1 cup	sliced pitted kalamata olives, well-drained	250 mL
2 to 3 tbsp	sweet rice flour	30 to 45 mL

1. In a large bowl or plastic bag, combine whole bean flour, amaranth flour, tapioca starch, sugar, xanthan gum, yeast, pepper and salt; mix well and set aside.

2. Pour water, oil, vinegar and goat cheese into the bread machine baking pan. Add eggs.

3. Select the **Dough Cycle**. As the bread machine is mixing, gradually add the dry ingredients, scraping bottom and sides of pan with a rubber spatula. Try to incorporate all the dry ingredients within 1 to 2 minutes. Stop bread machine as soon as the kneading portion of the cycle is complete. Do not let bread machine finish the cycle.

4. Remove baking pan from the bread machine and fold in olives.

5. Gently transfer dough to prepared pan and spread evenly to the edges, leaving the top rough and uneven. Generously dust top with sweet rice flour. With well-floured fingers, make deep indents all over the dough, pressing all the way down to the pan. Let rise, uncovered, in a warm, draft-free place for 30 minutes or until almost doubled in volume. Meanwhile, preheat oven to 375°F (190°C).

6. Bake for 30 to 33 minutes, tenting with foil after 15 minutes, until internal temperature of loaf registers 200°F (100°C) on an instant-read thermometer. Remove from the pan immediately and let cool on a rack. Cut into 8 wedges and serve warm.

Flatbread

MAKES
2 FLATBREADS,
8 PIECES EACH
(1 per serving)

We made this focaccia-like flatbread for those who enjoy more topping than base. Your most difficult decision will be to decide which two toppings you want to make.

Tips

To ensure success, see page 14 for information on using your bread machine and page 18 for general tips on bread machine baking.

Can't decide which topping to make? Make a different topping for each pan.

Reheat under the broiler to enjoy crisp flatbread.

Variation

Substitute any type of bean flour for the lentil flour.

NUTRITIONAL VALUES per serving	
Calories	70
Fat, total	2 g
Fat, saturated	0 g
Cholesterol	0 mg
Sodium	111 mg
Carbohydrate	12 g
Fiber	1 g
Protein	2 g
Calcium	11 mg
Iron	1 mg

◆ **Two 8-inch (20 cm) square baking pans, lightly greased**

²/₃ cup	amaranth flour	150 mL
½ cup	lentil flour	125 mL
⅓ cup	potato starch	75 mL
¼ cup	cornstarch	60 mL
1 tsp	granulated sugar	5 mL
2 tsp	xanthan gum	10 mL
1 tbsp	bread machine or instant yeast	15 mL
¾ tsp	salt	3 mL
1½ cups	water	375 mL
1 tbsp	extra virgin olive oil	15 mL
1 tsp	cider vinegar	5 mL
	Topping (pages 269–272)	

1. In a large bowl or plastic bag, combine amaranth flour, lentil flour, potato starch, cornstarch, sugar, xanthan gum, yeast and salt; mix well and set aside.

2. Pour water, oil and vinegar into the bread machine baking pan.

3. Select the **Dough Cycle**. As the bread machine is mixing, gradually add the dry ingredients, scraping bottom and sides of pan with a rubber spatula. Try to incorporate all the dry ingredients within 1 to 2 minutes. Stop bread machine as soon as the kneading portion of the cycle is complete. Do not let bread machine finish the cycle.

4. Gently transfer dough to prepared pans and spread evenly to the edges, leaving the tops rough and uneven. Let rise, uncovered, in a warm draft-free place for 20 minutes. Meanwhile, preheat oven to 375°F (190°C).

5. Bake for 15 minutes or until bottoms are golden.

6. Cover with preferred topping mixture. Bake according to instructions in topping recipe.

7. Cover a small cooling rack with parchment paper. Place rack, parchment paper side down, over hot baking pan. Immediately tip pan upside down, then quickly invert right side up onto a second small cooling rack. Cut each flatbread into 8 pieces and serve hot.

Florentine Flatbread Topping

This vegetarian Greek-style topping has generous amounts of spinach, feta cheese and kalamata olives.

Tips

You'll need about 5 oz (150 g) feta cheese for 1 cup (250 mL) crumbled.

For instructions on roasting garlic, see the Technique Glossary, page 307.

Flatbread can be reheated in just a few minutes in a toaster oven set to 375°F (190°C).

2 cups	fresh baby spinach, washed and trimmed	500 mL
1/2 cup	freshly grated Parmesan cheese	125 mL
1 tbsp	extra virgin olive oil	15 mL
2 tsp	dried oregano	10 mL
3	cloves roasted garlic, minced	3
1 cup	crumbled feta cheese	250 mL
1/2 cup	pitted kalamata olives, sliced	125 mL

1. In a microwave-safe bowl, microwave spinach, uncovered, on High for 2 to 3 minutes, stirring halfway through. Drain, place between layers of paper towels and pat dry. Spread over partially baked flatbread.

2. In a small bowl, combine Parmesan, oil and oregano; spread over spinach. Sprinkle with garlic, feta and olives.

3. Bake for 15 to 20 minutes or until top is golden. Remove from the pan, cut into 8 pieces and serve hot.

NUTRITIONAL VALUES per serving	
Calories	96
Fat, total	7 g
Fat, saturated	3 g
Cholesterol	15 mg
Sodium	337 mg
Carbohydrate	2 g
Fiber	1 g
Protein	6 g
Calcium	158 mg
Iron	1 mg

Pesto Flatbread Topping

When fresh basil is plentiful, make lots of pesto sauce and freeze it to use in the winter.

Tips

If you don't have a mini food processor, finely chop the garlic, basil and parsley with a sharp knife. Fold in the remaining ingredients.

Flatbread can be reheated in just a few minutes in a toaster oven set to 375°F (190°C).

Variation

Substitute 1 to 2 tbsp (15 to 30 mL) dry red wine for the vegetable broth.

◆ **Mini food processor**

1	large clove garlic	1
½ cup	packed fresh basil leaves	125 mL
2 tbsp	packed fresh parsley leaves	30 mL
2 tbsp	freshly grated Parmesan cheese	30 mL
1½ tsp	extra virgin olive oil	7 mL
1 to 2 tbsp	GF vegetable broth	15 to 30 mL

1. With the motor of a mini food processor running, drop garlic through the feed tube and process until chopped. Add basil, parsley, Parmesan and oil; process until well mixed, stopping once or twice to scrape down the sides of the bowl with a rubber spatula. With the motor running, gradually add broth through the feed tube until pesto is desired consistency.

2. Spread pesto over partially baked flatbread.

3. Bake for 15 to 20 minutes or until top is golden. Remove from the pan, cut into 8 pieces and serve hot.

Sun-Dried Tomato Flatbread Topping

*The fresh herbs enhance
the flavor of the sun-dried
tomatoes. Be sure you
have fresh basil on hand
before making this
topping.*

Tips

If you like a chunkier
topping, pulse only until
mixture is crumbly.

If you use oil-packed
sun-dried tomatoes, omit
the olive oil.

Flatbread can be reheated
in just a few minutes in a
toaster oven set to 375°F
(190°C).

NUTRITIONAL VALUES per serving	
Calories	104
Fat, total	8 g
Fat, saturated	2 g
Cholesterol	8 mg
Sodium	270 mg
Carbohydrate	4 g
Fiber	1 g
Protein	5 g
Calcium	103 mg
Iron	1 mg

◆ **Food processor**

1	large clove garlic	1
1 cup	snipped dry-packed sun-dried tomatoes	250 mL
¹⁄₂ cup	freshly grated Parmesan cheese	125 mL
¹⁄₄ cup	walnuts	60 mL
2 tbsp	packed fresh basil leaves	30 mL
2 tbsp	packed fresh parsley leaves	30 mL
2 tbsp	extra virgin olive oil	30 mL

1. In a food processor, combine garlic, tomatoes, Parmesan, walnuts, basil, parsley and oil; pulse until almost smooth and quite thick.

2. Press topping into partially baked flatbread.

3. Bake for 15 to 20 minutes or until top is golden. Remove from the pan, cut into 8 pieces and serve hot.

Vegetarian Flatbread Topping

All vegetarians, including vegans, love this recipe, because it makes lots of topping.

Tip
Flatbread can be reheated in just a few minutes in a toaster oven set to 375°F (190°C).

Variation
Substitute 1/2 cup (125 mL) thinly sliced zucchini or very small broccoli florets for the eggplant.

1	small Italian eggplant (about 8 oz/250 g), sliced	1
1 cup	sliced mushrooms	250 mL
1/2 cup	snipped dry-packed sun-dried tomatoes	125 mL
1/4 cup	finely chopped bell pepper (any color)	60 mL
1/4 cup	coarsely chopped onion	60 mL
1/2 cup	packed parsley leaves, coarsely chopped	125 mL
1 to 2 tbsp	extra virgin olive oil	15 to 30 mL

1. Spread eggplant, mushrooms, tomatoes, bell pepper and onion evenly over partially baked flatbread. Sprinkle with parsley. Drizzle with oil.

2. Bake for 20 to 25 minutes or until vegetables are tender. Remove from the pan, cut into 8 pieces and serve hot.

NUTRITIONAL VALUES
per serving

Calories	40
Fat, total	2 g
Fat, saturated	0 g
Cholesterol	0 mg
Sodium	74 mg
Carbohydrate	5 g
Fiber	2 g
Protein	1 g
Calcium	13 mg
Iron	1 mg

Sugar-Topped Orange Raisin Focaccia

No reason not to make a focaccia with a sweet topping. We sweetened up the dough as well.

Tips

Don't be surprised by the small amount of batter this recipe makes.

Focaccia can be reheated in just a few minutes in a toaster oven set to 375°F (190°C).

Variations

Substitute any type of bean flour for the pea flour.

Substitute walnuts or dried cranberries for the raisins.

NUTRITIONAL VALUES per serving	
Calories	142
Fat, total	3 g
Fat, saturated	1 g
Cholesterol	0 mg
Sodium	152 mg
Carbohydrate	27 g
Fiber	3 g
Protein	3 g
Calcium	18 mg
Iron	1 mg

◆ **8-inch (20 cm) round baking pan, lightly greased and lined with parchment paper**

⅓ cup	amaranth flour	75 mL
¼ cup	pea flour	60 mL
3 tbsp	potato starch	45 mL
2 tbsp	tapioca starch	30 mL
1 tbsp	granulated sugar	15 mL
1 tsp	xanthan gum	5 mL
1 tbsp	bread machine or instant yeast	15 mL
½ tsp	salt	2 mL
2 tsp	ground nutmeg	10 mL
⅔ cup	raisins	150 mL
¾ cup	water	175 mL
2 tbsp	grated orange zest	30 mL
2 tsp	extra virgin olive oil	10 mL
1 tsp	cider vinegar	5 mL

Sugar Topping

2 tsp	extra virgin olive oil	10 mL
1 tbsp	granulated sugar	15 mL

1. In a bowl or plastic bag, combine amaranth flour, pea flour, potato starch, tapioca starch, sugar, xanthan gum, yeast, salt, nutmeg and raisins. Mix well and set aside.

2. Pour water, orange zest, oil and vinegar into the bread machine baking pan.

3. Select the **Dough Cycle**. As the bread machine is mixing, gradually add the dry ingredients, scraping bottom and sides of pan with a rubber spatula. Try to incorporate all the dry ingredients within 1 to 2 minutes. Stop bread machine as soon as the kneading portion of the cycle is complete. Do not let bread machine finish the cycle.

4. Gently transfer dough to prepared pan and spread evenly to the edges, leaving the top rough and uneven. Drizzle with oil, then sprinkle with sugar. Let rise, uncovered, in a warm, draft-free place for 30 minutes or until almost doubled in volume. Meanwhile, preheat oven to 400°F (200°C).

5. Bake for 18 to 22 minutes or until bottom is golden. Cut into 8 pieces and serve warm.

Panini Sandwich Loaf

Cut this loaf into slices the traditional shape and size of panini sandwiches, then choose a filling (pages 276, 278 and 279).

Tips

To ensure success, see page 14 for information on using your bread machine and page 18 for general tips on bread machine baking.

Thoroughly mix the dry ingredients before adding them to the liquids — they are powder-fine and could clump together.

1 cup	sorghum flour	250 mL
¾ cup	whole bean flour	175 mL
⅔ cup	quinoa flour	150 mL
½ cup	tapioca starch	125 mL
3 tbsp	packed brown sugar	45 mL
1 tbsp	xanthan gum	15 mL
1 tbsp	bread machine or instant yeast	15 mL
1¼ tsp	salt	6 mL
1¼ cups	water	300 mL
2 tbsp	vegetable oil	30 mL
1 tsp	cider vinegar	5 mL
2	eggs, lightly beaten	2
2	egg whites, lightly beaten	2

1. In a large bowl or plastic bag, combine sorghum flour, whole bean flour, quinoa flour, tapioca starch, brown sugar, xanthan gum, yeast and salt; mix well and set aside.

2. Pour water, oil and vinegar into the bread machine baking pan. Add eggs and egg whites.

3. Select the **Gluten-Free Cycle**. As the bread machine is mixing, gradually add the dry ingredients, scraping bottom and sides of pan with a rubber spatula. Try to incorporate all the dry ingredients within 1 to 2 minutes. When the mixing and kneading are complete, remove the kneading blade, leaving the bread pan in the bread machine. Quickly smooth the top of the loaf. Allow the cycle to finish.

4. At the end of the cycle, take the temperature of the loaf using an instant-read thermometer. It is baked at 200°F (100°C). If it's between 180°F (85°C) and 200°F (100°C), leave machine on the **Keep Warm Cycle** until baked. If it's below 180°F (85°C), turn on the **Bake Cycle** and check the internal temperature every 10 minutes. (Some bread machines are automatically set for 60 minutes; others need to be set by 10-minute intervals.)

5. Once the loaf has reached 200°F (100°C), remove it from the pan immediately and let cool completely on a rack.

6. Cut loaf into slices, choose a filling (see pages 276, 278 and 279) and follow the filling recipe instructions to make panini.

NUTRITIONAL VALUES per serving	
Calories	342
Fat, total	9 g
Fat, saturated	1 g
Cholesterol	55 mg
Sodium	533 mg
Carbohydrate	55 g
Fiber	7 g
Protein	13 g
Calcium	34 mg
Iron	3 mg

Use a knife with a long serrated edge or an electric knife to slice this loaf evenly.

Always store bread at room temperature or wrapped airtight in the freezer. The refrigerator accelerates the staling process.

Dough Cycle and Bake Cycle

If your bread machine does not have a Gluten-Free Cycle, use the Dough Cycle followed by the Bake Cycle.

1. In a large bowl or plastic bag, combine sorghum flour, whole bean flour, quinoa flour, tapioca starch, brown sugar, xanthan gum, yeast and salt; mix well and set aside.

2. Pour water, oil and vinegar into the bread machine baking pan. Add eggs and egg whites.

3. Select the **Dough Cycle**. As the bread machine is mixing, gradually add the dry ingredients, scraping bottom and sides of pan with a rubber spatula. Try to incorporate all the dry ingredients within 1 to 2 minutes. When the mixing and kneading are complete, remove the kneading blade, leaving the bread pan in the bread machine. Quickly smooth the top of the loaf. Allow the cycle to finish. Turn off the bread machine.

4. Select the **Bake Cycle**. Set time to 60 minutes and temperature to 350°F (180°C). Allow the cycle to finish. Do not turn machine off before taking the internal temperature of the loaf with an instant-read thermometer. It should be 200°F (100°C). If it's between 180°F (85°C) and 200°F (100°C), leave machine on the **Keep Warm Cycle** until baked. If it's below 180°F (85°C), turn on the **Bake Cycle** and check the internal temperature every 10 minutes. (Some bread machines are automatically set for 60 minutes; others need to be set by 10-minute intervals.)

5. Once the loaf has reached 200°F (100°C), remove it from the pan immediately and let cool completely on a rack.

6. Cut loaf into slices, choose a filling (see pages 276, 278 and 279) and follow the filling recipe instructions to make panini.

Grilled Ham and Cheese Panini

Panini is the "in" sandwich today! Here's our grilled version.

Variations

Use 1 Golden Panini Bun (page 277), sliced in half horizontally, in place of the 2 slices of Panini Sandwich Loaf.

Feel free to pile on lots of thinly sliced GF cold cuts.

◆ **Panini press or contact grill, preheated to medium-high**

2	slices Panini Sandwich Loaf (page 274)	2
1 tbsp	GF mayonnaise	15 mL
1 to 2 tsp	Dijon mustard	5 to 10 mL
2 oz	GF smoked ham, thinly sliced	60 g
2 oz	Swiss cheese, thinly sliced	60 g
1	medium tomato, sliced	1
	Nonstick cooking spray	

1. Spread one slice of bread with mayonnaise and mustard. Layer with ham, cheese and tomatoes. Cover with remaining slice of bread. Lightly spray the outside of each slice with cooking spray.

2. Grill for 3 to 5 minutes or until cheese melts.

NUTRITIONAL VALUES per serving	
Calories	711
Fat, total	34 g
Fat, saturated	10 g
Cholesterol	118 mg
Sodium	2,084 mg
Carbohydrate	65 g
Fiber	9 g
Protein	41 g
Calcium	484 mg
Iron	4 mg

Golden Panini Buns

Make these buns for a more gourmet panini.

Tips

To ensure success, see page 14 for information on using your bread machine and page 18 for general tips on bread machine baking.

These buns freeze well. Freeze them individually, and pull them out as you need them for sandwiches. They thaw quickly at room temperature.

◆ **9-inch (23 cm) square baking pan, lightly greased**

1 cup	brown rice flour	250 mL
1 cup	whole bean flour	250 mL
1 cup	tapioca starch	250 mL
3 tbsp	granulated sugar	45 mL
2 tsp	xanthan gum	10 mL
1 tbsp	bread machine or instant yeast	15 mL
¾ tsp	salt	3 mL
1½ cups	water	375 mL
3 tbsp	extra virgin olive oil	45 mL
2 tsp	cider vinegar	10 mL
4	eggs, lightly beaten	4

1. In a large bowl or plastic bag, combine brown rice flour, whole bean flour, tapioca starch, sugar, xanthan gum, yeast and salt; mix well and set aside.

2. Pour water, oil and vinegar into the bread machine baking pan. Add eggs.

3. Select the **Dough Cycle**. As the bread machine is mixing, gradually add the dry ingredients, scraping bottom and sides of pan with a rubber spatula. Try to incorporate all the dry ingredients within 1 to 2 minutes. Stop bread machine as soon as the kneading portion of the cycle is complete. Do not let bread machine finish the cycle.

4. Gently transfer dough to prepared pan and spread evenly to the edges. Let rise, uncovered, in a warm, draft-free place for 40 to 50 minutes or until almost doubled in volume. Meanwhile, preheat oven to 425°F (220°C).

5. Bake for 28 to 30 minutes or until top is golden. Remove from the pan immediately and let cool on a rack. Cut into eight 4- by 2-inch (10 by 5 cm) rectangles.

6. Choose a filling (see pages 276, 278 and 279) and follow the filling recipe instructions to make panini.

NUTRITIONAL VALUES per serving	
Calories	297
Fat, total	9 g
Fat, saturated	1 g
Cholesterol	82 mg
Sodium	254 mg
Carbohydrate	46 g
Fiber	3 g
Protein	9 g
Calcium	27 mg
Iron	2 mg

Up-to-Date Grilled Cheese

This cheese-filled panini is perfect for kids — big or little!

Variations

Use 2 slices of Panini Sandwich Loaf (page 274) in place of the Golden Panini Bun.

Brie, Havarti and Monterey Jack are also good cheese options for this sandwich.

◆ **Panini press or contact grill, preheated to medium-high**

1	Golden Panini Bun (page 277), sliced in half horizontally	1
2 tbsp	pesto	30 mL
1 oz	Asiago cheese, sliced	30 g
1 oz	fontina cheese, sliced	30 g
1 oz	mozzarella cheese, sliced	60 g
	Nonstick cooking spray	

1. Spread the cut side of bottom half of panini bun with pesto. Layer with Asiago, fontina and mozzarella. Cover with top half of bun. Lightly spray the outside of bun with cooking spray.

2. Grill for 3 to 5 minutes or until cheeses melt.

NUTRITIONAL VALUES
per serving

Calories	778
Fat, total	47 g
Fat, saturated	19 g
Cholesterol	170 mg
Sodium	1,208 mg
Carbohydrate	54 g
Fiber	5 g
Protein	39 g
Calcium	1,056 mg
Iron	3 mg

Turkey and Cranberry Panini

We tasted a sandwich just like this at a bakery, and liked it so much we modified it for you.

Variations

Use 2 slices of Panini Sandwich Loaf (page 274) in place of the Golden Panini Bun.

Substitute chicken for the turkey and pesto for the cranberry sauce.

◆ **Panini press or contact grill, preheated to medium-high**

1	Golden Panini Bun (page 277), sliced in half horizontally	1
1 tsp	Dijon mustard	5 mL
2 tbsp	cranberry sauce	30 mL
1 tbsp	chopped toasted pecans	15 mL
2 oz	GF cooked turkey, thinly sliced	60 g
1 oz	Camembert, thinly sliced with rind	30 g
1	small green onion, finely chopped	1
	Nonstick cooking spray	

1. Spread the cut side of bottom half of panini bun with mustard and cranberry sauce, then sprinkle with pecans. Layer with turkey, cheese and green onion. Cover with top half of bun. Lightly spray the outside of bun with cooking spray.

2. Grill panini for 3 to 5 minutes or until cheese melts.

NUTRITIONAL VALUES per serving	
Calories	574
Fat, total	23 g
Fat, saturated	7 g
Cholesterol	129 mg
Sodium	1,219 mg
Carbohydrate	68 g
Fiber	5 g
Protein	27 g
Calcium	158 mg
Iron	3 mg

Cheesy Onion Rolls

You asked us for a filled roll you could serve for lunch. Here it is!

Tips

To ensure success, see page 14 for information on using your bread machine and page 18 for general tips on bread machine baking.

This dough is thicker than that of most gluten-free breads.

We don't recommend using a springform pan unless you want to clean your oven and test your smoke alarm battery — ours leaked! You can use a regular metal 9-inch (23 cm) round cake pan as long as the sides are at least 2 inches (5 cm) high.

◆ **9-inch (23 cm) round silicone baking pan with 2-inch (5 cm) sides**

1½ to 1⅔ cups	sorghum flour, divided	375 to 400 mL
¾ cup	whole bean flour	175 mL
⅔ cup	tapioca starch	150 mL
½ cup	cornstarch	125 mL
2 tbsp	potato flour (not potato starch)	30 mL
¼ cup	granulated sugar	60 mL
1 tbsp	xanthan gum	15 mL
4 tsp	bread machine or instant yeast	20 mL
1¼ tsp	salt	6 mL
1 cup	milk, warmed to room temperature	250 mL
2 tbsp	vegetable oil	30 mL
1 tsp	cider vinegar	5 mL
2	eggs, lightly beaten	2

Cheese Onion Filling

2 cups	shredded GF Tex-Mex cheese blend	500 mL
½ cup	finely chopped onion	125 mL
¼ cup	dried chives	60 mL
1½ tsp	garlic powder	7 mL
¼ cup	GF mayonnaise	60 mL

1. In a large bowl or plastic bag, combine 1 cup (250 mL) sorghum flour, whole bean flour, tapioca starch, cornstarch, potato flour, sugar, xanthan gum, yeast and salt; mix well and set aside.

2. Pour milk, oil and vinegar into the bread machine baking pan. Add eggs.

3. Select the **Dough Cycle**. As the bread machine is mixing, gradually add the dry ingredients, scraping bottom and sides of pan with a rubber spatula. Try to incorporate all the dry ingredients within 1 to 2 minutes. Stop bread machine as soon as the kneading portion of the cycle is complete. Do not let bread machine finish the cycle.

NUTRITIONAL VALUES per serving	
Calories	284
Fat, total	9 g
Fat, saturated	3 g
Cholesterol	40 mg
Sodium	454 mg
Carbohydrate	40 g
Fiber	4 g
Protein	12 g
Calcium	174 mg
Iron	2 mg

Tips

Be sure to prepare the filling before removing the first square of dough from the refrigerator. Work quickly when rolling out the dough and assembling the buns. Return the dough to the refrigerator for a few minutes if it becomes sticky.

We prefer to cut the dough into buns with a pizza wheel, but kitchen shears or a sharp knife work well too. You may have to dip the cutter in hot water between cuts.

Freeze wrapped squares of dough for up to 1 month. Thaw overnight in the refrigerator.

Variation

Substitute GF Italian cheese blend for the Tex-Mex blend.

4. Generously coat 2 large sheets of plastic wrap with some of the remaining sorghum flour. Divide dough in half and place each half on a sheet of plastic wrap. Generously dust each with sorghum flour. Fold plastic wrap to cover dough and pat dough out to a square about $1/2$ inch (1 cm) thick. Wrap airtight and refrigerate for at least 2 hours, until chilled, or overnight.

5. For the filling: In a bowl, combine cheese blend, onion, chives and garlic powder; set aside.

6. Remove a square of dough from the refrigerator. Unwrap and place on a sheet of parchment paper generously dusted with sorghum flour. Generously dust dough with sorghum flour and cover with another sheet of parchment paper. Lightly roll out to a 9-inch (23 cm) square, about $1/4$ inch (0.5 cm) thick. Remove top sheet of parchment paper.

7. Spread dough with half the mayonnaise and sprinkle with half the cheese mixture. Beginning at one side, roll up like a jelly roll, lifting the parchment paper to help the dough form a roll. Using your fingers, brush off excess sorghum flour. Using a pizza wheel dipped in hot water, cut into 6 equal pieces. Place cut side up, fairly close together, in pan. Repeat steps 6 and 7 with second square of dough.

8. Let rise, uncovered, in a warm, draft-free place for 60 to 75 minutes or until doubled in volume. Meanwhile, preheat oven to 350°F (180°C).

9. Bake for 50 to 60 minutes, tenting with foil after 40 minutes, until internal temperature of rolls registers 200°F (100°C) on an instant-read thermometer. Immediately invert onto a serving platter. Let stand for 5 minutes before removing pan. Serve warm.

Ham and Cheese Buns

These savory buns can be a bit tricky to prepare, but they are worth the time and effort.

Tips

To ensure success, see page 14 for information on using your bread machine and page 18 for general tips on bread machine baking.

This dough is thicker than that of most gluten-free breads.

We don't recommend using a springform pan, as it could leak. You can use a regular metal 9-inch (23 cm) round cake pan as long as the sides are at least 2 inches (5 cm) high.

◆ **9-inch (23 cm) round silicone baking pan with 2-inch (5 cm) sides**

1½ to 1⅔ cups	sorghum flour, divided	375 to 400 mL
¾ cup	whole bean flour	175 mL
⅔ cup	tapioca starch	150 mL
½ cup	cornstarch	125 mL
2 tbsp	potato flour (not potato starch)	30 mL
⅓ cup	buttermilk powder	75 mL
¼ cup	granulated sugar	60 mL
1 tbsp	xanthan gum	15 mL
4 tsp	bread machine or instant yeast	20 mL
1¼ tsp	salt	6 mL
1 cup	water	250 mL
2 tbsp	vegetable oil	30 mL
1 tsp	cider vinegar	5 mL
2	eggs, lightly beaten	2

Ham and Cheese Filling

½ cup	GF mayonnaise	125 mL
2 tbsp	Dijon mustard	30 mL
16	slices GF deli cooked ham, chopped	16
1 cup	shredded Swiss cheese	250 mL

1. In a large bowl or plastic bag, combine 1 cup (250 mL) sorghum flour, whole bean flour, tapioca starch, cornstarch, potato flour, buttermilk powder, sugar, xanthan gum, yeast and salt; mix well and set aside.

2. Pour water, oil and vinegar into the bread machine baking pan. Add eggs.

3. Select the **Dough Cycle**. As the bread machine is mixing, gradually add the dry ingredients, scraping bottom and sides of pan with a rubber spatula. Try to incorporate all the dry ingredients within 1 to 2 minutes. Stop bread machine as soon as the kneading portion of the cycle is complete. Do not let bread machine finish the cycle.

NUTRITIONAL VALUES
per serving

Calories	297
Fat, total	11 g
Fat, saturated	3 g
Cholesterol	45 mg
Sodium	595 mg
Carbohydrate	39 g
Fiber	3 g
Protein	12 g
Calcium	141 mg
Iron	2 mg

4. Generously coat 2 large sheets of plastic wrap with some of the remaining sorghum flour. Divide dough in half and place each half on a sheet of plastic wrap. Generously dust each with sorghum flour. Fold plastic wrap to cover dough and pat dough out to a square about $1/2$ inch (1 cm) thick. Wrap airtight and refrigerate for at least 2 hours, until chilled, or overnight.

5. For the filling: In a small bowl, combine mayonnaise and mustard until smooth. Set aside.

6. Remove a square of dough from the refrigerator. Unwrap and place on a sheet of parchment paper generously dusted with sorghum flour. Generously dust dough with sorghum flour and cover with another sheet of parchment paper. Lightly roll out to a 9-inch (23 cm) square, about $1/4$ inch (0.5 cm) thick. Remove top sheet of parchment paper.

7. Spread half the mayonnaise mixture over the dough. Sprinkle with half each of the ham and cheese. Beginning at one side, roll up like a jelly roll, lifting the parchment paper to help the dough form a roll. Using your fingers, brush off excess sorghum flour. Using a pizza wheel dipped in hot water, cut into 6 equal pieces. Place cut side up, fairly close together, in pan. Repeat with second square of dough.

8. Let rise, uncovered, in a warm, draft-free place for 60 to 75 minutes or until doubled in volume. Meanwhile, preheat oven to 350°F (180°C).

9. Bake for 50 to 60 minutes, tenting with foil after 40 minutes, until internal temperature of buns registers 200°F (100°C) on an instant-read thermometer. Immediately invert onto a serving platter. Let stand for 5 minutes before removing pan. Serve warm.

Sandwich Wraps

Here's the perfect on-the-go wrap to send in your kids' lunch.

Tips

To ensure success, see page 14 for information on using your bread machine and page 18 for general tips on bread machine baking.

Roll these wraps around your favorite sandwich fillings.

Dipping the spatula repeatedly into warm water makes it easier to spread this dough thinly and evenly. You cannot use too much water — it just evaporates as the dough bakes.

Variation

Try adding 1 to 2 tbsp (15 to 30 mL) dried herbs to the soft dough.

NUTRITIONAL VALUES per serving	
Calories	176
Fat, total	3 g
Fat, saturated	1 g
Cholesterol	5 mg
Sodium	486 mg
Carbohydrate	34 g
Fiber	4 g
Protein	6 g
Calcium	125 mg
Iron	1 mg

◆ **15- by 10-inch (40 by 25 cm) jelly roll pan, lightly greased and lined with parchment paper**

¼ cup	amaranth flour	60 mL
¼ cup	teff flour	60 mL
¼ cup	potato starch	60 mL
¼ cup	tapioca starch	60 mL
¼ cup	buttermilk powder	60 mL
1 tsp	granulated sugar	5 mL
2 tsp	xanthan gum	10 mL
1 tbsp	bread machine or instant yeast	15 mL
¾ tsp	salt	3 mL
¾ cup	water	175 mL
1 tsp	extra virgin olive oil	5 mL
2 tsp	cider vinegar	10 mL

1. In a large bowl or plastic bag, combine amaranth flour, teff flour, potato starch, tapioca starch, buttermilk powder, sugar, xanthan gum, yeast and salt; mix well and set aside.

2. Pour water, oil and vinegar into the bread machine baking pan.

3. Select the **Dough Cycle**. As the bread machine is mixing, gradually add the dry ingredients, scraping bottom and sides of pan with a rubber spatula. Try to incorporate all the dry ingredients within 1 to 2 minutes. Stop bread machine as soon as the kneading portion of the cycle is complete. Do not let bread machine finish the cycle.

4. Meanwhile, preheat oven to 400°F (200°C).

5. Remove dough to prepared pan. Using a moistened rubber spatula, spread evenly to the edges. Bake for 12 to 14 minutes or until edges are brown and top begins to brown. Let cool completely on pan on a rack. Remove from pan and cut into quarters.

Teff Pizza Crust

Try this flavorful, warm brown crust the next time you feel like pizza.

Tips

To ensure success, see page 14 for information on using your bread machine and page 18 for general tips on bread machine baking.

Variation

Vary the herb depending on the topping you select.

♦ **12-inch (30 cm) pizza pan, lightly greased and generously sprinkled with cornmeal**

¾ cup	teff flour	175 mL
½ cup	quinoa flour	125 mL
¼ cup	cornmeal	60 mL
¼ cup	cornstarch	60 mL
1 tsp	xanthan gum	5 mL
1 tbsp	bread machine or instant yeast	15 mL
¾ tsp	salt	3 mL
2 tsp	dried oregano	10 mL
1¼ cups	water	300 mL
1 tbsp	extra virgin olive oil	15 mL
1 tsp	cider vinegar	5 mL

1. In a large bowl or plastic bag, combine teff flour, quinoa flour, cornmeal, cornstarch, xanthan gum, yeast, salt and oregano; mix well and set aside.

2. Pour water, oil and vinegar into the bread machine baking pan.

3. Select the **Dough Cycle**. As the bread machine is mixing, gradually add the dry ingredients, scraping bottom and sides of pan with a rubber spatula. Try to incorporate all the dry ingredients within 1 to 2 minutes. Stop bread machine as soon as the kneading portion of the cycle is complete. Do not let bread machine finish the cycle.

4. Meanwhile, preheat oven to 400°F (200°C).

5. Gently transfer dough to prepared pan and, using a moistened rubber spatula, spread evenly to the edges. Do not smooth top.

6. Bake for 10 minutes or until bottom is golden and crust is partially baked.

7. Use right away to make pizza (for toppings, see page 287–290) or wrap airtight and store in the freezer for up to 1 month. Thaw overnight in the refrigerator before using.

NUTRITIONAL VALUES per serving	
Calories	127
Fat, total	3 g
Fat, saturated	0 g
Cholesterol	0 mg
Sodium	225 mg
Carbohydrate	22 g
Fiber	4 g
Protein	3 g
Calcium	27 mg
Iron	2 mg

Beer Pizza Crusts

MAKES 16 WEDGES
(1 per serving)

Love a tender pizza crust? This recipe is for you. It's also great when you're in a hurry, as the dough is so thin you can swirl it to spread it on the pans.

Tips

To ensure success, see page 14 for information on using your bread machine and page 18 for general tips on bread machine baking.

As the volume of beer in a bottle or can varies among brands, pour GF beer into measuring cup and add enough water to reach 1¾ cups (425 mL).

Yes, you're reading right: this dough is thin enough to pour. It can be spread with a rubber spatula if you prefer.

Expect slight shrinkage from the edges and small cracks in the dough.

NUTRITIONAL VALUES
per serving

Calories	100
Fat, total	4 g
Fat, saturated	0 g
Cholesterol	0 mg
Sodium	147 mg
Carbohydrate	14 g
Fiber	2 g
Protein	3 g
Calcium	10 mg
Iron	1 mg

◆ **Two 12-inch (30 cm) pizza pans, lightly greased and generously dusted with cornmeal**

1 cup	chickpea flour	250 mL
1 cup	sorghum flour	250 mL
⅓ cup	tapioca starch	75 mL
½ tsp	xanthan gum	2 mL
1½ tsp	bread machine or instant yeast	7 mL
1 tsp	salt	5 mL
1¾ cups	GF beer + water (see tip, at left)	425 mL
3 tbsp	vegetable oil	45 mL

1. In a large bowl or plastic bag, combine chickpea flour, sorghum flour, tapioca starch, xanthan gum, yeast and salt; mix well and set aside.

2. Pour beer mixture and oil into the bread machine baking pan.

3. Select the **Dough Cycle**. As the bread machine is mixing, gradually add the dry ingredients, scraping bottom and sides of pan with a rubber spatula. Try to incorporate all the dry ingredients within 1 to 2 minutes. Stop bread machine as soon as the kneading portion of the cycle is complete. Do not let bread machine finish the cycle.

4. Pour dough onto prepared pans, dividing evenly. Immediately swirl each pan to coat bottom, lifting and tilting pan to ensure entire bottom is covered. Let rise in a warm, draft-free place for 15 minutes. Meanwhile, preheat oven to 400°F (200°C).

5. Bake for 12 to 15 minutes or until bottom is golden and crust is partially baked.

6. Use right away to make pizza (for toppings, see page 287–290) or wrap airtight and store in the freezer for up to 1 month. Thaw overnight in the refrigerator before using.

Vegetarian Pizza

This pizza has lots of veggies — vegetarians will love it.

Tip

Choose from Rice-Free Brown Pizza Crust (page 202), Teff Pizza Crust (page 285) or Beer Pizza Crust (page 286).

◆ **Preheat oven to 400°F (200°C)**

1	partially baked pizza crust (see tip, at left)	1
3 tbsp	extra virgin olive oil	45 mL
1 tbsp	minced garlic	15 mL
2	plum (Roma) tomatoes, thinly sliced	2
1	red bell pepper, thinly sliced	1
1½ cups	sliced cremini mushrooms	375 mL
1 cup	broccoli florets	250 mL
½ cup	thinly sliced red onions	125 mL
1 cup	shredded mozzarella cheese	250 mL
½ cup	freshly grated Parmesan cheese	125 mL

1. Brush crust with oil. Sprinkle with garlic. Arrange tomatoes, red pepper, mushrooms, broccoli and red onion over top. Sprinkle with mozzarella and Parmesan.

2. Bake in preheated oven for 15 to 20 minutes or until crust is brown and crisp and cheese is bubbly. Transfer to a cutting board, let cool slightly, then cut into 8 pieces.

NUTRITIONAL VALUES
per serving

Calories	287
Fat, total	15 g
Fat, saturated	5 g
Cholesterol	15 mg
Sodium	452 mg
Carbohydrate	27 g
Fiber	4 g
Protein	12 g
Calcium	209 mg
Iron	2 mg

Mediterranean Pizza

**MAKES
8 SERVINGS**

*This filling takes longer
than most to prepare,
as you have to grill the
vegetables first. But the
results are more than
worth it!*

Tips

Choose from Rice-Free
Brown Pizza Crust
(page 202), Teff Pizza Crust
(page 285) or Beer Pizza
Crust (page 286).

Grilling the vegetables on
the barbecue intensifies
their flavors. If you're
barbecuing the night before,
grill them then.

For information on
roasting bell peppers, see
the Technique Glossary,
page 306.

NUTRITIONAL VALUES
per serving

Calories	204
Fat, total	8 g
Fat, saturated	2 g
Cholesterol	9 mg
Sodium	371 mg
Carbohydrate	26 g
Fiber	4 g
Protein	10 g
Calcium	232 mg
Iron	2 mg

◆ **Preheat oven to 400°F (200°C)**

3 tbsp	GF tomato pasta sauce	45 mL
1	partially baked pizza crust (see tip, at left)	1
3	grilled eggplant slices	3
1 cup	grilled zucchini slices	250 mL
1 cup	grilled shiitake mushroom caps	250 mL
1/2 cup	chopped roasted red bell peppers	125 mL
1/3 cup	packed fresh basil leaves, chopped	75 mL
1 cup	shredded mozzarella cheese	250 mL
1/4 cup	crumbled feta cheese	60 mL

1. Spread pasta sauce over crust. Top with eggplant, zucchini, mushrooms, roasted peppers and basil. Sprinkle with mozzarella and feta.

2. Bake in preheated oven for 15 to 20 minutes or until crust is brown and crisp and cheese is bubbly. Transfer to a cutting board, let cool slightly, then cut into 8 pieces.

Margherita Pizza

Donna's four-year-old grandniece orders a pizza just like this when she eats out at a favorite restaurant.

Tips

Choose from Rice-Free Brown Pizza Crust (page 202), Teff Pizza Crust (page 285) or Beer Pizza Crust (page 286).

Fresh mozzarella is often called bocconcini. Instead of the balls, you could purchase two 8-oz (250 g) discs and slice into ½-inch (1 cm) rounds.

For fast, easy cutting, use a pizza wheel.

Variation

Use ¼ cup (60 mL) basil pesto and 4 thinly sliced plum (Roma) tomatoes in place of the tomato sauce and fresh basil.

NUTRITIONAL VALUES per serving	
Calories	208
Fat, total	8 g
Fat, saturated	2 g
Cholesterol	8 mg
Sodium	444 mg
Carbohydrate	23 g
Fiber	4 g
Protein	12 g
Calcium	198 mg
Iron	1 mg

◆ **Preheat oven to 400°F (200°C)**

1	partially baked pizza crust (see tip, at left)	1
1 tbsp	extra virgin olive oil	15 mL
¼ cup	GF tomato pizza sauce	60 mL
¼ cup	packed snipped fresh basil	60 mL
4	1-inch (2.5 cm) balls fresh mozzarella cheese, thinly sliced	4
⅓ cup	freshly grated Parmesan cheese	75 mL

1. Brush crust with oil, then spread pizza sauce over crust. Top with basil, mozzarella and Parmesan.

2. Bake in preheated oven for 15 to 20 minutes or until crust is brown and crisp and cheese is bubbly. Transfer to a cutting board, let cool slightly, then cut into 8 pieces.

Tuscan Chicken Pizza

**MAKES
8 SERVINGS**

Why just stick with pepperoni? Shake things up and try our delicious chicken pizza. It's an opportunity to use up some of the cooked chicken breasts in the freezer!

Tips

Choose from Rice-Free Brown Pizza Crust (page 202), Teff Pizza Crust (page 285) or Beer Pizza Crust (page 286).

Use any or all of the following cheeses: Havarti, fontina, smoked Gouda or mozzarella.

Variation

Add 2 to 3 cloves of minced garlic.

◆ **Preheat oven to 400°F (200°C)**

½ cup	GF barbecue sauce	125 mL
1	partially baked pizza crust (see tip, at left)	1
2	boneless skinless chicken breasts (each 6 oz/175 g), cooked and chopped	2
½	medium red onion, sliced crosswise and separated into rings	½
½	yellow bell pepper, coarsely chopped	½
1½ cups	shredded cheese (see tip, at left)	375 mL

1. Spread barbecue sauce over crust. Top with chicken, red onion, yellow pepper and cheese.

2. Bake in preheated oven for 15 to 20 minutes or until crust is brown and crisp and cheese is bubbly. Transfer to a cutting board, let cool slightly, then cut into 8 pieces.

NUTRITIONAL VALUES per serving	
Calories	310
Fat, total	13 g
Fat, saturated	5 g
Cholesterol	55 mg
Sodium	557 mg
Carbohydrate	26 g
Fiber	3 g
Protein	23 g
Calcium	169 mg
Iron	2 mg

Lemon Pepper Lavosh

*These savory crackers
are perfect dippers
for hummus, chutney
or salsa.*

Tips

To ensure success, see
page 14 for information on
using your bread machine
and page 18 for general tips
on bread machine baking.

Store in an airtight
container at room
temperature for up to
3 months. If necessary,
crisp the lavosh in a 300°F
(150°C) oven for 5 minutes
before serving.

◆ 15- by 10-inch (40 by 25 cm) jelly roll pan, lightly greased

¾ cup	brown rice flour	175 mL
⅓ cup	tapioca starch	75 mL
1 tsp	granulated sugar	5 mL
1½ tsp	xanthan gum	7 mL
1½ tsp	bread machine or instant yeast	7 mL
½ tsp	salt	2 mL
½ tsp	freshly ground black pepper	2 mL
1 cup	packed snipped fresh parsley	250 mL
¾ cup	water	175 mL
2 tbsp	grated lemon zest	30 mL
1 tbsp	extra virgin olive oil	15 mL
1 tsp	cider vinegar	5 mL
½ cup	freshly grated Parmesan cheese, divided	125 mL

1. In a large bowl or plastic bag, combine brown rice flour, tapioca starch, sugar, xanthan gum, yeast, salt, pepper and parsley; mix well and set aside.

2. Pour water, lemon zest, oil and vinegar into the bread machine pan.

3. Select the **Dough Cycle**. As the bread machine is mixing, gradually add the dry ingredients, scraping bottom and sides of pan with a rubber spatula. Try to incorporate all the dry ingredients within 1 to 2 minutes. Stop bread machine as soon as the kneading portion of the cycle is complete. Do not let bread machine finish the cycle.

4. Meanwhile, preheat oven to 375°F (190°C).

5. Sprinkle prepared pan with half the Parmesan. Transfer dough to prepared pan. Using a moistened rubber spatula, spread out the dough to fill the pan evenly, sprinkling with Parmesan if dough becomes too sticky to handle. Sprinkle with the remaining Parmesan and press lightly into dough.

6. Bake for 20 to 25 minutes or until lightly browned. Turn off oven and let cool in the oven for 1 hour. Remove from oven and let cool, then break into large pieces.

NUTRITIONAL VALUES per serving	
Calories	62
Fat, total	2 g
Fat, saturated	1 g
Cholesterol	4 mg
Sodium	140 mg
Carbohydrate	9 g
Fiber	1 g
Protein	2 g
Calcium	52 mg
Iron	0 mg

Three-Cheese Lavosh

**MAKES ABOUT
32 CRACKERS**
(¹⁄₁₆ recipe per
serving)

These dark golden, crisp crackers have a sharp, cheesy tang. Try to eat just one!

Tips

To ensure success, see page 14 for information on using your bread machine and page 18 for general tips on bread machine baking.

The thinner the dough is spread, the more authentic the cracker will be. To more easily spread the dough, moisten the rubber spatula as needed. Don't worry: you can't use too much water.

Store in an airtight container at room temperature for up to 3 months. If necessary, crisp the lavosh in a 300°F (150°C) oven for 5 minutes before serving.

NUTRITIONAL VALUES
per serving

Calories	92
Fat, total	5 g
Fat, saturated	2 g
Cholesterol	11 mg
Sodium	194 mg
Carbohydrate	7 g
Fiber	1 g
Protein	5 g
Calcium	94 mg
Iron	0 mg

◆ **15- by 10-inch (40 by 25 cm) jelly roll pan, lightly greased**

½ cup	sorghum flour	125 mL
⅓ cup	whole bean flour	75 mL
¼ cup	tapioca starch	60 mL
1 tsp	granulated sugar	5 mL
½ tsp	xanthan gum	2 mL
1½ tsp	bread machine or instant yeast	7 mL
½ tsp	salt	2 mL
1 tsp	dry mustard	5 mL
⅓ cup	shredded Asiago cheese	75 mL
⅓ cup	shredded smoked Gouda cheese	75 mL
¾ cup	water	175 mL
2 tbsp	extra virgin olive oil	30 mL
1 tsp	cider vinegar	5 mL
½ cup	freshly grated Parmesan cheese, divided	125 mL

1. In a large bowl or plastic bag, combine sorghum flour, whole bean flour, tapioca starch, sugar, xanthan gum, yeast, salt, mustard, Asiago and Gouda; mix well and set aside.

2. Pour water, oil and vinegar into the bread machine baking pan.

3. Select the **Dough Cycle**. As the bread machine is mixing, gradually add the dry ingredients, scraping bottom and sides of pan with a rubber spatula. Try to incorporate all the dry ingredients within 1 to 2 minutes. Stop bread machine as soon as the kneading portion of the cycle is complete. Do not let bread machine finish the cycle.

4. Meanwhile, preheat oven to 375°F (190°C).

5. Sprinkle prepared pan with half the Parmesan. Transfer dough to prepared pan. Using a moistened rubber spatula, spread out the dough to fill the pan evenly, sprinkling with Parmesan if dough becomes too sticky to handle. Sprinkle with the remaining Parmesan and press lightly into dough.

6. Bake for 14 to 16 minutes or until golden brown. Turn off oven and let cool in the oven for 1 hour. Remove from pan to a cooling rack and let stand for 10 minutes. Break into pieces.

Soy-Free Golden Sesame Wafers

These wafers qualify as health food: sesame seeds provide calcium, omega-6 fats and antioxidants.

Tips

To ensure success, see page 14 for information on using your bread machine and page 18 for general tips on bread machine baking.

Watch these carefully during baking — even as little as 1 minute too long can cause the bottoms to burn.

Store in an airtight container at room temperature for up to 3 weeks.

It may not seem like enough, but this dough really does make 4 dozen wafers.

Variation

For a stronger sesame flavor, substitute sesame oil for the vegetable oil.

NUTRITIONAL VALUES per serving	
Calories	64
Fat, total	5 g
Fat, saturated	0 g
Cholesterol	0 mg
Sodium	12 mg
Carbohydrate	4 g
Fiber	1 g
Protein	2 g
Calcium	22 mg
Iron	1 mg

◆ **Baking sheets, lined with parchment paper**

⅔ cup	amaranth flour	150 mL
1 tsp	bread machine or instant yeast	5 mL
½ cup	granulated sugar	125 mL
2 cups	golden sesame seeds	500 mL
2 tbsp	cracked golden flaxseed	30 mL
½ cup	water	125 mL
⅓ cup	vegetable oil	75 mL

1. In a large bowl or plastic bag, combine amaranth flour, yeast, sugar, sesame seeds and flaxseed; mix well and set aside.

2. Pour water and oil into the bread machine pan.

3. Select the **Dough Cycle**. As the bread machine is mixing, gradually add the dry ingredients, scraping bottom and sides of pan with a rubber spatula. Try to incorporate all the dry ingredients within 1 to 2 minutes. Stop bread machine as soon as the kneading portion of the cycle is complete. Do not let bread machine finish the cycle. Set dough aside for 10 minutes.

4. Meanwhile, preheat oven to 325°F (160°C), with oven rack placed in the top position.

5. Drop dough by small spoonfuls at least 2 inches (5 cm) apart onto prepared baking sheets. Using a small square of parchment paper, cover each mound, then flatten with a flat-bottomed drinking glass. Using the flat edge of a metal spatula to assist, carefully peel away the parchment paper.

6. Bake, one sheet at a time, on top rack for 11 to 13 minutes or until dark brown on top and bottom. Let cool on baking sheet for 2 to 3 minutes. Transfer to a rack and let cool completely.

Pecan Crisps

These yummy treats look almost like large cookies. A bonus: they don't need refrigeration, so you can carry them anywhere you go.

Tips

To ensure success, see page 14 for information on using your bread machine and page 18 for general tips on bread machine baking.

Be sure to prepare both the filling and the topping before removing the first square of dough from the refrigerator. Work quickly when rolling out the dough and assembling the crisps. Return the dough to the refrigerator for a few minutes if it becomes sticky.

NUTRITIONAL VALUES
per serving

Calories	217
Fat, total	7 g
Fat, saturated	2 g
Cholesterol	18 mg
Sodium	160 mg
Carbohydrate	36 g
Fiber	2 g
Protein	4 g
Calcium	31 mg
Iron	1 mg

◆ **Baking sheets, lightly greased**

1½ to 1⅔ cups	sorghum flour, divided	375 to 400 mL
¾ cup	whole bean flour	175 mL
⅔ cup	tapioca starch	150 mL
½ cup	cornstarch	125 mL
2 tbsp	potato flour (not potato starch)	30 mL
½ cup	granulated sugar	125 mL
1 tbsp	xanthan gum	15 mL
4 tsp	bread machine or instant yeast	20 mL
1¼ tsp	salt	6 mL
2 tsp	ground cinnamon	10 mL
1 cup	milk, warmed to room temperature	250 mL
2 tbsp	vegetable oil	30 mL
1 tsp	cider vinegar	5 mL
2	eggs, lightly beaten	2

Cinnamon Filling

½ cup	packed brown sugar	125 mL
½ cup	granulated sugar	125 mL
2 tsp	ground cinnamon	10 mL
¼ cup	butter, melted	60 mL

Pecan Topping

¾ cup	chopped pecans	175 mL
⅔ cup	granulated sugar	150 mL
1 tsp	ground cinnamon	5 mL
2 tbsp	butter, softened	30 mL

1. In a large bowl or plastic bag, combine 1 cup (250 mL) sorghum flour, whole bean flour, tapioca starch, cornstarch, potato flour, sugar, xanthan gum, yeast, salt and cinnamon; mix well and set aside.

2. Pour milk, oil and vinegar into the bread machine baking pan. Add eggs.

3. Select the **Dough Cycle**. As the bread machine is mixing, gradually add the dry ingredients, scraping bottom and sides of pan with a rubber spatula. Try to incorporate all the dry ingredients within 1 to 2 minutes. Stop bread machine as soon as the kneading portion of the cycle is complete. Do not let bread machine finish the cycle.

We prefer to cut the dough into slices with a pizza wheel, but kitchen shears or a sharp knife work well too. You may have to dip the cutter in hot water between cuts.

Freeze wrapped squares of dough for up to 1 month. Thaw overnight in the refrigerator.

Be sure you use potato flour and not potato starch. One cannot be substituted for the other.

4. Generously coat 2 large sheets of plastic wrap with some of the remaining sorghum flour. Divide dough in half and place each half on a sheet of plastic wrap. Generously dust each with sorghum flour. Fold plastic wrap to cover dough and pat dough out to a square about $1/2$ inch (1 cm) thick. Wrap airtight and refrigerate for at least 2 hours, until chilled, or overnight.

5. For the filling: In a bowl, combine brown sugar, granulated sugar, cinnamon and butter. Set aside.

6. For the topping: In a bowl, combine pecans, sugar and cinnamon. Set aside.

7. Preheat oven to 400°F (200°C).

8. Remove a square of dough from the refrigerator. Unwrap and place on a sheet of parchment paper generously dusted with sorghum flour. Generously dust dough with sorghum flour and cover with another sheet of parchment paper. Lightly roll out to a 9-inch (23 cm) square, about $1/4$ inch (0.5 cm) thick. Remove top sheet of parchment paper.

9. Sprinkle half the filling over the dough. Beginning at one side, roll up like a jelly roll, lifting the parchment paper to help the dough form a roll. Using your fingers, brush off excess sorghum flour. Using a pizza wheel dipped in hot water, cut into 12 equal slices. Place cut side up, 3 inches (7.5 cm) apart, on prepared baking sheets.

10. Cover slices with a sheet of parchment paper. Flatten with a rolling pin to $1/8$ inch (3 mm) thick. Remove parchment, brush with half the softened butter and sprinkle with half the pecan topping. Cover with parchment paper and reroll lightly with a rolling pin.

11. Bake for 10 to 15 minutes or until crisps are golden brown. Remove from baking sheets to a cooling rack and let cool completely.

12. When baking sheets have cooled, repeat with the remaining dough, filling and topping.

Super-Thin Breadsticks

You'll love these crispy breadsticks with a real crunch!

Tips

For 24 equal strips, cut the dough in half, then cut each half lengthwise into 3 equal strips. Cut each strip in half lengthwise, then cut in half again.

To keep breadsticks crisp, store them in a paper bag.

◆ **9-inch (23 cm) square baking pan, lightly greased and generously dusted with cornmeal**
◆ **Baking sheet**

1 cup	brown rice flour	250 mL
1/3 cup	potato starch	75 mL
1 tsp	granulated sugar	5 mL
1 tsp	xanthan gum	5 mL
1 1/2 tsp	bread machine or instant yeast	7 mL
3/4 tsp	salt	3 mL
3/4 cup	water	175 mL
2 tsp	cider vinegar	10 mL
1	egg white, lightly beaten	1
1/4 cup	cornmeal	60 mL

1. In a large bowl or plastic bag, combine brown rice flour, potato starch, sugar, xanthan gum, yeast and salt; mix well and set aside.

2. Pour water and vinegar into the bread machine baking pan. Add egg white.

3. Select the **Dough Cycle**. As the bread machine is mixing, gradually add the dry ingredients, scraping bottom and sides of pan with a rubber spatula. Try to incorporate all the dry ingredients within 1 to 2 minutes. Stop bread machine as soon as the kneading portion of the cycle is complete. Do not let bread machine finish the cycle.

4. Meanwhile, preheat oven to 425°F (220°C).

5. Drop dough by spoonfuls over the cornmeal in baking pan. Using a moistened rubber spatula, spread dough evenly to the edges of the pan. Sprinkle with cornmeal.

6. Bake for 12 minutes or until light brown. Remove from the pan and transfer immediately to a cutting board, leaving oven on. Using a pizza wheel, cut bread into 24 equal strips (see tip, at left).

7. Arrange slices, cut side down, at least 1/4 inch (0.5 cm) apart on baking sheet. Bake for 10 minutes. Turn slices over and bake for 4 minutes or until golden brown. Remove from the pan immediately and let cool completely on a rack.

NUTRITIONAL VALUES per serving	
Calories	41
Fat, total	0 g
Fat, saturated	0 g
Cholesterol	0 mg
Sodium	76 mg
Carbohydrate	9 g
Fiber	0 g
Protein	1 g
Calcium	0 mg
Iron	0 mg

Parmesan Sticks

A lovely lingering taste of Parmesan enhances these bread sticks.

Tips

For 24 equal strips, cut the dough in half, then cut each half lengthwise into 3 equal strips. Cut each strip in half lengthwise, then cut in half again.

To keep breadsticks crisp, store them in a paper bag.

NUTRITIONAL VALUES
per serving

Calories	50
Fat, total	1 g
Fat, saturated	1 g
Cholesterol	4 mg
Sodium	140 mg
Carbohydrate	8 g
Fiber	0 g
Protein	2 g
Calcium	46 mg
Iron	0 mg

◆ **9-inch (23 cm) square baking pan, lightly greased and generously dusted with Parmesan cheese**
◆ **Baking sheet**

1 cup	brown rice flour	250 mL
1/3 cup	potato starch	75 mL
1 tsp	granulated sugar	5 mL
1 tsp	xanthan gum	5 mL
1 1/2 tsp	bread machine or instant yeast	7 mL
3/4 tsp	salt	3 mL
1/2 tsp	dry mustard	2 mL
3/4 cup	grated Parmesan cheese, divided	175 mL
3/4 cup	water	175 mL
2 tsp	cider vinegar	10 mL
1	egg white, lightly beaten	1

1. In a large bowl or plastic bag, combine brown rice flour, potato starch, sugar, xanthan gum, yeast, salt, mustard and 1/2 cup (125 mL) of the Parmesan; mix well and set aside.

2. Pour water and vinegar into the bread machine baking pan. Add egg white.

3. Select the **Dough Cycle**. As the bread machine is mixing, gradually add the dry ingredients, scraping bottom and sides of pan with a rubber spatula. Try to incorporate all the dry ingredients within 1 to 2 minutes. Stop bread machine as soon as the kneading portion of the cycle is complete. Do not let bread machine finish the cycle.

4. Meanwhile, preheat oven to 425°F (220°C).

5. Drop dough by spoonfuls over the Parmesan in baking pan. Using a moistened rubber spatula, spread dough evenly to the edges of the pan. Sprinkle with the remaining Parmesan.

6. Bake for 8 minutes or until light golden. Remove from the pan and transfer immediately to a cutting board, leaving oven on. Using a pizza wheel, cut bread into 24 equal strips (see tip, at left).

7. Arrange slices, cut side down, at least 1/4 inch (0.5 cm) apart on baking sheet. Bake for 10 minutes. Turn slices over and bake for 4 minutes or until golden brown. Remove from the pan immediately and let cool completely on a rack.

Equipment Glossary

Baguette pan. A metal baking pan divided into two sections shaped like long, thin loaves. The bottom surface may be perforated with small holes to produce a crisp crust and reduce the baking time.

Cooling rack. Parallel and perpendicular thin bars of metal at right angles, with feet attached, used to hold hot bread off the surface to allow cooling air to circulate.

Hamburger bun pan. A baking pan that makes six 4-inch (10 cm) hamburger buns.

Instant-read thermometer. See page 20.

Jelly roll pan. A rectangular baking pan that measures 15 by 10 by 1 inches (40 by 25 by 2.5 cm), used to bake wraps and crackers.

Loaf pan. Container used for baking loaves. Common pan sizes are 9 by 5 inches (23 by 12.5 cm) and 8 by 4 inches (20 by 10 cm).

OXO angled measuring cups. Made to give an accurate measure while set on the counter. There's no need to hold the measuring cup at eye level — you can look straight down as you fill it, and the angled insert lets you know when it is full enough. These cups are dishwasher-safe, but not microwaveable. Sizes available include $1/4$ cup (60 mL), 1 cup (250 mL), 2 cups (500 mL) and 4 cups (1 L). All sizes indicate metric and imperial amounts.

Panini press. Made of anodized aluminum, the two-piece panini press includes a thick nonstick pan for fast, even heating. It works much like an outdoor grill, but is faster. It gives sandwiches a delicious crunch, even browning and blackened grill marks. You can cook oil-free. It has an extra-large floating hinge so you can grill thick sandwiches easily.

Parchment paper. Heat-resistant paper similar to waxed paper, usually coated with silicon on one side; used with or as an alternative to other methods (such as applying vegetable oil or spray) to prevent baked goods from sticking to the baking pan.

Pastry brush. Small brush with nylon or natural bristles used to apply glazes or egg washes to dough. Wash thoroughly after each use. To store, lay flat or hang on a hook through the hole in the handle.

Pizza wheel. A sharp-edged wheel (without serrations) anchored to a handle.

Portion scoop. A utensil similar to an ice cream scoop, used to measure equal amounts of batter. For some recipes in this book, we use a muffin scoop, which has a $1/4$-cup (60 mL) capacity.

Rolling pin. A smooth cylinder of wood, marble, plastic or metal; used to roll out dough.

Sieve. A bowl-shaped utensil with many holes, used to drain liquids from solids. Also called a colander or a strainer.

Spatula. A utensil with a handle and a blade that can be long or short, narrow or wide, flexible or inflexible. It is used to spread, lift, turn, mix or smooth foods. Spatulas are made of metal, rubber, plastic or silicone.

Zester. A tool used to cut very thin strips of outer peel from citrus fruits. One type has a short, flat blade tipped with five small holes with sharp edges. Another popular style of zester is made of stainless steel and looks like a tool used for planing wood in a workshop.

Ingredient Glossary

Almond flour (almond meal). See Nut Flours and Meals on page 31.

Almonds. An ivory-colored nut with a pointed oval shape and a smooth texture. Almonds have a thin, medium-brown skin that adheres to the nut. Sweet almonds have a delicate taste that is delicious in breads. Blanched (skin off) and natural (skin on) almonds are interchangeable in recipes. Almonds are available whole, sliced, slivered or ground.

Amaranth. See page 23.

Apricots. A small stone fruit with a thin, pale yellow to orange skin and meaty orange flesh. Dried unpeeled apricot halves are used in baking.

Arrowroot starch. See page 32.

Asiago cheese. A pungent grayish-white hard cheese from northern Italy. Cured for more than 6 months, its texture is ideal for grating. Weight/volume equivalents are:

4 oz (125 g) = 1 cup (250 mL) shredded
2 oz (60 g) = 1/2 cup (125 mL) shredded
1 1/2 oz (45 g) = 1/3 cup (75 mL) shredded

Bean flours. See Legume Flours on page 30.

Bell peppers. The sweet-flavored members of the capsicum family (which includes chiles and other hot peppers), these peppers have a hollow interior lined with white ribs and seeds attached at the stem end. They are most commonly green, red, orange or yellow, but can also be white or purple.

Blueberries. Wild low-bush berries are smaller than the cultivated variety and more time-consuming to pick, but their flavor makes every minute of picking time worthwhile. They are readily available year-round in the frozen fruit section of most grocery stores.

Brown rice flour. See page 25.

Brown sugar. A refined sugar with a coating of molasses. It can be purchased coarse or fine and comes in three varieties: dark, golden and light.

Buckwheat. See page 23.

Butter. A spread produced from dairy fat and milk solids. Butter is interchangeable with shortening, oil or margarine in most recipes.

Buttermilk powder. A dry powder, low in calories, that softens the texture of breads and heightens the flavor of ingredients such as chocolate. It is readily available at bulk- or health-food stores. Store in an airtight container, as it lumps easily. To substitute for 1 cup

(250 mL) fresh buttermilk, use 1 cup (250 mL) water and $^1/_3$ cup (75 mL) buttermilk powder. If unavailable, substitute an equal amount of skim milk powder.

Cardamom. This popular spice is a member of the ginger family. A long green or brown pod contains the strong, spicy, lemon-flavored seed. Although native to India, cardamom is used in Middle Eastern, Indian and Scandinavian cooking — in the latter case, particularly for seasonal baked goods.

Cheddar cheese. Always select a sharp (old), good-quality Cheddar for baking recipes. (The flavor of mild or medium Cheddar is not strong enough for baking.) Weight/volume equivalents are:

4 oz (125 g) = 1 cup (250 mL) shredded
2 oz (60 g) = $^1/_2$ cup (125 mL) shredded
$1^1/_2$ oz (45 g) = $^1/_3$ cup (75 mL) shredded

Chickpea (garbanzo bean) flour. See page 30.

Cilantro. This herb has a flavor reminiscent of lemon, sage and caraway. To increase flavor in a recipe, substitute cilantro for parsley.

Cornmeal. See page 24.

Cornstarch. See page 32.

Coconut. The fruit of a tropical palm tree, with a hard, woody shell that is lined with a hard white flesh. There are three dried forms available, which can be sweetened or not: flaked, shredded and the smallest, desiccated (thoroughly dried).

Coconut flour. See page 29.

Cranberries. Grown in bogs on low vines, these sweet-tart berries are available fresh, frozen and dried. Fresh cranberries are available only in season — typically from mid-October until January, depending on your location — but can be frozen right in the bag. Substitute dried cranberries for sour cherries, raisins or currants.

Currants. See Dried currants.

Dates. The fruit of the date palm tree, dates are long and oval in shape, with a paper-thin skin that turns from green to dark brown when ripe. Eaten fresh or dried, dates have a very sweet, light brown flesh around a long, narrow seed.

Dried currants. Similar in appearance to small dark raisins, currants are made by drying a special seedless variety of grape. Not the same as a type of berry that goes by the same name.

Egg replacer. See page 220.

Eggs. Liquid egg products, such as Naturegg Simply Whites, Break-Free and Omega Pro liquid eggs and Just Whites, are available in the United States and Canada. Powdered egg whites, such as Just Whites, can be used by reconstituting with warm water or as a powder. A similar product is called meringue powder in Canada. Substitute $1/4$ cup (60 mL) liquid whole eggs for each large egg, and 2 tbsp (25 mL) liquid egg whites for each large egg white.

Fava bean flour. See page 30.

Fennel seeds. Small, oval, green-brown seeds with prominent ridges and a mild anise (licorice-like) flavor and aroma. Available whole or ground, they are used in Italian and Central European cookery, particularly in rye and pumpernickel breads.

Feta cheese. A crumbly white Greek-style cheese with a salty, tangy flavor. Store in the refrigerator, in its brine, and drain well before using. Traditionally made with sheep's or goat's milk in Greece and usually with cow's milk in Canada and the U.S. A lactose-free flavored soy product is also available.

Figs. Pear-shaped fruit with thick, soft skin, available in green and purple. Eaten fresh or dried, the tan-colored sweet flesh contains many tiny edible seeds.

Filberts. See Hazelnuts.

Flaxseed. See page 30.

Garbanzo bean flour. See page 30.

Garfava (garbanzo-fava bean) flour. See page 30.

Garlic. An edible bulb composed of several sections (cloves), each covered with a papery skin. An essential ingredient in many styles of cooking.

Gluten. A natural protein in wheat flour that becomes elastic with the addition of moisture and kneading. Gluten traps gases produced by leaveners inside the dough and causes it to rise.

Glutinous rice flour. See Sweet Rice Flour, page 26.

Golden raisins. See Raisins.

Granulated sugar. A refined, crystalline, white form of sugar that is also commonly called white sugar, table sugar or just sugar.

Guar gum. A white, flour-like substance made from an East Indian seed high in fiber, this vegetable substance contains no gluten. It may have a laxative effect for some people. It can be substituted for xanthan gum.

Havarti. A Danish semi-soft cheese, creamy white in color. Havarti melts easily in breads. Weight/volume equivalents are:

4 oz (125 g) = 1 cup (250 mL) shredded
2 oz (60 g) = $1/2$ cup (125 mL) shredded
$1^1/2$ oz (45 g) = $1/3$ cup (75 mL) shredded

Hazelnut flour (hazelnut meal). See Nut Flours and Meals on page 31.

Hazelnuts. Slightly larger than filberts, hazelnuts have a weaker flavor. Both nuts have a round, smooth shell and look like small brown marbles. They have a sweet, rich flavor and are interchangeable in recipes.

Herbs. Plants whose stems, leaves or flowers are used as a flavoring, either dried or fresh. To substitute fresh herbs for dried, a good rule of thumb is to use three times the amount of fresh as dried. Taste and adjust the amount to suit your preference.

Honey. Sweeter than sugar, honey is available in liquid, honeycomb and creamed varieties. Use liquid honey for baking.

Kalamata olives. See Olives, kalamata.

Linseed. See Flaxseed, page 30.

Maple syrup. A very sweet, slightly thick brown liquid made by boiling the sap from North American maple trees. Use pure maple syrup, not pancake syrup, in baking.

Millet. See page 24.

Mixed candied fruit. A mixture of dried candied orange and lemon peel, citron and glazed cherries. Citron, which can be expensive, is often replaced in the mix by candied rutabaga.

Molasses. A by-product of refining sugar, molasses is a sweet, thick, dark brown (almost black) liquid. It has a distinctive, slightly bitter flavor. It is available in the United States in light, dark and blackstrap varieties. In Canada, these varieties are called fancy, cooking and blackstrap. Use light (fancy) molasses for baking unless blackstrap is specified. Store in the refrigerator if used infrequently.

Nut flour (nut meal). See page 31.

Nonfat dry milk. See Skim milk powder.

Oats. See page 24.

Olive oil. Produced from pressing tree-ripened olives. Extra virgin oil is taken from the first cold pressing; it is the finest and fruitiest, pale straw to pale green in color, with the least amount of acid, usually less than 1%. Virgin oil is taken from a subsequent pressing; it contains 2% acid and is pale yellow. Light oil comes from the last pressing; it has a mild flavor, light color and up to 3% acid. It also has a higher smoke point. Product sold as "pure olive oil" has been cleaned and filtered; it is very mild-flavored and has up to 3% acid.

Olives, kalamata. A large, flavorful variety of Greek olive, typically dark purple in color and pointed at one end.

Parsley. A biennial herb with dark green curly or flat leaves used fresh as a flavoring. Substitute parsley for half the amount of a strong-flavored herb such as basil.

Pea flour. See page 30.

Pecan meal. See Nut Flours and Meals on page 31.

Pecans. This sweet, mellow nut is smooth and oval, golden brown on the outside and tan on the inside. You can purchase pecans whole, halved, chopped or in chips.

Peppers. See Bell peppers.

Pinto bean flour. See page 30.

Poppy seeds. These tiny, kidney-shaped seeds have a mild, sweet, nutty, dusty flavor. They are available whole or ground. They are most flavorful when roasted and crushed.

Potato flour. See page 32.

Potato starch (potato starch flour). See page 32.

Provolone cheese. An Italian cheese with a light ivory color, mild mellow flavor and smooth texture that cuts without crumbling. Available shapes are sausage, squat pear and piglet. Weight/volume equivalents are:

4 oz (125 g) = 1 cup (250 mL) shredded
2 oz (60 g) = 1/2 cup (125 mL) shredded
1 1/2 oz (45 g) = 1/3 cup (75 mL) shredded

Pumpkin seeds. Available roasted or raw, salted or unsalted, and with or without hulls. Raw pumpkin seeds without hulls — often known as pepitas ("little seeds" in Spanish) — are a dull, dark olive green. Roasted pumpkin seeds have a rich, almost peanuty flavor.

Quinoa. See page 25.

Raisins. Dark raisins are sun-dried Thompson seedless grapes. Golden raisins are treated with sulfur dioxide and dried artificially, yielding a moister, plumper product.

Rice bran. See page 25.

Rice flours. See page 25.

Rice polish. See page 25.

Salt. See page 32.

Sesame seeds. These flat oval seeds, which can be ivory, red, brown, pale gold or black, have a nutty, slightly sweet flavor. Black sesame seeds have a more pungent flavor and bitter taste than white or natural sesame seeds.

Skim milk powder. The dehydrated form of fluid skim milk. Use 1/4 cup (60 mL) skim milk powder for every 1 cup (250 mL) water.

Sorghum flour. See page 26.

Sour cream. A thick, smooth, tangy product made by adding bacterial cultures to pasteurized, homogenized cream containing varying amounts of butterfat. Check the label: some lower-fat and fat-free brands may contain gluten.

Soy flour. See page 31.

Starches. See page 32.

Sun-dried tomatoes. Available either dry or packed in oil, sun-dried tomatoes have a dark red color, a soft, chewy texture and a strong tomato flavor. Use dry, not oil-packed, sun-dried tomatoes in recipes. Use scissors to snip. Oil-packed and dry are not interchangeable in recipes.

Sunflower seeds. These plump, nutlike kernels grow in teardrop shapes within gray-and-white shells. They are sold raw or roasted, and salted, seasoned or plain. Shelled sunflower seeds are sometimes labeled "sunflower kernels" or "nutmeats." When buying seeds in the shell, look for clean, unbroken shells.

Sweet peppers. See Bell peppers.

Sweet potato flour. See page 33.

Sweet rice flour. See page 26.

Tapioca starch. See page 32.

Tarragon. An herb with narrow, pointed, dark green leaves and a distinctive anise-like flavor with undertones of sage. Use fresh or dried.

Teff. See page 26.

Vegetable oil. Common oils used are canola, corn, sunflower, safflower, olive, peanut, soy and walnut.

Walnuts. Inside a tough shell, a walnut's curly nutmeat halves offer a rich, sweet flavor, and the edible, papery skin adds a hint of bitterness to baked goods. Walnuts are available whole (shelled and unshelled), halved and chopped.

White (navy) bean flour. See page 30.

Whole bean flour. See page 30.

Wild rice. Not actually rice at all but a marsh grass seed. The long, shiny black or dark brown grains take longer to cook than white rice and triple or quadruple in size when cooked. In its natural state, wild rice is gluten-free, but when found in boxed wild rice/white rice mixes, it is best avoided.

Xanthan gum. See page 33.

Yeast. See page 33.

Yogurt. Made by fermenting cow's milk using a bacteria culture. Plain yogurt is gluten-free, but not all flavored yogurt is.

Zest. Strips from the outer layer of rind (colored part only) of citrus fruit. Avoid the bitter part underneath. Used for its intense flavor.

Technique Glossary

Almond flour (almond meal). *To make:* See Nut flour. *To toast:* Spread in a 9-inch (23 cm) baking pan and bake at 350°F (180°C), stirring occasionally, for 8 minutes or until light golden.

Almonds. *To blanch:* Cover almonds with boiling water and let stand, covered, for 3 to 5 minutes. Drain. Grasp the almond at one end, pressing between your thumb and index finger, and the nut will pop out of the skin. Nuts are more easily chopped or slivered while still warm from blanching. *To toast:* see Nuts.

Baking pan. *To prepare, or to grease:* Either spray the bottom and sides of the baking pan with nonstick cooking spray or brush with a pastry brush or a crumpled-up piece of waxed paper dipped in vegetable oil or shortening.

Bananas. *To mash and freeze:* Select overripe fruit, mash and package in 1-cup (250 mL) amounts in freezer containers. Freeze for up to 6 months. Defrost and warm to room temperature before using. About 2 to 3 medium bananas yield 1 cup (250 mL) mashed.

Beat. To stir vigorously to incorporate air, using a spoon, whisk, handheld beater or electric mixer.

Bell pepper. *To roast:* Place whole peppers on a baking sheet, piercing each near the stem with a knife. Bake at 425°F (220°C) for 18 minutes. Turn and bake for 15 minutes or until the skins blister. (Or roast on the barbecue, turning frequently, until skin is completely charred.) Place in a paper or plastic bag. Seal and let cool for 10 minutes or until skin is loose. Peel and discard seeds.

Blueberries, frozen. *To partially defrost:* Place 1 cup (250 mL) frozen blueberries in a single layer on a microwave-safe plate and microwave on High for 80 seconds.

Blanch. To completely immerse food in boiling water and then quickly in cold water, to loosen and easily remove skin, for example.

Bread crumbs. *To make fresh:* For best results, the GF bread should be at least 1 day old. Using the pulsing operation of a food processor or blender, process until crumbs are of the desired consistency. *To make dry:* Spread bread crumbs in a single layer on a baking sheet and bake at 350°F (180°C) for 6 to 8 minutes, shaking pan frequently, until lightly browned, crisp and dry. (Or microwave, uncovered, on High for 1 to 2 minutes, stirring every 30 seconds.) *To store:* Package in airtight containers and freeze for up to 3 months.

Combine. To stir two or more ingredients together for a consistent mixture.

Cream. To combine softened fat and sugar by beating to a soft, smooth, creamy consistency while trying to incorporate as much air as possible.

Drizzle. To slowly spoon or pour a liquid (such as icing or melted butter) in a very fine stream over the surface of food.

Dust. To coat by sprinkling GF confectioner's (icing) sugar, unsweetened cocoa powder or any GF flour lightly over food or a utensil.

Eggs. *To warm to room temperature:* Place eggs in the shell from the refrigerator in a bowl of hot water and let stand for 5 minutes.

Egg whites. *To warm to room temperature:* Separate eggs while cold. Place bowl of egg whites in a larger bowl of hot water and let stand for 5 minutes.

Flaxseed. *To grind:* Place whole seeds in a coffee grinder or blender. Grind only the amount required. If necessary, store extra ground flaxseed in the refrigerator. *To crack:* Pulse in a coffee grinder, blender or food processor just long enough to break the seed coat but not long enough to grind completely.

Garlic. *To peel:* Use the flat side of a sharp knife to flatten the clove of garlic. Skin can then be easily removed. *To roast:* Cut off top of head to expose clove tips. Drizzle with $\frac{1}{4}$ tsp (1 mL) olive oil and microwave on High for 70 seconds, until fork-tender. Or bake in a pie plate or baking dish at 375°F (190°C) for 15 to 20 minutes, or until fork-tender. Let cool slightly, then squeeze cloves from skins.

Glaze. To apply a thin, shiny coating to the outside of a baked food to enhance the appearance and flavor.

Grease pan. See Baking pan.

Hazelnut flour (hazelnut meal). *To make:* See Nut flour. *To toast:* Spread in a 9-inch (23 cm) baking pan and bake at 350°F (180°C), stirring occasionally, for 8 minutes or until light golden. Let cool before using.

Hazelnuts. *To remove skins:* Place hazelnuts in a 350°F (180°C) oven for 15 to 20 minutes. Immediately place in a clean, dry kitchen towel. With your hands, rub the nuts against the towel. Skins will be left in the towel. Be careful: hazelnuts will be very hot.

Herbs. *To store full stems:* Fresh-picked herbs can be stored for up to 1 week with stems standing in water. (Keep leaves out of water.) *To remove leaves:* Remove small leaves from stem by holding the top and running fingers down the stem in the opposite direction of growth. Larger leaves should be snipped off the stem using scissors. *To clean and store fresh leaves:* Rinse under cold running water and spin-dry in a lettuce spinner. If necessary, dry between layers of paper towels. Place a dry paper towel along with the clean herbs in a plastic bag in the refrigerator. Use within 2 to 3 days. Freeze or dry for longer storage. *To measure:* Pack leaves tightly into correct measure. *To snip:* After measuring, transfer to a small glass and cut using the tips of sharp kitchen shears/scissors to avoid bruising the tender leaves. *To dry:* Tie fresh-picked herbs together in small bunches and hang upside down in a well-ventilated location with low humidity and out of sunlight until the leaves are brittle and fully dry. If they turn brown (rather than stay green), the air is too hot. Once fully dried, strip leaves off the stems for storage. Store whole herbs in an airtight container in a cool, dark place for up to 1 year and crushed herbs for up to 6 months. (Dried herbs are stored in the dark to prevent the color from fading.) Before using, check herbs and discard any that have faded, lost flavor or smell old and musty. *To dry using a microwave:* Place ¹/₂ to 1 cup (125 to 250 mL) herbs between layers of paper towels. Microwave on High for 3 minutes, checking often to be sure they are not scorched. Then microwave for 10-second periods until leaves are brittle and can be pulled from stems easily. *To freeze:* Lay whole herbs in a single layer on a flat surface in the freezer for 2 to 4 hours. Leave whole and pack in plastic bags. Herbs will keep in the freezer for 2 to 3 months. Crumble frozen leaves directly into the dish. Herb leaves are also easier to chop when frozen. Use frozen leaves only for flavoring and not for garnishing, as they lose their crispness when thawed. Some herbs, such as chives, have a very weak flavor when dried, and do not freeze well, but they do grow well inside on a windowsill.

Instant-read thermometer. *To test baked goods for doneness:* See page 20.

Milk. *To warm to 80°F to 90°F (27°C to 32°C):* Pour into a microwave-safe container and microwave on High for 1 minute for each 1 cup (250 mL). Stir and check the temperature with an instant-read thermometer.

Mix. To combine two or more ingredients uniformly by stirring or using an electric mixer on a low speed.

Nut flour (nut meal). *To make:* Toast nuts (see Nuts), cool to room temperature and grind in a food processor or blender to desired consistency. *To make using ground nuts:* Bake at 350°F (180°C) for 6 to 8 minutes, cool to room temperature and grind finer.

Nuts. *To toast:* Spread nuts in a single layer on a baking sheet and bake at 350°F (180°C) for 6 to 8 minutes, shaking the pan frequently, until fragrant and lightly browned. (Or microwave, uncovered, on High for 1 to 2 minutes, stirring every 30 seconds.) Nuts will darken upon cooling.

Oat flour. *To make:* In a food processor or blender, pulse oats until finely ground, or to desired consistency.

Olives. *To pit:* Place olives under the flat side of a large knife; push down on knife until pit pops out.

Peaches. *To blanch:* See Blanch.

Pecan flour (pecan meal). *To make:* See Nut flour.

Pumpkin seeds. *To toast:* See Seeds.

Quinoa. *To rinse:* Before cooking, quinoa seeds need to be rinsed to remove their bitter, toxic resin-like coating, called saponin. Quinoa is often rinsed before it is sold, but rinse it again to remove any soapy residue that remains. The presence of saponin is obvious by the appearance of soapy-looking "suds" when the seeds are swished in water. Place quinoa seeds in a fine-mesh sieve and rinse thoroughly with water. *To soak:* In a fine-mesh sieve, rinse ⅔ cup (150 mL) quinoa well under cold running water. Transfer to a small bowl, add 1 cup (250 mL) water, cover and refrigerate overnight. Drain well. Yields 1 cup (250 mL) soaked quinoa. *To cook:* For 1 cup (250 mL) cooked quinoa, bring ¼ cup (60 mL) quinoa and ¾ cup (175 mL) water to a boil over high heat. Reduce heat to low, cover and simmer for 15 to 20 minutes. Fluff with a fork. Remove from heat and let stand, covered, for 5 to 10 minutes or until water is absorbed, quinoa grains have turned from white to transparent and the tiny spiral-like germ is separated.

Sauté. To cook quickly at high temperature in a small amount of fat.

Seeds. *To toast:* There are three methods you could use: 1) Spread seeds in a single layer on a baking sheet and bake at 350°F (180°C) for 6 to 10 minutes, shaking the pan frequently, until aromatic and lightly browned; 2) Spread seeds in a single layer in a large skillet and toast over medium heat for 5 to 8 minutes, shaking pan frequently; or 3) Microwave seeds, uncovered, on High for 1 to 2 minutes, stirring every 30 seconds. Seeds will darken upon cooling.

Sesame seeds. *To toast:* See Seeds.

Sunflower seeds. *To toast:* See Seeds.

Wild rice. *To cook:* Rinse 1 cup (250 mL) wild rice under cold running water. Add to a large saucepan, along with 6 cups (1.5 L) water. Bring to a boil and cook, uncovered, at a gentle boil for 35 minutes. Reduce heat, cover and cook for about 10 minutes or until rice is soft but not mushy. Makes about 3 cups (750 mL). Store in the refrigerator for up to 1 week.

Yeast. *To test for freshness:* See page 34.

Zest. *To zest:* Use a zester, the fine side of a box grater or a small sharp knife to peel off thin strips of the colored part of the skin of citrus fruits. Be sure not to remove the bitter white pith below.

About the Nutritional Analysis

The nutrient analysis done on the recipes in this book was derived from The Food Processor SQL Nutrition Analysis Software, version 10.9, ESHA Research (2011).

Where necessary, data were supplemented using the following references:

1. Shelley Case, *Gluten-Free Diet: A Comprehensive Resource Guide*, Expanded Edition (Regina, SK: Case Nutrition Consulting, 2006).
2. USDA National Nutrient Database for Standard Reference, Release #25 (2012). Retrieved June 2013 from www.nal. usda.gov/fnic/foodcomp/search/.

Recipes were evaluated as follows:

- Where alternatives are given, the first ingredient and amount listed were used.
- Optional ingredients and ingredients that are not quantified were not included.
- Calculations were based on imperial measures and weights.
- Nutrient values were rounded to the nearest whole number.
- Defatted soy flour and brown rice flour were used, including where these ingredients are listed as soy flour and rice flour.
- Canola oil was used where the type of oil was not specified.

It is important to note that ingredient substitutions and differences among brand-name products may alter the nutrient content per serving.

Library and Archives Canada Cataloguing in Publication

Washburn, Donna, author
    Great gluten-free whole-grain bread machine recipes : featuring 150 delicious recipes /
Donna Washburn & Heather Butt.

Includes index.
ISBN 978-0-7788-0463-5 (pbk.)

    1. Gluten-free diet—Recipes. 2. Cooking (Bread). 3. Automatic bread machines.
4. Cookbooks. I. Butt, Heather, author II. Title.

RM237.86.W3737 2013   641.5'638   C2013-903327-0

Index